Lessons Learned
During a
Wasted Youth

Lessons Learned During a Wasted Youth

A selection of writings by

Judd Arnett

Thomas P. Stewart
Publisher

Boca Raton, Fla—Harbor Springs, Mich.

Printed in U.S.A

ISBN 0-9625276-1-0

Library of Congress Cataloging-in-Publication Data
Card Number: 95-078932
Main entry under title: Lessons, Selected
    Writings by Judd Arnett
    1. Essays.   2. Human interest.
    3. Family values.
    I. Judd Arnett

For distribution information call 1-800-338-8211

Cover Art by Pierre Bittar
Paris, France—Birmingham, MI, USA
1-810-433-9917

Contents

Author's Notes

Indeed, time marches on. This may be especially noticeable to one who has spent an adulthood dealing in words, for in backtracking he may discover that what was written ten or more years ago falls under the heading of "Did I write that?"

The files show that he did. They go back to late 1959 and continue through 1990, approximately 9,000 in all.

Happily, throughout the search for "book-size" pieces there has been constant admiration for the determination of the citizens to support the common good of our country. Despite instances of arouse and beware—and all of our history has been marked by such events—Americans have retained the ability to sort the good from the bad, the wheat from the chaff, and that is the best news to come out of the decades capsuled in the following pages.

This effort would not have been possible without the unflagging support of the partner known as "Irish"; the importance of suggestions of Frank Ross, retired professor of English at Eastern Michigan University; and the constant assistance of Tom Stewart, golf professional, author and publisher, who retained faith in the undertaking even though he has never been able to cure this hacker's built-in-slice.

Kudos to the poet and my friend Margaret Rorke for sharing her words. And a special thanks to Pierre Bittar whose wonderful art adorns my walls and the cover of this book.

And out there, bless them, are the faithful friends and readers who have been asking, "Where is the book you promised?" Here it is—some of the impressions recorded as society responded to shifting moods and manners.

JUDD ARNETT

Dedicated to Rosemary Dolan Arnett; to the memory of Fern (1983); to our devoted pets who added spice to life; and to the most valuable constituents a writer can have—faithful readers.

ONE
Jughandle and Pals

Honeybunch, My Eye

I was hoofing down the street the other day when all at once I came upon this big youngun, eight or thereabouts, who had his nose pressed against a display window, watching a mechanical toy perform.

From up the street the boy's mother called out—"Come on, Honeybunch, we have to go"—so without batting an eye, or flinching or blushing, the lad answered—"All right, Mother"—and then he trotted to her side.

Honeybunch, I kept thinking. Honeybunch? Holy Toledo, what is happening to nicknames in this day and age? . . .

When Old Arney was a moppet, the bestowing of nick-names was a solemn affair in which, likely as not, our elders participated.

A nickname was supposed to indicate something of a fellow's character; or it treated upon some memorable occasion from his past; or it indicated that he had a special talent; or, sometimes but not too often, it was an expression of the community's affection.

Once you were nicknamed, the handle stayed with you through thick and thin. In other words, you were stuck with it.

One afternoon a bunch of us sprouts were playing football with a sock stuffed with leaves, when all at once Orville Minnich started wiggling his hips like he had been told that college players did, and none of us could tackle him good and clean.

Among the onlookers was Billy Yaney, the town paperhanger, and he called out: "Attaboy, Snake!"

Well, sir, right then and there Snake Minnich was born, and nothing he could do thereafter, including fist fighting or Indian rassling, could change his name. It was Snake this and Snake that all the way through school and finally he became more or less resigned to it.

Years later, during the war, he returned to town with a chest full of campaign ribbons and captain's bars on his shoulders, and I guess he was as close to a real, live hero as our community had at the moment.

Still, I am told that when he walked down the street his old friends called out, "Hiya, Snake,!" just as though time had stood still for all of those years.

We also had a fellow in our town by the name of Arthur Hoeffer, only everybody called him "Dummy," thus proving that we could be subtle in our nicknaming, too. For Dummy Hoeffer was about as smart as anyone then extant, being sort of a one-name calculating department.

Dummy Hoeffer was a lumber buyer, meaning that he purchased trees in the raw, and it was said that he could size-up an elm or an oak and come within three board feet of telling how many two-by-fours would be sawed out of it. In a town full of pool sharks he could also hold his own with the top seven or eight, playing a wild, break-'em-open game that gained him admiration even in defeat.

The high school pitcher, name of Fred McVetta, was known as "Curveball" from the first day he came in from the country, for his stock in trade was a sweeping outshoot that he started at the batter, making him scrootch in fear, only it zoomed over the plate and, four out of nine times, thudded off the catcher's knee. I have seen Rocky Colàvito strike out on less.

I have forgotten the reasons for some of the nicknames—Fatsy Crum, Nano Sharpe, Gunny Burgoon, Winnie Kershner—but there was good cause behind them, no doubt, for as I have already said a nickname was an honorable thing and you did your best to be worthy of it.

Honeybunch, indeed, twice over! A kid would have died of mortification had his Mom called him that in public or private.

Why heavens-to-Betsy, my Mom called me "Jughandle" for years, that being the title Bill Yaney bestowed on me the day he christened Snake Minnich!

Funny Sorta Christmas

Reverie . . .

Now it is the morning after Christmas and you are young again, cherie, with no bills to pay, no bales to tote, no accounting to make for the sorry condition in which mankind finds itself. What a wonderful state, youth, and what a pity to waste it on the young, as Mark Twain once said. Anyhow, now you are eight and your name is Henry and this is what you think as daylight filters through your bedroom window:

Well, I guess I'll get up and go down and have a glass of milk and six or seven cookies. I know I'm not supposed to eat so many cookies because of my teeth, but there won't be any breakfast for another two hours and a growing boy has to keep his strength up doesn't he? ha, ha. That's what Pop keeps telling me when we have string beans for supper. I hate string beans. But he says, eat your string beans, son, you hafta keep you're strength up. Oh, boy.

—————————————————

This has been a funny Christmas, sorta. I guess it has been because everybody knows I'm too old to believe in Santa Claus, but I've been too smart to admit it, ha, ha. If I'da said, I don't believe in Santa Claus anymore, folks, I'da got a bunch of shirts and sweaters and other dumb stuff for Christmas, just like happened to

Petey Brown. Boy, was he stupid. Just couldn't keep his big mouth shut. But because I didn't say it, I got the shirts and sweaters, all right, which I couldn't do nothing about, honest, but I also got some valuable stuff, too. Boy, when you're only 8 going on 9 you hafta be real cool about this Santa Claus bit, believe me, ha, ha.

Kids aren't the only ones who have to play it cool, though. Mom played it real cool this Christmas, too. From about the middle of November on she kept saying, John—that's my Pop, John—John, she would say, let's have a practical Christmas this year. We need a new chair in the living room. So why don't we buy a new chair, dear, and that will be our Christmas? Ha ha.

Pop bought the new chair, all right, but the closer it got to Christmas the more he realized that he hadn't gotten anything for Mom's Christmas, yet, so two days before he dashed out and bought her a new coat and a fuzzy-wuzzy sweater.

She acted real surprised yesterday morning. Why John, dear, she said, the chair was my Christmas. I didn't expect another thing. And then she gave him a kiss, which was mushy. Later on, when he went out into the kitchen, she gave me a big wink and I gave her one right back. We have lots of secrets, Mom and me. Ha, ha. Poor Pop.

I guess this has been one of the best Christmases we have ever had even though I did kinda feel like bawling at the dinner table when Pop got to talking about the people who don't have it so good.

For a while I felt sorry about that Santa Claus bit, and the new bicycle stuff, when there are kids who don't even have sweaters and shirts. But Pop sorta smoothed things over by saying, Son, always do your best to make it a Merry Christmas for those you love, but remember those less fortunate, too. I said, Yes sir. And I will, too.

———◆◆◆———   ———◆◆◆———

Well, I guess I'll ride the new bike over to Petey Brown's house and let him take a look at it. Boy, will he turn green with envy, ha. ha. He wanted a new bike, too, but about three weeks ago he got to blabbering about how he didn't believe in that kid stuff, Santa Claus, and it really cooked his goose. He got shirts and sweaters and stuff, ha. ha.

Oh, oh—Mom is calling. No, M'am. I'm not eating cookies. Not now . . .

Yes, M'am. I'll be back in time for brunch. I love you, too, Mom . . .

Everybody's Got It

Notes and Comment . . .

When the Young Curmudgeon had designs on a baseball career with the Toledo Mud Hens, being then approximately 10 years old and unaware of the terrors of the outcurve followed by a high hard one under the chin, he diligently participated in practice sessions on what was loosely called the "athletic field" at the rear of the school house.

Any day in March with sufficient warmth to dissipate the last of the snow drifts signalled the beginning of the workouts, with Coach hitting grounders and pop flies in rotation to aspirants large and small. Those sessions were completely democratic, open to anyone who had a fielder's mitt or the nerve to tackle a sizzler bare-handed, and one recalls them with that sense of youth relived which gladdens the Golden Years, as some fool once termed the approach of senility.

Anyhow, that early in the season the infield had been tufted, hummocked and potted by the wild winds of winter, so one hoped that when his turn came Coach would favor him with a pop fly or, next best, a soft liner. Leastwise, such were the sentiments of the Young Curmudgeon, who had suffered more than one ill experience with grounders which took unexpected hops. Moreover, he had a two-dollar filling—dentists were upper middle class in those days, too—in one of his front teeth, and he knew the loss of it would bring consternation on the home front. So pray for a pop fly.

And here it came, towering in the general direction of first base, which was the Young Curmudgeon's preferred station, bright against a sky not yet committed to eternal spring, soaring a bit as the wind caught it, sailing; leveling, reaching the peak of its arc, holding its pattern for a split second, then plummeting earthward, picking up speed, a lethal object bound in horsehide and dedicated to your embarrassment.

———

And there you were, head thrown back, eyes bulging, running in a few steps, then retreating, reeling to the right, veering to the left, circling, your companions shouting advice—most of it bad—and finally, by grace of pure accident, you would settle under it, beat your right hand in your fielder's mitt and yell: "I've got it!"

Whereupon Coach would greet with scorn what you considered a triumph of mind and body over a flying object. He would stand at home plate, bat akimbo, and he would mimic your cry of achievement. " 'I've got it!' he would bellow, 'I've GOT it!' Where do you attend school? Mudville? You're supposed to say, 'I HAVE it!' Remember that!"

Yes, sir, Coach. Sorry, Coach . . .

———

How times have changed. Today, everybody's got it. Chevy's got it. He's got it. She's got it. We've got it. The bank's got it and try and get it. Got has become the word of the minute in television commercials, and it clangs against these ancient ears and impresses a permanent frown on the fun-loving face of dear old Coach.

This latest torrent started with Chevrolet, we think, and surely the corporation should be ashamed of itself. "Chevy's got it!," the commercial proclaimed, and thereafter the inelegant phrase seemed to race through every advertising agency. Got it, got it, got it, got it, got it—it has become an echo in the Rockies, bouncing off a thousand peaks and distorting the language from Main to California. So rarely do you hear, "I have it!," that you are tempted to rush out and buy a tube of it in support of reasonable usage. "Chevy's got it!" Good grief. Ten million youngsters, soon to circle under the pop flies of this latter-day spring, will have got it, too. It says so on television, Coach.

Thanks, advertising agencies. One wonders how we ever got along without you. Got it, got it, got it, got it, got it, got it! Pass

the Old Slippery Elm, chum, and don't pretend you haven't got any.
Much obliged. I've got it!

A Day to Remember

School's First Day

*Some bluster in with surface pride
That covers qualms deep down inside.
Some hang to Mom with quivering knees
And give her skirt a death-like squeeze.
Some greet the change with downright sobs,
Decrying how this moment robs
The future of the past's great joys:
The playpen, crib, and box of toys.
This day in every mortal's span
Becomes a "giant step for man."*

—Margaret Rorke

Herewith comes the opinion that there will be three days you
will remember as long as you live: your first day at school; the first
time you were married (in this society a bit of elasticity is required
here!); and the first time the doctor said, "I don't think there's anything seriously wrong with you," or, "Your trouble is that you're
pregnant!" You may add to this list of memorable events as you see
fit, but it is eight-to-one, as George Puscas keeps offering, that the
three mentioned will be included.

Before she was caught in the web of the Young Curmudgeon's
dazzling charms (hoo, boy!), Miss Fern taught country school and
then first grade, so she is an expert on the openings of new terms.
When she read Margaret Rorke's poem a few minutes ago she said,
"That's delightful. That's the way it was."

Indeed.

One remembers Miss Baker, who taught first grade at a salary of approximately $700 per annum. Of course, those were 1917 dollars, and thank you Lord for such a lengthy tenure, but even so it was an arrangement bordering on the outrageous and the board of education should have been ashamed of itself.

Still, Miss Baker was guaranteed other and perhaps more important compensations. Very shortly she earned the slavish affection of the children who filled her desks; she had the absolute support of parents ("If you get a licking at school, Young Curmudgeon, you will get a worse one when you come home!"); and as a teacher she was guaranteed a high place in the community's pecking order.

It was true that in those days female teachers were likely to have been recent graduates of high school, with only six months or so of "normal school" to their additional academic credit, but it was accepted that they possessed an unusual flair for getting along with children, that they would seek additional college training as time and money permitted, and that in the meantime they were so dedicated to education and so morally sound they would not run off with a traveling salesman or a fireman employed by the Wabash Railroad.

Perhaps three-fourths of our grade school teachers came from such an educational background, male as well as female, and we did not feel stinted then nor do we now. For what they had in common was a zeal for fundamentals, mainly reading, writing, arithmetic, and geography, and when they had finished with you there was little mystery left in long division, you knew the capital city of Oregon, among others, and you could quote Longfellow by the yard. How much better things are today we will leave to your own determination.

———⊷•⊶——— ———⊷•⊶———

We went to school that first day under duress, as the lawyers put it, bawling and sniffling and thereby shaming a sister, Geneva, an assigned custodian, to such an extent that she remembered the experience all of her life and never tired of recounting it. Within a week, however, we had become so stuck on Miss Baker that she became sort of a second Momma, and had she told us to run through a brick wall carrying a dishpan full of hot coals, we would have attempted it.

Is there a comparable degree of fidelity left among today's moppets? In truth we do not know, for our lifetime has either been cursed or blessed, take your pick, by a dearth of offspring. One would hastily add, too, that he can not recall a time when the public schools were not accused of "spending too much money," so what we hear today is neither new nor memorable.

But even from a distance dictated by fate, or whatever, it is obvious that something is missing from the old relationship involving teachers, pupils, parents, and the total concept of education. The children to one side, no one seems very happy these days and that is too bad, for the school house is still the most important structure in our society, and we will not regain our balance as a people until harmony is restored to public education.

No Riots, Hatred or Cops

All right, Arn baby, what would your sainted mother have done to keep you under control had there been a riot in Liberty Center while you were growing up?

A fair question, this, in view of a recent tirade in which it was said that parents should be held accountable for what has been going on in various areas. So what would she have done, dear mother of mine?

The answer must be based largely on supposition since we never had any riots in Liberty Center. Whoops, there, that isn't quite true. Every two years, when we played Napoleon at home in football, about 14 of our farmers would try to whip 22 of theirs, and I guess you could have called those encounters "riots." The law was never involved, however, the sheriff being a knowledgeable sort who knew when it was wise for him to be in a different part of the county, and property damage was invariably held to the trampling of a few shocks of corn or an acre of two pasture land.

What they really had was a biennial testing of community will and with women and children barred, and to call them "riots" is stretching the meaning of the word to the uttermost, but it is only fair, nonetheless, that you should know such affairs did happen in Liberty Center, which was otherwise dominated by peace, quiet, tranquility and law and order to the brightest ray supreme, whatever that means.

But supposing there had been a riot, a tearing through the night, a flinging of objects jagged and lethal, a screaming and a caterwauling, a pounding of feet and a hurling of obscenities, a snarling hatred of adversaries and a contempt for the innocent—what would she have done?

Well, she would doubtless have called me into the parlor, which was the room in our house reserved for occasions bordering on affairs of state, and she would have issued an ultimatum in the following temper:

"Hiram," she would have said, "some of the helions hereabouts have decided that they despise what the community and their parents have been trying to do for them.

"To express their displeasure, I hear they are going to take to the streets tonight. They will damage property, they will flaunt Marshal Flim Mueller, they will disturb the peace and they will sully the good name of our town.

"Now, Hiram," she would have concluded, "I know you do not plan on taking part in this shameful affair. But just in case you do, I want you to understand that I will slap you into a peak—and then knock the peak off!"

That was her favorite warning: "I will slap you into a peak—and then knock the peak off!" She never went that far, obviously. Oh, a few times she waltzed me around real good, switch flailing, but she was never one for slapping or cuffing, probably figuring that the youngest of her brood was too weak up there to run the risk of permanent damage.

After about the age of 12, when I probably outweighed her, fear of being "slapped to a peak" faded somewhat, but I never put it past her and to have given her cause to try would have been more painful than the punishment.

Aside from not having any riots truly worthy of the word, we had other advantages in those days. It was not then incumbent upon young people, meaning those below the age of 18, to shoulder the responsibility for the conduct of national or international affairs. This may have limited our horizons, and it may be one of the reasons why my generation has been so dumb about so many things, but there was a definite benefit in that we did not get all nervous or unstrung when things went wrong.

If there was a war, somebody fought it—maybe we did. If there was a depression, we struggled through it. If there was an epidemic, we took our aspirin and hoped for the best.

We did not blame our elders that these things were occurring, we did not stand on the street corners damning our leaders and plotting their overthrow, it never struck us that breaking the windows in the school house or the drug store would emphasize the sorry plight of mankind, including us: We simply loved our country and our people and we were content to await our turn at adulthood, when the responsibilities would be ours.

A hell of a way to grow up, wasn't it? No riots, no hatred or cops, no disdain of parents. No wonder you are such an old fool, Arn baby.

Run, Sheepy, Run

The other evening on the telly the little shaver who plays the sheriff's son in the Andy Griffith program came home all tuckered out, with his shirttail flapping and the bill of his cap turned toward the northeast, and when his Old Man asked him where he had been and what he had been doing, he said he had been playing Run, Sheepy, Run.

Holy Toledo! That was the first time I had heard anyone mention Run, Sheepy, Run for at least 35 years, more like 40, maybe, and the news that the game still lives, that kids still have the legs for it, so enthralled me that I sat there and watched two commercials before going out to get a drink of water, ha.

Since Then . . .

. . . I have been thinking about Run, Sheepy, Run, Liberty Center style, and this has led to considerable private embarrassment, for if you were to ask me what the rules of the game were, I would be hard put to explain them to you.

Run, Sheepy, Run, as I remember it, was something like Hide-And-Go-Seek, except that a whole bunch of nippers were "it." Not just one was "it," like in Hide-And-Go-Seek, is what I am trying to say.

No, this was a team exercise, in Liberty Center, at least, and you all took it on the lam at the same time, and tried to sneak back to base at the same time, yelling Run, Sheepy, Run when you were going and coming but not when you were hiding, for Pete's sake.

Does that sound like Run, Sheepy, Run? Well, that's the way I recall it, dimly.

It was a spring and fall game, as I remember, because in the summer was when you went swimming or camping, while in the winter you played basketball in the Town Hall every time the gang could scrounge together 50 cents to pay for the lights. We were terribly underprivileged in those days, there being no Youth Movement in Our Town, and kids were known to actually work in order to get money to pay Flynn Mueller, the Marshal, who had the renting of the Town Hall. Ye gods, what a backward era to have sprung from . . .

Anyhow, during a split season of Run, Sheepy, Run you hit upon favorite places to hide, you and your blood-brother buddies, and for a long time—until the Management became aware of what was going on—four or five of us headed for the cob room at the elevator.

The cob room, dummy, was where they stashed the corn cobs after they had shelled the corn, and then they would use them the next day to stoke the furnace so they could make some steam to run the machinery that shelled the corn. The whole operation was about as close to Perpetual Motion as anyone ever came in those times.

There Was a Vent . . .

. . . or opening in the outer wall of the cob room, about ears high to a tall horse, and the biggest guy would make shoulders for the next biggest guy, who would climb in the opening and then lean down and help the next littlest guy, and finally we would all be in except the biggest guy, and we would pull him up by his arms and the scruff of his neck, saying criminently, Elmer, what did you have for supper, fried bricks? Real funny kids in those days.

We would hunker there in the utter darkness, not smoking or anything, even though the Management later accused us of it, just talking of things of great consequence, or how to do the Australian crawl.

And finally, when it was obvious the "its" were getting tired of looking for us, and were about to go home to their Mommas, the sissies, we would drop to the ground and go tearing toward home base, yelling Run, Sheepy, Run! . . . Oh, how sweet it was.

A Fiddle Riddle

It seems to me that one of the most amazing pieces of news to show up in the Morning Friendly since the invention of movable type was the revelation on Saturday last that Dave Rubinoff and his violin had been named the parties of the second part in a $1,506,000 damage suit filed in Wayne County Circuit Court.

That the part of the first part, in this instance the management of the Wolverine Hotel, should even imagine that a violin player could scratch together $1,506,000 leaves me absolutely flabbergasted.

I realize, of course, that in most legal actions the party of the first part throws caution to the winds when he sics his attorneys on the party of the second part.

The Price . . .

. . . for the assuaging of wounds named in the initial petition is usually a bit inflated. The plaintiff will ordinarily settle out of court with alacrity for something less than his original figure. There is a good deal of bluff and bluster in "lawing," as we used to call it, and you can't tell from his opening move whether the party of the first part has an ace in the hole, or a deuce.

Even so, as a frustrated fiddle player I remain awestruck by the mere suggestion that Dave Rubinoff has chattels and other assets in the amount of $1,506,000. There is also the second thought that mine was, indeed, a wasted youth . . .

In the Golden Era . . .

. . . to which the time machine has now transported us there were rigid standards of culture for the young.

A boy of approximately 12, for example, was considered well on his way toward a proper upbringing if he could play a tune upon a musical instrument and recite Henry Wadsworth Longfellow's doleful poem, "A Psalm of Life."

In respect to the latter . . . ("Tell me not in mournful numbers, Life is but an empty dream!, etc.") . . . William Feather reminds us that as late as 1929 a nationwide newspaper poll indicated that it lead all other poems in popularity, far and away. What, if anything, has replaced "A Psalm of Life" in the cultural caches of modern youth?

Anyway, while mastering "A Psalm of Life," with suitable gestures, and perhaps "Thanatopsis" for an encore, a lad also was expected to show some proficiency as a maker of music. There was a choice, in this instance, between the piano and the violin, and I was influenced to the latter by a series of circumstances.

In the first place, I had heard a violin played one morning at Methodist Sunday School, and the results sounded reasonably pleasant and gave the appearance of having been easily attained. If you could do the Australian crawl, or throw an outcurve, you ought to be able to play the fiddle. And secondly, I had heard enough scale practicing on the piano, chiefly "Peter, Peter Pumpkin Eater," to realize that in such a direction threatened madness.

So a violin was procured and a series of lessons arranged and Young Arn set upon the road to complete culture. In those days there were no accepted short cuts no matter what instrument you assaulted. Teachers were totally committed to scales and there was the feeling that if you attempted to play any honest-to-Pete music it would ruin you.

But there came a day, at long last, when Young Arn was entrusted with "Old Black Joe," and by Jove, he did it! The family rejoicing reached such proportions that we had beef and noodles for supper, with raisin pie.

A few weeks later, however, it was suggested that portions of "Old Black Joe" might be rendered on two strings simultaneously, thus increasing the sheer delight of both performer and audience. That really did it! By common consent it was agreed that such tortured melody was inhuman to all concerned, and since then it has been inconceivable to me that a man could accumulate $40 playing the violin, let alone $1,506,000.

A Very Scientific Game

At this season of the year, with the backbone of winter long since relegated to the soup pot, with the warm winds blowing and the dandelions flourishing—now more than at any other time it always comes home to your commentator that he had a deprived childhood.

Very soon now, if not already the Little League baseball teams will go into training under the supervision of managers, coaches, trainers and anxious fathers.

These kids will have more equipment than the Detroit Tigers—bats, balls, uniforms, windbreakers, shoes, masks, gloves, the whole works. They will be put through setting-up exercises, speed drills, endurance runs, double play maneuvers and strategy sessions. Then the first time they get into an honest-to-goodness game they will either win or lose, 18 to 17, on six hits, 14 walks and seven errors. A very scientific game, baseball, and to play it properly you must start early under expert guidance.

We had no such tender loving care when your commentator was a nipper. In fact, we had barely enough equipment to shield the catcher and glove the first baseman. Otherwise, it was every stalwart for himself and if you got your fingers jammed snagging a line drive, tough luck.

In the spring we would scrounge together a dime, usually from the sale of bottles to an understanding druggist, and then we would go to the hardware and buy a baseball. Leastwise, the manufacturer marketed this object as a baseball, but it had a peculiar characteristic in that if you dropped it on the sidewalk, the down side went flat.

Anyhow, from the hardware we migrated to the garage where our great and good friend, Tommy Bichan, would wrap about five yards of black tape around the spheroid. Now we had a baseball worthy of the name, a lethal weapon, really, and we treasured it because we knew it would be the only one we would have that season.

We would repair then to a large lot inhabited by three or four sheep and a spavined horse and spring training would begin.

In the main, this consisted of the two biggest kids nominating themselves as pitchers, whereupon they would warm up. They would throw two or three fast ones followed by a dozen or so out-curves, big sweeping benders that would scare the wadding out of a batter. Sweet Maria, how your commentator dreaded the out-curve! But nature provided revenge, although somewhat delayed. By the age of 14 most of those pitchers would have arms so sore they could scarcely deal a hand of pinochle.

But now to the organization of the teams, which would remain more or less constant for the rest of the season.

The time-honored ritual was for the two biggest kids, the pitchers, to serve as captains and selectors of their team mates. They would aim to get a catcher who could hang on to the out-curve, a first baseman unafraid of low throws—but after that it was pretty much potluck. The lowliest position was right field, usually filled by a sissy britches who let everything hit his way fall in front of him. I have no recollection of a right fielder ever catching a fly. It just wasn't heard of or expected of him.

The bases were gunny sacks with a light loading of sand and home plate was the bottom out of a bean crate, turned cattywampus. The umpire, usually a kid recuperating from the mumps or measles, stood back of the pitcher, where his view was blocked and he was available for intimidation as needed. Anything within a foot of the plate, from the ankles to the eyebrows, was a strike and the batter knew it before-hand. Fair for both sides, come to think of it.

Thus arrayed, we would have at it. The big kids hit the ball and the little kids chased it. Anything well stroked between third and short was apt to get lost in the weeds, whereupon it became an inside-the-park homer. We had kids in our town who probably hit two or three hundred homers a season. If a well set-up youngster didn't go six-for-eight he considered it a bad day and could hardly eat more than thirds for supper. Boy, we had some real sluggers down in Liberty Center.

After a few games, that baseball was so squishy the pitcher had to mold it back into shape before he could throw another out-curve. It never dawned on us that our folks would pop for a new ball, let alone full uniforms and fringe benefits. What a bunch of dumb, deprived kids. No wonder the world has gone to you-know-where in a hand basket.

Spring's Easier Now

In the lifetime of your commentator, who has now achieved the age when it is considered complimentary to say of him that he remains young at heart, many scientific miracles have eased the lot of the common man and his faithful spouse.

I can remember, for instance, when the only doctor in our village did a flourishing business in the setting of bones fractured whilst the unfortunate victims were cranking their cars. The engine of a Model T would put you in orbit if you neglected to adjust the spark lever before twisting her tail. The electric starter ended this threat to wrist, forearm and even elbow.

Further . . .

. . . there was a time when the washing machine wringer worked on the same relentless principle as a rolling mill at Great

Lakes Steel. To the best of my recollection a whole housewife was never squashed in a wringer, but many an unwary attendant was drawn shoulder-deep into one of the contrivances, which had great power due to the need for sufficient constriction to wring out a pair of long-handled underwear.

Now, thank heaven, these appliances are equipped with the automatic cut-off, or kick-out, and a measure of tranquility has settled over the land.

Yes, indeed, on all fronts—life is better than it used to be, and anyone who turns prosaic about the "good old days" is being sentimental, at best. Take me back in memory, if you insist, but leave me here in the flesh. And most particularly at this time of the year I don't want to have anything to do with that orgy, that family travail, that annual displacement known as Spring Housecleaning. Holy Toledo!

When it came April in the days of which we are speaking, the lady of the house abandoned all grace, relinquished all charm, forfeited all kindliness and approached spring housecleaning with the fury of a hurricane moving inland against Miami Beach.

Husband, children, friends, pets—none escaped the wrath which was released against dirt and dust, real or imagined. Little girls were taught that the only way to clean house was to demolish it, room by room and when they grew large enough to command establishments of their own they vied in the extravagances of their exertions.

The well-appointed living room, or parlor, had carpeting tacked to the floor. In retrospect, it seems to me that the proper ratio of tacks to carpeting was about 100 per running yard. These had to be pried loose, with hammer claw or screw driver, gently but firmly, so as not damage the material. This ordeal fell to the lot of small boys and husbands who were not alert enough to have an emergency at store or office. And then after you got the darned thing untacked, you had to beat it.

A carpet beater was a loop of strong wire affixed to a wooden handle, the whole contraption being somewhat larger than a tennis racket. You draped the carpet over a clothesline, being careful that the ends did not dangle in the grass, and then you went after it with the beater, thump and wallop.

Then . . .

. . . the living room floor having been scrubbed with a solution of water, soap and ammonia strong enough to bring tears to your eyes, it was time for re-tacking the danged carpet.

Curtains were washed and stretched on frames which had needle-like protrusions for piercing and securing the cloth. All of the dishes came out of the cupboards, which were washed and re-lined with fresh paper. Bedsteads were disassembled and mattresses and springs were lugged outside for washing, beating or airing as the situation required. Two wagonloads of flora and fauna were fetched out of the basement and the discards in the attic were sorted and rearranged.

Those were days of great exertion and ferocity and the food was always bad.

Well, times have changed. Next week we are going to have an outfit come in and wash the living room rugs, tacks and all. The Golden Age, this!

Dumb and Happy

July

July is a patriot, see him salute!
His is an ardor that's hard to refute.
Always he talks of sweet liberty's birth,
Bringing to mankind the best of earth.
July wears the colors so dear to this land,
Marches down Mainstreet ahead of the band;
Picnics and hotdogs and Mom's apple pie:
Really as months go, July's quite a guy!

—Margaret Rorke

All in a Lifetime . . .

Some thought has been given to a procession of Julys, and the conclusion supports Ms. Rorke's contention that the month is "quite a guy!" One would probably not swap it even-up for October, but in this market of opinion it is worth two Januaries; and all of February and March, with the first 10 days of April to boot.

This enthusiasm for our seventh month is no doubt a carry-over from those salad years when the Young Curmudgeon was footloose, fancy-free and probably headed at this very moment for a swim in the Maumee River. Oh, those were the days, Alfie, and don't you let anyone sell you a different bill of life.

When you were young you were dumb and happy and then the transformation occurred, as it does to all mortals: One day it dawned on you that you were just dumb. There is much, very much indeed, to be said in support of the assertion that ignorance is bliss.

Now we see the Young Curmudgeon—he is in his 10th year, let us say—padding beside the road which leads to the river. He walks there because he is barefoot and there are fewer sharp stones to cause him anguish. When he puts his feet down, plunkity-plunkity, small puffs of white dust erupt between his toes and he has the feeling that he is walking in talcum powder. It does not bother him.

Nothing bothers him. He does not know, for example, that the lush farmland through which he strolls is at risk to the bankers and the tax collectors. No one has told him that Warren G. Harding, who looks precisely as a president should, is over his handsome head with the Ohio gang, as it will later be called.

The Young Curmudgeon believes what he has been told—that the world has been made safe for democracy. He has not the slightest inkling that already in Europe the cauldron is simmering and out of it will bubble the Second World War. As he hears it at the family table, he accepts the judgment of college professors who proclaim that the era of prosperity will continue forever and ever. If someone used the word "depression" in his presence, he would not know the meaning of it.

He accepts without question the integrity of athletics. He believes in the medical profession, period. He goes to church twice on Sundays after Sunday School. Dull, he sometimes thinks, but being a Christian is important and that's how you get there.

He pads along, conquering the distance one short step at a time. The sun shines upon him. He sweats and itches in places. It does not occur to him that he is plodding away a day in his life, that this is part of the journey into an uncertain future.

Instead, he anticipates belly-whopping into the river, sputtering and spitting out large dollops of the muddy effluent, afraid neither of typhoid nor the skitters, basking in the merriment of his friends.

Ah, it is July. It is the time to be dumb and happy.

———

Was the world, largely speaking, happier when it was dumber? Probably. Being dumb did not prevent catastrophes, but at least we did not worry so much while they were brewing.

Now we have mass communications and we can spot catastrophes eight thousand miles away as they are forming, but they seem to happen just the same. Not a single catastrophe has been averted in recent times which would have occurred because we lacked mass communications. Think about that for a while and then go soak your head in July. It is a great month.

The Dangers of Dancing

One of the best annual conventions this department has ever heard of will be held on Friday and Saturday morning.

The Michigan Council of Square and Round Dance Clubs, 2,500 strong, will convene, and this is what the advance publicity promises:

"Only one business session will be conducted, including the annual election of officers. Most of the convention will be devoted to dancing: from 11 a.m. to 11 p.m., with after-parties to follow."

Sweet Betsy, it makes your feet hurt just to think of it! But they will have fun . . .

Speaking of Dancing . . .

. . . your orator recalls as though it had happened only yesterday the first time he ever set foot upon a floor made slick with corn meal. The time was mid-winter of 1927; the place was the Town

Hall in Liberty Center; and the orchestra (piano, banjo, drums, saxophone) was playing the song with that immortal line, "Ooooooh, I'll be down to gitcha in a taxi, honey! . . . "

Up until that moment there had been a rather stiff-necked resistance to dancing, as was common among the young swains of the era. Oh, we would show up at 50 cents per head on those gala evenings when the Town Hall rocked and shook to the stompings of the area's farmers, but we were content to stand against the walls, above and beyond the battle, so to speak, willing but uncommitted observers of the bunny-huggin' and two-steppin' performed in that swirling arena.

There was nothing wrong with dancing, understand; our reluctance to participate was not based on blue-nosery or provincialism. My goodness, Liberty Center in those days was one of the most progressive communities on the face of the earth—with movies on Sundays, a full lyceum course, and at least a week of medicine shows, hot ziggity-zam.

No, no. It was rather a matter of not wanting to get involved, as the saying went, for it was assumed that if you did not know how to dance, but a girl taught you to dance, and then you danced in public with her—well, you were just about two jerks from goin' steady forever, and a fellow had better live a little first, hadn't he?

(Note: How the girls learned to dance, I do not know. But they could, bless their pretty little heads, and they would teach you with great alacrity. Women! They have been leading men down the primrose path, as you shall see, ever since I can remember.)

Anyhow, on this particular night, with the orchestra playing such toe-ticklers as "Whispering," "My Blue Heaven," "Bye, Bye Blackbird" and "I'm Looking' Over a Four-Leaf Clover," I was just standing there with the fellas, doing nothing', so help me, when this little blond, name of Jerry, came whirling by in the arms of Freddie McVetta, who could throw the dangest out-curve with a baseball I ever saw, and the music stopped, bump, diddy, bump-bump, right then and there. Afterwards, I figured she had timed it that way, for women know when you are watching them out of the corners of your eyes . . .

Well, sir, Ol' Freddie moved away after a bit, saying as how he had the next dance with Maude Murray, and that left just Jerry and

me, Holy Toledo, and then the blasted orchestra started playin'
"Oooooooh, I'll be down to gitcha in a taxi, honey!" Later, I figured she had something to do with that, too, but I couldn't prove it.

Why Don't You . . .

. . . dance with me, she said, holding out her hands, and I said,
Jerry, I can't dance with you because I don't know how to dance a
single lick. I would be so happy to teach you, she said, smiling up
at me, and that was when terror set in and I said, oh, no; but she
said, just put your arm around me and start off on your left foot;
a-one and a-two, she said, moving close to me, oh sweet heaven;
and the first thing I knew we were out in the middle of the floor, a
two-steppin', and I was hooked, baby.

Springtime Nostalgia

It is said that the people have the need for nostalgia in these trying times, so here is a whole wagon load of it, fresh from Memory
Lane . . .

There was a certain day in late spring when you went barefooted
for the first time. How do the swallows know when to return to
Capistrano? Instinct, you say. Well, the same innate urge caused little boys to remove their shoes and peel off their socks when the moment was exactly right. It had something to do with air
temperature, the feel of the ground, the thickness of the grass, the
humming of the insects—somehow you were absolutely sure that
the hour had arrived, and you were right.

What a joy to commune with Mother Nature, skin to skin! You
wiggled your toes into the earth; you did strange, Indian-type
dances where the grass was the lushest; you pranced, and jumped,
and pirouetted and finally fell in a giggling heap, madly in love with
life itself. What a lovely day in spring that always was.

For a week or two you had to be careful where you walked, for
a sharp stone would cause you to wince and say "gol dang it," or

something equally ferocious. But by mid-summer your feet would have become so tough—so crusted!—that you could trod on gravel or a sidewalk baked by the sun and think nothing of it. The last thing Mom would say to you at night was: "Wash your feet before you go to bed." That was the worst part of it.

Going barefooted was for small and middling kids. After you had reached 10 or 11, you started wearing tennis shoes in the summertime. Don't ask me why: It was just part of the normal order of things, of the process of growing up.

The armed conflicts of these later years have had a tremendous bearing on the toys available to youngsters, but my generation literally took to the trenches as the result of World War I. Like father, like son? Perhaps. We heard a great deal about the fighting in France and our hero was a young chap around town who had won a medal for storming a German strongpoint.

So we dug trenches in our backyards, and constructed bunkers, and spent many a dramatic afternoon defending them against "the enemy." The racket of it, the pretend "machine-gunning" and "rifle firing" disturbed the naps of old ladies, who surely wished in their own genteel ways that the Huns would overrun us. But we never lost a battle.

It was about this time, too, that the Daisy Air Rifle came into our lives, and if you didn't have one you were dead, socially. By the sheerest of accidents I shot and killed a bird sitting on a telephone wire, a carry of some 30 or 40 feet, and from that moment on I never had much urge for hunting. But the Daisy was a beautiful piece of equipment, the answer to a boy's dream. I spent hours trying to become a marksman. No such luck.

To us, Zane Grey was the greatest writer who ever lived. (Fortunately, I didn't learn until a few days ago that he started adult life as a dentist in New York City.) What tales he told, of peerless white hunters and dusky Indian maids; and his cowboys were pillars of virtue and models of bravery. More than one kid in our town, influenced by Mr. Grey, hopped the afternoon Wabash freight train, headed west. Fort Wayne, Indiana, was as far as the boldest reached. Darkness, strange faces, a paucity of food and the knowledge that Mom would be worried sick took the starch out of running away.

We also built fleets of airplanes, keeping the grocery stores stripped of orange crates, which were perfect for the fuselage. Given wings, wheels and a wooden propellor, a fellow was almost inspired to test his creation off the roof of the barn. Fortunately, cooler heads prevailed, else some of us would long since have been plucking our harps in heaven.

What did girls do in those years? Gosh, I don't know. I can't remember seeing a girl until I was about 13, and then everything went blank for six months. You talk about a fellow walking around in a trance. Whooo—eee. If she had asked, I would have jumped off the barn without an airplane. Don't ever make fun of a kid with a bad case of puppy love, for chances are he is going through the torments of hell.

In the evenings we might sit around and do some singing, bearing down on such old favorites as "Down by the Old Mill Stream." It was funny—you could go to bed as a tenor and get up the next morning as a whisky baritone. Your voice changed just like that. One kid switched from bass to tenor and that ruined our quartet. But we enjoyed singing and we could do "Juanita" just about as pretty as you ever heard it if I do say so myself.

Well, that ought to be enough nostalgia for one day. The best of all was going barefooted, and I may try it again some evening if the temperature ever gets above 70.

Friends for Life

The other afternoon a new dining room table was delivered to the House on Grandmont, no cash down and a year to pay, on tick as we used to say, and in the evening we stood around, sizing it up, viewing it first from this angle and then from that, rubbing our hands over the wood and, in the main, just getting used to it.

The Girl Friend allowed as how it isn't quite the same color as the hutch, which was purchased several summers ago, also on tick, but the man who sold it to her had said that it would darken with age, she remembered, so we decided not to worry about that.

Then she allowed as how her old table cloths might not fit and I got weak from thinking, Oh, heavenly days, Magee, we have started another one of those chain reactions and it will cost a hunnert and fifty dollars before we get everything to match again, but she tried one, finally, fitting the linen to the glossy surface, and it was all right so that crisis passed, phew.

At last, without saying anything, we sort of drifted away from the table, thinking our own thoughts, and I am pretty sure that what both of us were thinking was the same thing; because you get that way after a while, and what we were thinking was: "There's a stranger in the house, but it may become a friend in due time. . . . "

When We Married . . .

. . . which was about 362 years ago I like to tell people, ha, ha, and slap my thigh, because it makes the smoke come out of her ears, we had approximately $12.50 in cash and no credit. (It was during the Depression, and who had credit then?)

Anyhow, my sainted Mother, who never threw anything away— she was one of the great all-time savers of busted-bottomed chairs, lampshades with hand-painted petunias and that sort of thing—she remembered that there was a table in the attic and we were welcome to it, for free, seeing as how we were just getting started and all that.

Well, sir, we dug out that table, which was minus a leg, and took it to an old fellow in town who had a lathe and was a craftsman to boot, and he made a new leg, out of cherry, you couldn't tell the difference, and refinished the whole thing, and the bill was $5.

So for the last 362 years, ha, ha, we have been eating off a $5 dining room table, but the food has been good, you can tell by looking at me sidewise, and there has been a little bit of Mom with us, bless her heart, and still will be, for now it has been moved into the living room.

You Really . . .

. . . shouldn't get sentimental about possessions, especially furniture, probably, but in addition to that $5 table we have a few other items I wouldn't part with for love or money.

In the den, for example, there is a red leather chair which is no better than 500 other models on the market today, but this one is very special because I traded a furniture dealer four pages of advertising for it one Christmas when I was a Country Editor out in Illinois.

If you have ever set four pages of advertising on a Model C Intertype, and then run them off on a hand-fed Miehle press—well then, and only then, will you know what that chair means to me.

There are some dishes "from the family"; and a water color of a red barn by Frank Williams; and a coffee table from one of the dearest friends we have ever had; these things, and a few others, are beyond price. . . .

When we still had our lovely old cocker spaniel, Scoop, and if he had to spend, say, a week-end in the kennel, why the first thing he did when he got home was take a tour of the house to make sure that everything was just as he had left it. He was a great one for old things, in familiar places.

Most men are like that, too, I think, which should be a warning to the young bride: Buy wisely, honey, because he will probably make you live with it the rest of your life!

Twenty-Year-Hitch

"That will be 6 per cent for 20 years," he warned, smiling frostily, so I took a deep breath, signed in triplicate—and all at once I was back in the Army again.

This is the Army of Mortgaged Souls—General Blood, commanding, General Foreclosure, chief of staff.

The terms of enlistment are brief but cruel. Everyone is a private as long as he lives; there is no such thing as a 30-day furlough; and the PX is permanently closed.

But it is an American axiom that "everyone should own his own home," so beat the drum and tootle the fife and off we go on a 20-year hitch, you'll never get rich, you'll never get rich, 'cause you're in the Army now.

I Went AWOL . . .

. . . from the Army about a year ago, jumping an enlistment in Florida and swearing by all eternal—"I'll never pay interest again!"—but freedom wasn't much fun . . .

Gone was the pleasure of "mowing our yard," or "transplanting our petunias," or "painting our front porch," or of saying, proudly, "come out to our house tonight."

Americans enjoy saying "ours" or "mine" even when the word is one part fact and nine parts fiction. How many homes are free and clear, actually "ours" or "mine"?

But we play at this game, payment by payment, and what a giddy day it is when the amount going for principal finally exceeds the sum—sweat and blood!—dedicated to interest. That takes about 10 years, I reckon. So hay foot, straw foot . . .

'Our' House . . .

. . . is out on Grandmont in a section that was first snatched away from the Indians in 1835 when President Andy Jackson approved a land grant to a Thomas Norton, who bought the whole area for approximately $100.

Thereafter, it was used as farm land and it passed from owner to owner as death, hard times, a bank failure and one divorce kept it in various stages of litigation.

The Grandmont Subdivision was the result of the industrial burgeoning of the City shortly before World War I, and today there are no vacant lots on "our" street.

Instead, there is block after block of old homes—"ours" was built in 1938—and we fell in love with it at first glance. Instantly we become putty in the hands of the real estate people, who can spot a wounded heart at 50 paces.

When You . . .

. . . turn off Grand River or Schoolcraft in the early evenings it is like moving into a new world. The graceful old trees form an archway high above, and gone is the roar of traffic.

Children play on the neat, green lawns and dogs frolic at their silly little games.

We shan't move in until late this month, but already we are playing the game. We call it "our" house. . . .

Oh, you'll never get rich, you'll never get rich, 'cause you're in the Army now!

A Walk in the Evening

Notes and Comment . . .

On a glorious night, to following Toby the Terrier through the neighborhood, and to seeing and hearing several things . . .

At a house up the block some youngsters had gathered for a jam session, live and direct from the living room, the ensemble including trumpet, trombone, clarinet and tuba. The doors and windows were open and the music swelled into the street, loud and clear, a happy sound.

What were these kids playing? A Beatle sonata? A moaner and wailer out of James Brown? A frug fantasia?

No, no, no! They were applying the Memphis Beat to "Alexander's Rag Time Band," tossing the lead back and forth between the trumpet and the trombone, with the clarinet tweetling and the tuba snorting at proper intervals. It was enough to cause Ol' Arn to lean against a tree and whisper into the darkness—"All is not lost . . . "

The cultural purists will take to the warpath over this, but it is contended, nonetheless, that Dixieland is one of our finest art forms, an expression of the American past which lives on despite the frequent distortions to which our popular music is subjected. Basically, Dixieland is a small part of our heritage which is true to reality and worthy of survival, and it was good to hear members of "this younger generation" working at it as the moon sailed through the sky and the stars glittered in infinity.

Walking Along . . .

. . . it was noted that several families had taken to their front stoops as spring finally fulfilled its promise, and there was a sudden nostalgia for the old-fashioned front porch, of which only a few remain and none on "modern houses."

What possessed our architects to eliminate the front porch, the sweetest sanctuary on a warm evening man has ever devised? To sit there at day's end, embraced by the soft night, caressed by playful breezes, was a moment borrowed from heaven for enjoyment on this earth. Today, we have the back porch, if there is any porch at all, but it is not the same, lacking the feeling of intimate yet sheltered proximity to the center of things.

On the old front porch you had the sense of holding the world at arm's length, being a part of it while still removed from the hustle and bustle, a contributor and yet an observer. Architects really blew it when they eliminated the front porch.

To passing the only new home constructed on our street in seven years, and to remembering a telephone call in the late winter from the wife of the owner, who complained of vandalism. I did not know what to say to her, or to do about it. Yet there is something wrong in American when builders have to figure theft and breakage into their estimates, as has been the case for some time.

A strange society, this, with peaks and valleys of greatness and pettiness. Most of our troubles stem from an improper sense of values, but how do you rectify this? It is beyond me . . .

To Wondering . . .

. . . why it is that dogs fenced-in invariably bark at dogs on-leash, whereas the latter pay only the slightest attention, if any, to the challenge being hurled.

Toby the Terrier will turn herself skinside inside if she is in the yard when one of her rivals strolls past, but when she is taking her constitutional she couldn't care less about the yapping and howling which greets her approach. Some form of snobbery, probably. If you want to make a bad joke, you might say that dogs are not above putting on the dog when the opportunity presents itself.

Turning for home and to trying to figure out why there is so much "white stuff" in lawns and fairways this year. Is it a form of clover of timothy? It is thick and tough and will spoil a five-iron shot unless you strike the ball with vigor. Oh, my golf! Mewling and puking it is, with wounded-swan drives and limpid approaches. Come on, Toby, let's go home and read Sam Snead's book one more time!

TWO
The Way It Used to Be

Why Go to School?

This morning your commentator sat at the kitchen window coffee cup in hand, and watched as the Young America of the neighborhood headed back to school.

If there was any enthusiasm in this return to the halls of learning, I failed to spot it. Usually there is a deplorable tendency among
these untamed wildcats to come yowling and screetching in prides
of threes and fours, tromping the lawn, heckling the dog and otherwise making a shambles of what should be an hour of peace and
harmony. But on this occasion they were splendidly subdued, as
though they realized that summer had slithered through their fingers and life would never again be quite the same.

Many were wearing stiff new clothes in rather somber shades—
dark blues, sedate greens, flat grays. I even noticed a scattering of
neckties, miracle of miracles. Well, give them two weeks and most
of them will look like unmade beds, thus returning the situation to
normalcy, as Warren G. Harding promised.

Why do kids have to go to school? Now that is a good question,
especially if you are between the ages of 6 and 18.

I seem to remember (man, this was a long time ago!) that one of
the reasons we had to go to school was so our parents could recover their tranquility.

Has this changed? I doubt it. Traditionally, mothers have cried
the first day Little Buster went toddling off to his classes—and cel-

ebrated every year thereafter. For Mom and Pop, school is a tranquilizer, a gentle fix that silences clangor and takes the edge off the screaming meamies. On the home front, the first day of school is like getting hit in the back of the head with a large, soft pumpkin, to quote my friend Willie the Sniffer.

Beyond aid and comfort to parents, why else do kids have to go to school? Well, it helps personnel directors, as I will now attempt to demonstrate.

The other day, having taken refuge from a series of double bogies in the 19th hole of the Pine Lake Hackery and Slashery, your commentator engaged in conversation with a chap who announced that he was quitting his company after many years of faithful service. Where should he turn for another job?

I suggested one of the automobile companies, giving a definite name and pointing out that it seemed to me the people there were making scads of money with a minimum of toil and sweat. If you have to work, go where the lettuce grows two feet high, baby. He thought this was a very sound idea based on irrefutable logic.

But then another fellow cast gloom on our planned assault on the makers of the Ramrod Eight. Do you have your degree, he asked of the man seeking a new career at higher pay.

No.

Has this company become degree-happy? I inquired.

They are not only degree-happy, he replied, but now they are becoming masters'-degree-happy. They won't hardly talk to you unless you have read Einstein in the original . . .

So there you are. That's why kids have to go to school these days until they are old enough to be vice president, U.S.A. Personnel directors.

It used to be that a personnel director was willing to take a flyer on a high school graduate because that's what the market was offering. Life was simple and sweet. The hiring man picked out a youngster with clean fingernails and a reasonably fresh shirt and started him through the company grinder. Office boy. Third assistant draftsman. A year in the tool shed. A stretch with the Minneapolis branch office. Upward and onward, step by step, learning the business.

Then college graduates become available and the personnel director decided he had better tone-up the company with some degrees. This was a gradual influx, but about five years ago you started finding fully-anointed Ivy Leaguers, or reasonable facsimiles, sharpening pencils and sorting out paper clips, just biding their time.

And now, at least at the company in question, they are talking with masters' degree-ers. That's what the market is—and that is where the personnel director has set his bench mark. He can't have his office cluttered with dropouts.

Is this good or bad? Who am I to say? But it is the way things are, Little Buster, so you had better crack those books or you will never make it to the Promised Land.

His Silence Served, Too

If this observer remains "typical" of the more than two million men who served under him against the Japanese, then it is proper to say that the rank and file of us have been brought up a bit short by the death of Chester William Nimitz.

He was our guy, the Admiral, along with Bull Halsey and a few others, and it is difficult now to accept the fact that old age was a factor in his passing. Yet, he would have been 81 this coming Thursday, and since this means that the rest of us are getting along, too, perhaps the best thing to do is to say that he lived a full life and let it go at that.

One of the best things about Chester William Nimitz was his ability to leave the stage after his date with history had been fulfilled. He fought his war, driving the Jap fleet off 65 million square miles of ocean, and then he just faded away; resisting all temptations and pressures to write his memoirs. He was one of our few major militarists who refused to contribute to the nation's "war literature," and for this he should be honored, too.

If all the rest of us—gobs and admirals, doughboys and generals, grease monkeys and pilots—had either kept quiet about war, or had told the unvarnished truth about it, there wouldn't be enough "glamor" left in mortal combat to fool anyone. A true patriot, I am now convinced, is a fellow who fights because it is necessary—and then clams up for the rest of his life. But they are rare birds, indeed.

The great majority of us, as a matter of fact, put aside the tedium, the terror, the hurrying-up-and-waiting, the waste and the sheer idiocy of war and remember only those episodes which provided momentary pleasure.

Talk . . .

. . . with an ex-sailor about liberty in San Francisco during the war, for example, and he will remember Market Street in the late afternoon; the sun shining on the Bay; the girls; the booze; the chow.

What he will have forgotten, of course, is that he shared Market Street with about 50,000 others just as lonely as he was; beyond the ferry to Oakland, there was no way for him to enjoy the Bay; there was a high rate of you-know-what among the ladies of the evening; the booze was apt to be watered; and in some of the best restaurants they practiced an obvious degree of snobbery on enlisted men.

There was no such thing as a "good liberty town," and I doubt if one has been invented to this day. The U.S.O. tried hard, and I do not mean to knock it, but the truth is that there is no substitute for home, sweet home.

As for the war itself, I am sometimes guilty of recalling nights at sea, with the ship knifing through the dark, swirling, all-claiming water, a billion stars carpeting the sky, and maybe after a session with this recalcitrant typewriter, or 60 minutes in traffic, it comes back as restful and peaceful. Oh, to be a sailor again!

Well, Nuts . . .

. . . What I have forgotten is the terrible, consuming loneliness of those endless journeys; and the fear which came to throat and stomach when the GQ buzzer sounded—whhhaaaaaaaaaa!—the worst noise ever produced by man in his extremities. I would run up and down those steel ladders and bark all the skin off my shins, panting and wheezing, scared silly, and that was the whole truth of war.

Sometimes I get to thinking about some of the islands I saw—Saipan, let us say—and perhaps one of them will come back as a green jewel tucked in an azure sea.

Well, nuts again! Saipan was a hell-hole and so was its sister island, Tinian, with dead Japs floating face down in the water, and buddy you can also have Okinawa, the Philippines, Ulithi, Eniwetok, Guadalcanal, the Russells and all the rest of them!

The "glamor" of war? There isn't any, Sonny. It is a game for madmen, and I'm happy Chester William Nimitz remained quiet about it after his service was over.

Slackers Dot History

There has been a good deal of public indignation of late concerning patriotism, or rather the lack of it, with the detractors of modern youth pointing to "draft-dodging through hasty marriage" (the hard way!) as a barometer of where this generation stands in respect to service to the flag.

Succinctly—oh, nuts! There are times when some of us who are old enough to know better act as though we represented the last surviving gasps of honor, decency, love of country, chivalry, patriotism and adventure-someness. Worse than that, we pretend that our age was "perfect," completely free of cowards and knaves. What rot!

Matter of Fact . . .

. . . if you will read the history of our major conflicts, and the public reaction to them, you will find that a good many Americans have always taken a jaundiced view of personal participation in war, and have gone to considerable lengths to avoid involvement. You may be amazed too, to learn that during the time of the initial crisis—the rebellion against Great Britain—there were occasions when patriotism knew its worst hours.

In "The War of The Revolution," for example, Christopher Ward deals in great detail with the situation around Boston in the winter of 1776, when General Washington was trying to hold an army together as enlistments ran out. An appeal was made to the 7,000 men of the 11 old regiments to extend their tours of duty— but only 966 agreed.

Worse, the Connecticut troops threatened to leave the encampment enmasse, insisting that their expiration date was Dec. 10. They resisted the suggestion that they stay four more days. Mr. Ward has written of the incident in this fashion:

"They were paraded on December 1. The men that were disinclined to stay even four days after their enlistments expired were formed in a hollow square, and Lee (General Charles) addressed them. 'Men,' said he, 'I do not know what to call you. You are the worst of all creatures.' Then he 'flung and curst and swore at us and said that if we would not stay he would order us to go to Bunker Hill (i.e., to attack the British stronghold) and if we would not go he would order the riflemen to fire at us.' They agreed to stay the four days. They got a drink of rum, and were promised another on the morrow . . . "

Washington wrote of the troops to Joseph Reed: "Such a dirty, mercenary spirit pervades the whole, that I should not be at all surprised at any disaster that may happen. I have often thought how much happier I should have been, if instead of accepting a command under such circumstances, I had taken my musket on my shoulder and entered the ranks, or, if I could have justified the measure to posterity and my own conscience, had retired to the back country, and lived in a wigwam."

In the Civil War, the wealthy of the North were permitted to "buy substitutes," a factor which contributed to eventual riots against the draft act, while in the south there were exemptions for slave-holders and sufficient other loopholes to prevent the full weight of manpower from being brought to the battle fronts.

In World War I . . .

. . . and again in World War II, it was absolutely amazing how many strapping young fellows suddenly were seized with an urge to go back to farming or found havens in other pursuits ruled "essential to the war effort." The Congress, you might also remember, failed by only one vote to kill the draft act on the very eve of Hitler's blitz of France and the Low Countries.

The point is that when it comes to patriotism, we had better be careful who hurls the first stone. Succeeding generations have looked both good and bad, but there have always been enough of the stalwarts to offset the slackers. The pattern will probably be repeated.

It is fair, too, I think, to note that in Vietnam, which is not an easy war, our youngsters have performed very well. And there will be more of them, if needed.

Give Life a Chance

A constituent who is 21 and a graduate of the University of Michigan has taken what he calls a "menial job" because it was the only employment that he could find. While at work the other day he read the column in which it was suggested that "life fades away and the truly intelligent among us are those who learn to savor each and every moment of it."

How is this possible in his case, he wants to know, when he is making no progress career-wise and when there seems little prospect that he will be able to provide the comforts of home for the young lady who has captured his affections?

The difficulty in responding to such an appeal for assurance that all will end well is that you must lean on personal convictions for which there is no hard and fast proof. How, for example, do you support your belief that there is a mystic flow to life that quite often has more to do with the attainment of happiness than all of your best-made plans? Perhaps the best way to put it is just to say that "things happen." Quite often the jigsaw puzzle that is every person's life simply "comes together." Looking back, there is no perceptible reason why it should have occurred in that particular manner, but it did. Was it fate? The hand of God? Happy chance?

Being in the right place at the right time? Select your own name for it, but "things happen."

————————

Will you permit the personal assumption that your commentator is happy in Detroit and in the work he is doing? Well, 16 years ago he was at loose ends, wondering which way he should jump. He was thinking of such places as New York, Chicago, Washington and San Francisco. In June of 1959, had you told him that he would wind up in Detroit, he would have replied that you had lost your mind. Impossible. Couldn't happen. You know the rest of it.

A dear friend came to this city during the Great Depression, armed with an engineering degree from a very fine university. He, too, took a "menial job"—because he could find nothing else—and stayed with it out of desperation. It was a matter of keeping body and soul together. A few years ago he retired as an executive from the same company without having practiced engineering a single day.

————————

Tony Delorenzo came to Detroit as a slashing and dashing bureau chief for United Press. Today he is a vice president of General Motors with responsibility for public relations. The publisher of this megaphone of free speech has a law degree, but to the best of my knowledge he has never chased a single tort around a court room. Another lawyer of this acquaintance made a career out of advertising. Charley Gehringer never sold anything until he retired from the Tigers, and then he became one of the brightest stars in our galaxy of manufacturers' representatives. The late Billy Rose, showman and songwriter, darned near cornered the market on one of the most important stocks offered on the New York exchange. What's it all about, Alfie? "Things happen," and life is not as nearly prescribed as the textbooks indicate. Something totally unexpected may be just around the corner, ready to alter the direction of your pursuit of happiness. Opportunity, some call it, but to me it is much more mystic than that.

————————

The recession has either side-tracked or slowed the careers of many Americans, a high proportion of them young. It always has been so during hard times. Wasn't there a letter to the editor the other day in which the writer pointed out that after he had graduated in the 1930s, it took him two years to find his first job?

It is so easy—so pat—to recommend "patience," and one is not surprised when the advice is rejected. But waiting is also part of life, and over the long haul you learn that to do it as gracefully as possible is best for you and those who have your interests at heart. For only a few is there instant success. The rest of us have to tough life out, day by day and step by step, hoping for that magic moment when "things happen."

The Spark of Youth

Among America's most pressing problems is the current breakdown in communications between its younger and older generations.

For the sake of convenience, let us say that the dividing line is the age of 40. There will be stragglers from both camps, of course, with some of the older claiming allegiance with the younger and some of the younger casting their lots with the older, but we have to start somewhere in the development of this drama of the diffused generations, so let it be at two-score, please.

Over the Easter weekend, representatives of the younger generation created headlines with a "love-in" at Los Angeles, a "be-in" at New York and a more traditional riot at Ft. Lauderdale. Elsewhere around the nation there were assorted other rallies and conclaves, many of them leading to brisk confrontations with the police, those unhappy and grossly unappreciated defenders of law, order and the status quo.

What Meant . . .

. . . these small unheavals? Among the older generation, there seem to be two reactions, neither studded with brilliant new thought. (1) The youngsters of today are a worrisome lot unworthy of the care and money being lavished upon them; (2) In the early spring the sap always flows, kids will be kids just as you and I once were Maggie, so simmer down and this, too, will pass.

But what of the younger generation? What did the weekend mean to them as an expression of their identities, as a symbol of their beings? Ah, now we approach the Never-Never, now we slip into Guess Land, now this journey across the Dividing Line becomes as uncharted as a flight into infinity. Nonetheless, we must risk it . . .

In the current number of Harper's Magazine there is an article by a brilliant young writer, Michael Harrington, entitled "Taking The Great Society Seriously." He makes this point:

"Perhaps the most ironic disappointment is that the United States in 1966 had not yet constructed the number of low-cost housing units which Senator Robert Taft, the leading conservative of this time, had targeted for 1955."

Every major big city in America, Mr. Harrington continues, "is in a financial, racial and social crisis. The present condition of our cities touches the very intangibles of the quality of our life, for here old age is lonelier, youth more rootless, the streets more chaotic."

And against this backdrop of social failure, we are producing the best educated and yet the most restless younger generation of our history—a newly-motivated class of Americans who are not at all certain that the pursuit of money for the sake of personal gain is the way to build a better society.

In Considering . . .

. . . the younger generation, you must remember that they are approaching the age of responsibility in an era of visibility and mobility which seemed "Buck Roger-ish" only a few years ago. The jet airplane, television, the new conscience in journalism—the strengths and weaknesses of our society are open to young people as never before, and they are seeing and studying America at the low ebb of its physical grandeur and at a time of stagnation in its social progress.

It is to their credit, I think, that they do not approve of much of what they see, and it is a hope of the future that their forms of protest will take a more substantial turn as they reach maturity.

America needs a "new revolution"—a dedication to the end of slums, and abject poverty and traffic congestion which is costing, at the rate of $1.50 an hour, more than $13 billion a year in lost time. The progress of the future can and should be accomplished within the framework of the free enterprise system, but patently we have reached the time when we require new energy, new drive, new blood.

If the younger generation responds to the challenge, we can well afford to forgive them the "love-in" or the "be-in."

Our Lindy

What follows will no doubt be awash with nostalgia before we are finished, for it will be a recounting of a hero as we once knew him, and of the simple machine he flew to glory.

On this 20th of May, 1973, we have Skylab floating around in outer space, a $475 million marvel of technology which has been crippled by the malfunctioning of some of its devices. Those of us who retain slight enthusiasm for exploration of this type have been left down-in-the-mouth by the development, especially since there seems no way to recover the financial investment. Certainly not from the manufacturer, who gave no warranty. A half-billion, give or take five percent, won't break us if squandered, but even so it would have kept the Head Start program going for a year or more and it is a considerable amount to kiss goodby when we are supposed to be on an economy kick.

—————————

Skylab's predicament, if that is the proper expression, is made even more poignant by the fact that this May 20th marks another anniversary of the flight of Charles A. Lindbergh from New York to Paris, a feat of such consequence that it left the whole world breathless and pulled aviation out of the Dark Ages.

That expedition, underwritten by private funds, cost approximately $15,000, including board and room and incidental expenses, with a bit more than $10,000 representing the investment in "The Spirit of St. Louis," which was handmade to specifications. It was quite an airplane.

————◆◆◆————   ————◆◆◆————

The wingspan was 46 feet; the overall length was 27 feet, eight inches; the power plant was a J-5C Wright Whirlwind engine capable of 1950 RPMs at maximum speed; the fuel tanks held 425 gallons of gasoline and 25 gallons of oil; and the gross weight at the time of take-off, including the pilot, was 5135 pounds.

In this primitive contraption, which now hangs in the Smithsonian Institution, Charles Lindbergh—Our Lindy—flew 3610 miles in 33 hours, 29 minutes and 30 seconds, and since then the world has rarely shared such joy, relief and exultation.

His receptions throughout Europe became a series of tumultuous triumphs and when he returned to the United States aboard a Navy cruiser dispatched by President Calvin Coolidge, he was caught up in an overwhelming swirl of hero worship. Late in that summer of 1927, Charles Lindbergh came to Detroit, his home town by birth, and two passengers were taken for flights of 10 minutes each—Henry Ford and Edsel Ford. The next April "The Spirit of St. Louis" was piloted to Washington and the Smithsonian. The log showed the plane had made 174 flights, covering a total flying time of 489 hours and 28 minutes. All of this for an original investment of $15,000.

————◆◆◆————   ————◆◆◆————

Some years later, in 1953, to be exact, Mr. Lindbergh published his autobiography, "The Spirit of St. Louis," to almost unanimous acclaim. The Chicago Daily news called it "A stunning, tremendously beautiful reading experience—a classic of adventure writing," and it received the Pulitzer Prize. It is well worth reading or re-reading today, for it reminds us that one of the virtues of the past was the independence and fierce pride of individuals, something we are apt to overlook in today's homogenized society.

At the outset no one, least of all a member of government, encouraged Charles Lindbergh to hop from New York to Paris. The idea occurred to him one night as he was flying the air mail between St. Louis and Chicago, in itself a repeated experience of such uncertainty and danger as to satisfy the lust for adventure of most young men.

He knew that $25,000 had been posted for the success of such a flight, but it wasn't a question of money or fame. It was something that had to be done, he felt, if aviation was to flourish.

The early difficulty of finding backers; the search for a plane and the decision, finally, to have it built by Ryan of San Diego; the shaking crashes—and deaths—of competitors; the sleepless night before a risky takeoff in overcast; the eerie flight during which "figures" joined him in the cockpit and helped ward off sleep; the dead reckoning landfall along the Irish Coast; his worry over the fact that he had no passport—all of this and much, much more became part of the saga of The Flying Eagle.

He was a trail blazer, of course, for aviation, for lunar exploration, for Skylab. For a few glorious years in a simpler era, he was an American hero. And if you insist on being penurious about it, what he did cost $15,000, private money.

16 Out of 32

Counting the one that falls on the morrow, there have been 32 Christmases since the attack on Pearl Harbor, and we have been at war during exactly half of them.

Add them up: Four Christmases during World War II; three during the Korean War; and nine in Vietnam. That is 16 out of 32, a record unequaled in this century by any other major Christian power. Not even the Germans, who are blamed for starting two world wars, come close to matching our endurance under arms. It is something to think about, isn't it?

We had hoped to be spared this Christmas, but evidently the peace that was "at hand" in October took sudden wing. Whose fault this was we may never know. In diplomacy gone awry there are countless opportunities for obfuscation of the truth, and both sides will doubtless work at it. Leave it, then, to the historians. Let us concentrate on the need for peace, the sooner the better.

America needs peace, and lots of it, because there is no way we can fulfill our destiny at home or abroad while we are at war.

War-stained as we are, and troubled though we may be by attacks on our fundamental liberties, this land remains the only beacon of hope for the oppressed throughout the world. We are losing this image because of our involvement in Vietnam, but we must regain it because of our responsibility to mankind.

For where else is the yoked peasant to turn for inspiration? To Russia, where gentle poets infuriate the keepers of discipline? To Red China, where the individual is fitted into the cogs of a vast and faceless society? To France or England, where the glories of the past fade into the realities of today? Where? Where shall he turn, this creature of God seeking a flicker of hope, except to America?

Over the years we have become numb to this responsibility. It is said, for example, that at the moment the President does not care what other people are saying about the resumption of bombing in North Vietnam.

But he must care and we must care, for if our not caring became the accepted response to those in desperate need of inspiration, then what would we have become? Another Russia with the pretense of brotherly love; another Red China wearing a false face?

No. We must care, all of us, about what the rest of the world thinks of us, and warrant the warmest of approbation, or else what little remains of the true spirit of Christmas will be endangered, here and elsewhere.

America also needs peace because the quality of life, spiritual as well as material, is being frayed by war.

It is an ancient cliche that had we spent on the advancement of our society what we have spent on the wars of this century, we would now be verging on Paradise. We could have given every family a new home, provided every youngster with a first-class education, spent billions on medical research and care; the statistics are staggering.

The cliche's weakness, of course, is the assumption that we might have remained aloof from conflict and retained our pre-eminence.

What the world might be like had Hitler prevailed is beyond rational estimate. You can make an argument for (as well as against) all wars, but once the lines had been drawn and the issues determined, our participation in the second European holocaust was probably essential to mankind.

It must be admitted, too, that only in war has this society, or any society, been able to inspire its people to efforts approaching the super-human. Survival is a basic instinct in all of us, and war promotes it.

Even so, there is much we could and should be doing in peace to advance public well-being. Surely if we were out of Vietnam there would be some additional money for education, health care, the environment, the movement of people, the planning of new and better cities. We should require no inspiration beyond common sense to improve our way of life.

Spiritually, the benefits of peace would be boundless. Vietnam has torn our people apart and has spawned a cynicism for leadership and morality that is beyond parallel in our history.

A Christmas with peace, please God, next year.

An American Pioneer

A family affair . . .

I remember the day in June when we went to the hospital to see his wife, Ruth, who had suffered the stroke destined to leave her a semi-invalid.

"This is the elevator," Jack said as we approached that mechanical marvel. "If you want to go up, you push the top button. And if you want to go down, you push the bottom button. You got it?"

I assured him that I had it, and there is the hope the lesson was well-learned. For now, these five months later, I must return to the hospital in Ironton, Ohio, and push the right button again. Jack has had a heart attack.

He is my only brother, at 82 the senior member of the clan, and all of these years he has defied Father Time at least where the rest of us were concerned. We have remained very young in his estimation, inept and in need of the surest guidance, and here I am with vivid recollections of the first Armistice Day, but still the baby of the family.

Push the right button. Don't smoke so much. Get more sleep. Eat your dinner. Beware of the vested interests. Turn right at the next corner. That's the Ohio River. You were born in this house. There's a traffic light in front of you. Don't work so hard. Stay another day. You only live once . . .

Yes, Jack. Yes, brother-who-was-also-father. And now hang on please, for the clan is gathering one more time.

———————

In him there has always been much of what America has been about. Before his retirement he was a working man, a railroader with 47 years of unbroken service to the Chesapeake & Ohio. It was a love-hate relationship, a very private affair, actually. It was all right for him to cuss "the operation" up and down, with special spleen reserved for "those damned rich stockholders in Norfolk," but if you joined in the indictment he might turn on you. The C. & O., as we always called it, was also part of his "family," and he reserved the right to determine who was entitled to kick it in the shins.

He was always typical of the working man, too, in that the closer he edged toward financial solvency, the more conservative he became. During his earlier years, when he was struggling to make ends meet, he fulminated against "the monopolies" and "Wall Street" in general and voted the straight Democratic ticket. You had to be touched in the head, he insisted, to do otherwise.

Later, however, things started coming together for him, and his view of politics changed. Softened. Maybe Wall Street had its problems, too. When he announced in 1972 that he had found McGovern "irresponsible" and would therefore vote for Nixon, he took pouting umbrage at my suggestion that perhaps he had fallen in with "the Ironton reactionaries." Young people—the baby of the family, again—should have more respect for the rights of property. There was quite a lecture on that subject before the day was done.

————————

In his heyday he was typical, too, of those who helped build the country with their strength and native inborn skills. Of public education he had eight grades, which was quite customary in those days, and then he went out and found a job. On the Baltimore & Ohio. Always he was a railroader, as our father before him. By employment or marriage, the whole family was tied to railroading. I was the only one who escaped, if that is the proper word for it.

We sometimes forget how recent as time is measured is the industrial development of America. The howling wilderness is only a few generations behind us. For better or worse, Jack helped tame it. In his own way, and in his own era, he was a pioneer.

These men burrowed the coal from the dark hills of Ohio, Kentucky and West Virginia. They hewed the ties, placed the rails and built the steel cars and the steam locomotives which transported the energy of mid-America.

What did they get out of it? A sense of history? One doubts that. Rare is the working man who understands that his blows with the hammer, or his straining against the fulcrum, will lead to a new order. One works because it is his lot in life and success is difficult to measure in the changing currencies of our system. When our father died in 1914 he was trainmaster for the C. & O. at Russell, Kentucky, and he was considered one of the middle class pillars of the community. His salary was $100 per month.

But now it is time to go and push that button. Up, we will go up to where the leader of the clan is stricken.

A Case of the Grumps

All in a Lifetime . . .

The other day there was a letter from a constituent raising Old Ned with the younger generation, meaning the lads and lassies between 15 and 20, and from the way he wrote I could tell he was 50, maybe a shade beyond, which is the dangerous age.

When a fellow gets to be 50, or thereabouts, he becomes inflicted with the grumps. He gets to thinking that while he is too young to die he is also too old to enjoy life the way he useter, so for a year or so he grumps around in what you might call the Neutral Zone.

His beer tastes flat; young people are all feet and mouths; all politicians are crooks; it will rain on his day off, sure as God made little green apples; there hasn't been a good novel since Moby Dick; they aren't building automobiles like they did 20 years ago; if you think Tommy Sands can sing, you oughta heard Jolson . . .

Oh, the Neutral Zone is hard on everyone, for the fellow caught in it and for those forced to live with him, and it is usually during this period that his wife takes up oil painting, or joins the Daughters of the American Revolution, or makes frequent trips to visit distant relatives. Anything to get out of the house.

But we have digressed, haven't we? Where were we? Oh, yes: I was fixing to tell you about my youth, so that you may have a point of comparison with what is going on today.

You Think Kids . . .

Wear silly clothes today, and affect hideous hair styles?

Well, when I was about 16 we went through the Black Hat Cycle. Every kid on the basketball team, which was practically every kid in school, bought a black hat. Adam West, who operated the town's only haberdashery, got rid of some merchandise he had had on the shelves for 30 years.

However, just having a black hat wasn't enough. You had to cut the brim to one-inch, no more, no less. For school, you wore it with a team sweater and corduroy pants.

For dress-up, you wore it with a double-breasted blue serge suit. You looked like an idiot. You knew you looked like an idiot. But blimey, it was the season for looking like an idiot. Can't you understand that, Mister? . . .

Just about that same time, the prevailing style in hair cuts was for the barber to run the clippers to within one-eighth of an inch of your cranium. It made your ears stick out like the opened doors on a Yellow Cab, but everybody was doing it.

Why? Darned if I know now. In fact, I didn't know then, either. It was just the style, Mister. You hafta be in style don'tcha, huh, Mister?

Cars . . .

Oh, yes . . .

About every two weeks, having scrounged together the money for gasoline, theatre tickets and incidentals, we would pile into a Model A, or a Chevy, and head out for Toledo.

It was only 30 miles, one way, but what with the difference in the roads and the equipment, it was the easy equivalent of 100 miles today.

And we made it wide open, the cut-out roaring, the fenders flapping, whooping and hollering, young, Mister, with the sap of youth sluicing through our veins, young and sassy, young and reckless, young and happy, young, young, young . . .

Did I say we went to the theatre? Well, it was vaudeville, really, a dozen acts to enthrall and entrance; there was this doll with a violin, see, and she came out on the stage holding it in her hands, and she said, If you will ask it to play something, anything, it will—and I'll be dad-burned if it didn't, Mister, and how did she do that?

Home through the night, then, roaring and flapping, young, young, young, and I reckon that's the way kids are today, too, Mister, they haven't changed much.

There Goes a Streaker

We are caught up in the phenomenon of "streaking" and all sorts of bright sayings are sprouting in response to this sudden burst of nakedness.

It is said, for example, that a "yellow streaker" is a lad who sprints across the campus while wearing his underpants. Other definitions are more pungent and must be excluded from this family journal. But surely we have a full-blown craze on our hands, or in our eyes, and when it will end no one knows.

Being of what are called "advanced years"; having sags, bulges and wrinkles in the wrong places, and having been nourished through puberty during an era when sin was clearly defined and often lamented—well, by all rights I should be against "streaking" with full might and main.

As a matter of fact, ghosts from my puritanical past now gather around this desk and point accusing fingers. "The least you can do is wring your hands," one of them says, but this is far from the consensus. The others want hellfire and damnation, a perfectly clear indictment of "streaking" in all its forms, fashions and foibles.

"Throw the book at 'em," one ghost exclaims, and this brings a murmur of approval. It is agreed, then, that "streaking" is an affront to decency, at the very least, and the meeting adjourns on that note. I am left with the task of composing the indictment.

———◦◦◦———   ———◦◦◦———

But for some reason the words will not flow. What is the matter with me, anyhow? Well, for one thing the appearance of the ghosts raised another specter. All at once from the dim and distant past there came the recollection of a hot summer's day when we went swimming, boys, and girls together, in the buff. Holy Toledo, that was "streaking" too, wasn't it? We kept that harmless little orgy very quiet, of course, and there were no cameras present, thank goodness. But in this instance, as in all others, where does "purity" begin and where does it end?

And then there is the matter of "an affront to decency." Is this what the young people intend? I have no way of knowing, precisely, but again we come to the root of the indictment system— you should not pre-judge guilt before the jury comes in with its verdict. In this case, it may take the psychiatrists 10 years to decide what brought on "streaking," and by then who will care? Further, one remembers that some of these "streakers" may be the offspring of those who engaged in "panty raids" and other hijinks, and the Republic did not collapse. In truth, every generation has produced those who fractured some of the rules of propriety, but somehow we managed to survive. We will overcome "streaking," too, although admittedly the cause of it intrigues me.

Could it have been brought on by the long winter during which activity was deadened by the gasoline shortage? Might it be a lemming-like protest against the failure of society to define and meet its responsibilities? Ah, we are painting ourselves into a corner. Only the individual "streaker" knows why he streaks, and for reasons already outlined I am incapable of performing a clinical experiment. Surely, slow motion would not count in "streaking."

———

Over the years, affronts to decency have taken strange and curious forms. One can recall when bobbed hair shocked society; when the knee-length dress was a ticket to perdition; when the theories of Darwin led to a celebrated court trial; when the rumble seat was considered the invention of the devil; when Hell awaited those innocent souls who had been sprinkled rather than immersed; when you read Sinclair Lewis with the shades drawn.

Are we any worse off now? Again, it is a matter of individual opinion—and I think not. In many ways not so cloyingly connected with "decency" we may be better off today than ever before. There is new and gathering support for the works of God, for the earth He created and bequeathed to us. Never have so many doubted the use of might as an extension of political policy. And there is the growing realization that society should be measured by the steps it takes to reduce poverty, disease, illiteracy. These are matters of "decency" which far, transcend "streaking" or any other passing fad.

Being beyond youth in years, I do not pretend to understand the young. So what else is new? My father did not understand his children, nor his father, either. What frowns, what signs of anguish, what remorse at the twig so weakly bent, what supplications for improvement! Ah, that perpetual torment of mankind, the generation gap.

Yet somehow we have moved from the old swimming hole, in the buff, to "streaking" across a college campus in the nip of winter. What has it been? Evolution? Who knows?

The Halls of Montezuma

As a taxpayer and a self-appointed patriot with an honorable discharge from the United States Navy, I would like to say a few words in favor of the Gyrenes. Okay?

This urge to speak out in behalf of the Halls of Montezuma and all that sort of razzmatazz has been sparked by a report that says the Marine Corps is obsolete and a burden on the Pentagon's budget. Well, horse feathers.

If the next war—and there will be another one, never fear—is fought with nuclear warheads, we won't need the Marines. But if it is a dirty little brawl featuring the bayonet to the short ribs and cannister at close range, why get rid of the one outfit we have which savors such intimate action? Oh, it is a sad day when an ex-sailor must toot the horn of the United States Gyrenes, but who else is there to do it? May they forgive me in the fo'c'sle and in heaven to boot.

It has been said that the marine, hitting the beach with his rifle and two cans of rations that might pass as dog food, is no longer relevant in modern warfare. Again, we get back to the question—how are we going to fight this war? This was a matter which troubled John F. Kennedy, incidentally, and was one of the reasons why he was so strong for the Green Berets, another gung-ho outfit.

Now as in the 1960s there has to be some substitute for the atomic bomb in case of a "brush war," or whatever you want to call it, and there is no better answer than the Marine Corps. Semper Fidelis! If boot camp is anything like it used to be, just to survive that planned hell makes you the best foot-slogger, pound for pound and dollar for dollar, on the face of the earth.

This we are going to give up as "old-fashioned" at a time when the predators are growling in the jungles? If the Gyrenes need more sophisticated weapons, provide them, for heaven's sake. But don't tamper with the pride or morale of a fighting force that has served this nation with distinction since its founding. We have always needed the Gyrenes and we will need them again. This is as bitter as gall coming from an old swabbie, but it is the truth. When it comes to war, the Marines are dead solid perfect. A fellow can sure get along without them on liberty, you understand, but if our assignment is to bash some enemies of the Republic in the teeth, bring on the United States Marines.

Let the Russians squander their money on ships, most of which wouldn't last 30 seconds in the event of all-out naval warfare. Give us a bigger and better-armed Marine Corps, enthused with the old-time spirit, and it will be easier to sleep nights.

In "our war" we put the regimental band ashore at Saipan and again at Tinian, and about 10 days later we brought them back. All eight or 10 of the survivors. But that first night, as we steamed toward Hawaii, they gave a concert on the fantail and when they closed with "The Hymn" there wasn't a dry eye on the ship. Ah, from the Halls of Montezuma to the Shores of Tripoli . . .

You don't dig it, you say? Well, it was difficult to understand, even then. How the Gyrenes have felt about their outfit has been a running mystery stretching over two centuries. There has always been something about those confounded people an outsider couldn't put his finger on. Meaner than a sackful of rattlesnakes—and in love with one another. Special. It was the only bunch I ever came across where the enlisted men ate before the officers. And yet the chain of command was inflexible. When the Old Man said jump, they jumped. And he jumped. Maybe that was it. He jumped, too. First.

One night on the trip home a little red-headed sergeant came to the yeoman's cubicle and I said to him, in effect, tell me about the Marines. And he said, I am not sure I can tell you about them, but maybe I can show you.

So we blindfolded him and he sat on the deck (!) and took his rifle apart, right down to the stock and the barrel, and we mixed the parts like stirring a cake and then he fumbled around and by "feel" he put the rifle together again, 50 or 60 or maybe even 100 nuts and bolts and assorted pieces, and when he was through he said, simply, that's part of the Marines for you.

He was not more than 20 years old and he had been through the Inferno, but he still believed in something. The United States Marines.

Thoughts for the Young

Having attained what is loosely called "maturity," does the Common Man possess any knowledge worth passing on to young people?

Probably not. Most of us learn only through wiggling out of small disasters, and how you escaped one in 1948 may not be relevant to how you should go about eluding one in 1971. Beyond that young people are resentful of those who try to tell them how to run their lives, and properly so. It is an important part of the process of living to surmount your own difficulties, and anyone who tries to interfere is an egotistical buttinski.

———————

Nevertheless, having started this chain of thought and being stuck with it, here are a few things I either would or wouldn't do if permitted to go around the track one more time.

1. I wouldn't buy anything I couldn't pay for within ten years. Not even a business or a house? Neither!

A business you cannot amortize within a decade, at least as far as the original investment is concerned, isn't worth the midnight oil you will burn in an effort to save it. If you can't make oodles of money in business, thus protecting yourself from changing conditions, shifting markets and the likelihood of fresh competition, for heaven's sake stay out of it and work for someone who can.

As for a house, at the end of a 25-year mortgage, let us say, the roof will probably be sagging, the fence will be falling down, the furnace will be on the Fritz and the neighborhood will have gone to pot. Then where are you? Broke in Hartford, as we used to say. In a very real sense, a householder is also in business, although few of us recognize this fact. Besides, if you will figure out how much a mortgage at six percent costs you over a protracted period, you will be so nauseated you won't be able to sign the contract. Hurrah for nausea.

2. I would recommend joining a political party at an early age and then fighting from within to seize it from the hands of the idiots who are currently running it.

Which political party? It doesn't make a bit of difference. Both of them are constantly in need of reform and either one is apt to sweep into power at the next election, so the dangers are equal and the opportunities for improvement likewise.

Working within a political party is the best way the Common Man has to insure a modicum of sanity in public affairs. He won't be able to accomplish much, granted, but anything is better than what we had two minutes ago.

In addition, politicians are fascinating people—some of them are even fun—if you are in a position to scare the wadding out of them every once in a while.

3. I would join a church and work from within, for some of the same reasons recommended in the political section of this tract, above.

4. Never—but never—would I sign anything without the advice of a lawyer, and preferably two, and I would never write a non-business letter to a lady toward whom I had other than the most pristine of intentions.

5. Under no circumstances would I keep a diary, for nine times out of ten those darned things come back to haunt you.

6. Every year I would take $500 and either bet it all on one horse or have a fling in the stock market, depending on which seemed the more promising at the moment. This would help disabuse you of the notion that there is a free lunch if you just go looking for it.

7. If I ever caught myself voting for a candidate who promised to lower taxes and increase spending, I would make an immediate appointment with a head shrinker.

8. As soon as possible I would start giving money to charity, depending on someone like Msgr. Clement Kern to decide where it should go.

9. When I could no longer play golf from a handicap of 10, I would hope to have sense enough to quit.

10. And I would never look back on life, never regret a moment of it, and to young people I would say, only: "You do likewise!"

The Missing Course

Before the plumber came, the toilet in the lavatory off the den had a bad case of post-nasal drip. "Tweedle—zinkle—gurgle—biddle—tweedle," it would go after we had flushed it, followed by "cloinky—dripple—groany—gurgle—weepy."

Over and over, with nerve-wracking persistence, until you went back and jiggled the handle. Then it would emit a mighty sigh and die a thousand gasping deaths. Very disturbing to television reception, especially when you were listening to the weather report. Did the man predict rain or snow, hail or shine? Who could say for sure?

After the plumber had gone, leaving behind $15 worth of new parts, the melody changed, "Zoink," it would say, "zinkity—zank—zoink—zoink." Once more to jiggling the handle and once more a thousand deaths. It got so we would walk a flight of stairs to avoid the discord and low-decibeled clanging.

Then, about a week ago, the lady of the house made a golden find while engaged in a shopping expedition. She came upon a Daisy natural rubber Tank Ball, with solid copper Rust-Proof Stem, produced by the Schacht Rubber Mfg. Company, Inc., of Huntington, Ind. Price, 51 cents. It was one of the greatest discoveries since oil in Pennsylvania.

We inserted the new Tank Ball and Rust-Proof stem the other evening, with your commentator working in cold water up to his elbows while the necessary detachments and attachments were made. Then it was necessary to fashion what you might call a "union link" out of a piece of coat hanger, connecting the loop at the top of the Rust-Proof Stem to the end of the flushing lever. A whole column could be devoted to the vagaries of toilet tank manufacturers whose lack of precision makes the hand-fashioned "union link" necessary, but let's not get into that. Suffice it to say that the link we replaced looked as though it had survived a fight between a Sherman tank and a battery of howitzers, so evidently previous owners had experienced a bit of difficulty, too.

The project finished, it was time for quality control, as they say in the automobile industry. So we flushed it. The water ran out; and water ran in. Steady, even cycles, both ways. Then silence. Gone was the "zoink-zinkity-zank-zoink-zoink." Just pure, pristine silence. It was eerie, actually, but we hope to get used to it.

All of this is sort of a prelude to the observation that the most useful citizen in our neighborhood is a sprightly retiree by the name of Adrian H. Cousino. Without him, some of us would wind up in debtor's prison.

Mr. Cousino—at our house we wouldn't think of calling him "Adrian"—is a quiet, serene man with many years of service at the Ford Motor Co. and with World War I under his belt. He is a fine companion under any circumstances, and in moments of emergency he is priceless.

For Mr. Cousino is that rare urbanite who can keep things running. He can replace a light switch; jolly the furnace back into operation; mend the downspouts; patch a screen door; or mix a batch of concrete. No crisis overwhelms him and few exceed his capabilities. He also keeps a small compost pile in his backyard, which explains why he has the best lawn in the block.

He can, in short, "work with his hands," and for him householding has no terrors. His advice and assistance are sought far and wide, so he leads a happy and busy life, beholden to neither plumber, nor electrician, nor stonemason, nor tinsmith. He is a free man, one of the few of this acquaintance.

Much has been written about the joys of home ownership—so much, in fact, that one hesitates to thrash against the tide. Still, the truth is that unless someone in the family is a fixer-upper of considerable skill and daring, deed-holding can be a pain in the neck as well as a pain in the wallet.

What the country needs, of course, are more citizens with the dexterity of Mr. Cousino. How do we get them? Why, we start training them at a tender age.

No student should be permitted a high school degree until he or she has completed a course in home repairs. This would do the country much more good than additional emphasis on foreign languages or speed reading. The happy family has a sink that runs, a toilet that flushes and a coffee pot that percolates. Think that over, Mister Educator, the next time you wonder what you should be doing to prepare Young America for a more blissful future.

Anyone for Nutting?

Aside from football, which was our meat and drink in the days of which this is a memory, there was something to be said in the early fall for going nutting.

After the leaves had turned, a tramp through the woods awakened an appreciation for beauty in even the most bumpkinish of us. We might have experienced difficulty in putting into words our reaction to a maple tree smitten by light frost, but it was lovely to see, nonetheless, and since when have you needed the gift of gab to be in favor of nature's handiwork?

Anyhow . . .

. . . beyond the beauty of the woods in autumn there was the prospect of a bushel or so of walnuts and/or hickory nuts stored away against the winter's need, and that was all the incentive any red-blooded, constantly-hungry American boy needed.

For either straight-away eating, or as additives in candy or cake, there has never been anything the equal of a hickory nut or a walnut you fetched home with your own hands. I do declare that the very thought of a piece of homemade chocolate candy, teeming with nut meats, makes the slobbers run down my chinny-chin-chin. Oh, the ecstasy of it all! True, too many hickory nuts or walnuts would give you canker sores in your mouth, but you had to take the bitter with the sweet, as the feller said.

Anyhow, of a bright and crisp morning, with the frost still sparkling on the grass, you would set forth for the woods, burlap bag in hand. The chances are you had spotted some trees weeks earlier, while picnicking in the woods. If not, you would head back to where fortune had smiled in years past, in the hope of being lucky once more. For sure, you would find some nuts; most years, they were plentiful.

Right enough, you came upon a clump of walnut trees at the far edge of the woods, and the ground was covered with the season's bountiful crop. It was a matter, then, of picking and choosing, of selecting the most likely offerings and of filling your sack half-full, leaving room for the hickory nuts you also desired.

These latter trees you found after a meandering walk, and sometimes you had to throw a club into the branches to dislodge the hickory nuts. Again came the luxury of selection, of accepting and rejecting, and then it was time to head home to complete the day's work.

This consisted of shucking the hickory nuts, which was relatively easy, and of hulling the walnuts, which was a pain in the neck. Walnut stain would stay on your hands for two weeks, resisting the strongest of soaps and the most persistent of scrubbings.

However, hulling was simplified if you could run the walnuts through a corn sheller. The kid who discovered this was considered a genius and it was said of him that he would certainly become an inventor of note. He didn't. He became a gandy dancer on the Wabash Railroad, which offered steady work.

After . . .

. . . you had removed the last of the outer wrappings, so to speak, you spread the walnuts and the hickory nuts out to dry, leaving them for maybe two weeks. Then you put them in baskets and stashed them in the attic where it was warm and dry.

Then, along about the middle of November, a great light would flash through your head one early evening and you would say— "Hey, Mom, how about some chocolate candy with walnuts?" How sweet it was! Or maybe some afternoon you would come home from school and there would be a cake as big around as a wash tub with carmel frosting sprinkled with hickory nuts. Holy Toledo!

A handful of walnut meats scattered through a batch of Jell-O made all the difference in the world, while hickory nuts gave pudding of any kind a shot in the arm, you might say.

Nothing paid more dividends than a day of nutting, as you can see, and if I knew a friendly farmer I would go right now.

The Symbol of Kennedy

The period of official mourning for John Fitzgerald Kennedy has ended and now Old Glory has been returned to full staff.

From this office, looking south along Washington Boulevard, you can see the flag at Cobo Hall snapping and fluttering in the breeze, a bright and brave splotch of color against an overcast sky. You watch it for a few moments and you say to yourself: "Good! . . . We can't live in the past forever. . . . We must look to the future. . . . "

But still the haunting love affair involving the memory of Jack Kennedy and the American people goes on and on. Do you know anyone who has been able to accept the "reality" of his death? I don't. It is as though we had been subjected to a mass nightmare, which will end tomorrow morning, surely.

This is all very strange inasmuch as Mr. Kennedy was elected by a very short whisker in 1960, and thereafter became one of our most "controversial" presidents.

He was in hot water with someone most of the time: there was scarcely a month during his three years when he was not embroiled

with the Russians, or Congress, or Fidel Castro, or the segrega-
tionists, or the far right, or a reluctant ally.

———

It varied as to "what he couldn't carry in 1964." Some people
said he "couldn't carry the South," while others proclaimed that he
"was in difficulty in the West." There were times when even Michigan was "doubtful," or so it seemed. A state official, who shall remain nameless, told me shortly after the assassination that "I had
been receiving dozens of letters from suburbanites complaining of
his civil rights program. He was in trouble in some sections of
Wayne County. . . . "

Was he, actually? One wonders. It could have been, rather, that
many people saw in Jack Kennedy the symbol of intelligent opposition. He was a man you could argue with, or against, heatedly,
even violently, and yet retain full respect for him.

I think he would have won in 1964 "going away," as they say at
the race track, for when that young fellow got on the TV and
pounded the podium, and pointed his finger right smack at you—
well, he was mighty effective. I shudder to think what he would
have done to one or two of the candidates who were mentioned by
the Republicans as "hopefuls."

———

But we digress. . . . There is still the matter of the love affair. . . .

When his face is shown on television, or when his voice is trans-
mitted across the land, there is a poignant remembrance not just of
a man, but of an era.

This was the youngest elected President we had ever had, a
leader entirely of this century, and he came along at a time when
America was growing a bit fat around the middle.

There had been eight years of Ike, God love him, of the old shoe
approach to problems at home and abroad, and then—zoom! The
young fellow started talking, and shaming us and infuriating us,
and all at once America was the place where they were talking politics and issues and people from the salons to the saloons, literally.
We hadn't seen or heard anything like it since 1933, and even that
was different.

It was different because of the young fellow, who said "vigah," and "Cuber," and "Latin Americer" and things like that, all the time pointing that finger, shaming, shaming, shaming. You felt the back of your neck if you didn't try to live up to SOMETHING. . . .

Well, the flag is back at full staff, the official mourning is ended, we shall never mention this subject again in this column. As they say in the Army: Eyes Front! Forward March. . . .

THREE
On the Home Front

Well, Son

There is a letter here, doctor, from a young man who says he does not understand his father.

(So what else is new, Arn? So he thinks he's unique, maybe? So what's his beef against his old man, who ought to slough him across the mouth, probably? . . .)

Well, doctor, what this young man has with his father isn't a beef, really. It is more like a puzzlement or an inability to identify. It is not quite a breakdown in communications, but it borders on it. Perhaps you would like to hear excerpts from the letter?

(Not necessarily, but go ahead . . .)

"My father is in his early fifties," the young man writes, "while "I have just reached twenty-five. We have always been quite close—one reason being that I am the only son—and it goes without saying that I love him very much.

"However, of recent years, the last two or three in particular, he has developed what seems to me to be a very narrow attitude. Whenever I try to talk with him about current events or the people involved in them, he invariably drags in something or somebody from his generation and makes a comparison unfavorable to mine.

"If I mention The Supremes, for example, he will snort and tell me that I should have heard the Andrews Sisters when they were in their prime. If we get to talking baseball and I praise Willie Mays or Al Kaline, he breaks in to say sure, sure, but you should have seen Joe DiMaggio or Ducky Medwick.

"It is the same way in politics, literature, music—anything in my generation can do, his generation did better. This is very trying, and I am wondering if there is anything you can suggest that I might do about it? Sincerely, James L. . . . ."

There You Have It . . .

. . . doctor, the whole story of the young man who is growing weary of being put down by his pater. Do you have any advice for him? Free, of course.

(The only time you ever come around here, Arn, is when you want something for nothing. How do you expect us psychiatrists to keep up with the obstetricians if we give it away? I haven't had a new Cadillac since February and the neighbors are starting to talk. Worse than that, my wife is encouraging them. Money, money.

(The trouble between that father and son, Arn, is that the old boy is suffering from the Golden Era Syndrome. He lived his most fruitful and impressive years during a time in our history when greatness was rampant, and I doubt if he ever adjusts to modern circumstances. He sounds as though he is rather strong-minded, and that's the worst type when the Golden Era Syndrome hits them.

(You take popular music, for example. The father probably remembers Frankie Carle playing "Rose Room," and after he had heard that, and had dug it, as the saying goes, what was left to him? Elvis Presley? Fred Grimm?

(Or how about golf, Arn? The boy feels that Arnold Palmer is the king of the wheelers and dealers, what with his jet plane and such, but the father probably recalls Walter Hagen, who really had a touch of class. He used to show up at a snooty country club in a chauffeured limousine as long as a freight car, The Haig did and he lifted professional golfers out of the pool hustler class and made them respectable. Walter Hagen could spend more money in a week than Palmer can earn in a year, then go out and shoot a 67 with wooden-shafted clubs and a ball with a cottage cheese center.

(The worst thing about the Golden Era Syndrome, Arn, is that there is no cut-off point. In other words, you are hooked on the whole spectrum of activities and those prominent in them. Red Grange, Joe Louis, Lou Gehrig, Odd McIntyre, Clark Gable, Bing Crosby . . .)

Yes, doctor . . .

(. . . W.C. Fields, Eddie Cantor, Al Jolson, Gary Cooper, Hank Greenberg, Will Rogers, Wiley Post, Jimmy Doolittle, Irving Berlin, Richard Byrd, Ted Husing . . . Don't interrupt me . . .)

Three Cheers for Pills

For a long time, perhaps even longer than donkey's years, the operator of this keyboard took no medicine whatsoever, not so much as an aspirin. His innards were as pure as the driven snow, to coin a phrase, and if ever he fell asleep at the wheel of a car (he did once) it was not because of licit drugs. O, those were the days, when hearts were young and gay and you could buy a fine pair of britches at Sears, Roebuck for less than five dollars.

Now the day starts, and ends, and is interrupted betimes by the taking of medicine. At last count, thanks to the invasion of a virus that the doctor prefers to honor by calling it an infection, the daily dosage had climbed to 10 pills, two of them the size of peach pits, four in the heavyweight category, the rest welterweights. Keeping track of when to take what is quite often a bungled chore, but somehow life goes on and the liver does not leap out of place and upset the whole gearbox.

Taking medicine has become a national assignment, and one would be pleased to hear from constituents who consider themselves in the championship class as pill swallowers. We can tell you in advance that unless you can beat 19, you are not going to win the title, for that is the daily intake of a friend who lives in the Bloomfield Hills area. His lovely wife acts as his computer and is forever standing in front of him with a glass of water and at least two capsules in hand. He admits that Michigan winters are hard on him, but he can't go to Florida because there isn't room in the car for all of his medicine and allied paraphernalia.

———

It is said, and one believes it, that we—meaning those of us still breathing in and breathing out—are the healthiest of All Americans, putting the likes of Daniel Boone, Old Hickory Jackson and Robert E. Lee in the shade. There are reasons for this.

If you will permit your doctor to tinker with you long enough, and expose you to an almost endless array of high-tech machinery, the chances are at least nine out of ten that he will discover what ails you. There may be times, when all the results are tabulated, that you will wish he hadn't been so dad-burned persistent and nosy, but more often than not you will be thankful for knowledge that will permit you to stay in this vale of tears for another few years. Some of us are critical of the lives we lead, but hush at the thought of the alternative. Some very thoughtful folks, including Eleanor Roosevelt, have been quizzical of the quality of life hereafter, if any. But who knows? This may be Hell, with Heaven to be anything that comes hereafter. For a whole lot of the world's unfortunates, it wouldn't take much to be an improvement.

———

One remembers being 12, lighting up third off a match—you should never do that!—jumping off a roof and breaking his left arm. It has been sensitive lately because of drizzly weather. But the thing was that the doctor had to set it three times, breaking it twice more, and what yelling that brought on, before he got it right.

Over the years, a number of friends died because of lockjaw, appendicitis, diphtheria, consumption, pneumonia and assorted other ailments that could now be handled in stride by the medical profession. Sometimes we give the doctors Hail Columbia for what they still can't do, such as heading off arthritis or lumbago, but if you have been around since the end of World War II, you have been the beneficiary of miracles in medicine.

One even knows a doctor who advocates a bit of drinking now and then. What more could you want this side of the Blue Yonder?

Soaked at the Source

Some things learned during a lifetime, including a wasted youth (Part II) . . .

1. The supposition that Big Business is being taxed to its knees is piffle, pure and simple. Corporations generate huge tax returns for government at all levels, but this does not necessarily mean that they are being bled white by the IRS and satellites.

In 1976, as an illustration, General Motors had world-wide revenue of 47.1 billion dollars, with profits of 2.9 billion. How were the receipts from sales distributed?

Well, depreciation accounted for 2 percent; use in business required 2.7 percent; stockholders received 3.4 percent; employes were paid 32.4 percent, and payments to suppliers amounted to 51 percent. The slice of the pie reserved for taxes amounted to only 8.5 percent. (Note: These figures come from "GM 1977 Information Handbook," just released to the news media.)

Government was enriched, of course, by the taxes levied on dividends to stockholders, wages to workers and profits realized by suppliers. The easiest and surest taxes came from the employes, who were "soaked at the source."

2. The advantage women have held in length of life will be lost, it says here, when they become fully involved in business and industry. Homemaking may not be one of the more exciting or glamorous pursuits, but it exacts less wear and tear on the constitution than the daily rat race. Incidentally, the heroine of our times may well be the working wife, who manages to keep both boss and husband under control. How she does it is a miracle beyond the savvy of yours truly.

3. Given a rerun of his life and times, your commentator would follow an early instinct and become connected with baseball, even

as an umpire. While the game has been deteriorating in recent years, there is still the feeling that Jimmy Campbell, general manager of the Tigers, has the most fascinating job in Detroit.

4. The "science" with the largest feet of clay is meteorology. Weather forecasting doesn't seem to have improved one iota in 20 years, although admittedly this attitude may have been prompted by the recent experience of being caught on a golf course in a pelting rain after a promise of "sunny and clear." Unless you are bald and wear spectacles, the rain in Spain holds no pain.

5. It is disturbing how many ailments common five or six decades ago are still prevalent and without cure. Rheumatism, the "simple" cold, lumbago, arthritis, ingrown toenails(!), influenza, high and low blood pressure, sore throat, tendonitis, catarrh (how long has it been since you heard catarrh instead of sinus trouble?), bone spurs, fallen arches, sugar diabetes—shoot, modern medicine is just getting warmed-up to meet the challenges which have been around since bleeding was abandoned as a standard practice.

6. The first World War produced enough bad generalship to last humanity into eternity.

7. Civilization would have been better off without the jet engine, atomic energy, television, rock'n'roll, pornography, the sack dress and 535 congressmen.

8. It is impossible for the average duffer to cure a slice in golf without developing a hook. And vice versa.

9. Soapy Williams stirred the natives, pro and con, more than any other governor in Michigan's history.

10. We are still waiting to see and hear a lefthanded violinist!

No Wedding Bells

Of recent weeks your commentator has been a spectator at two weddings, one of the High Methodist variety, with a female vocalist, a full pipe organ and communion after the knot had been tied; and one with less ritual inasmuch as the Protestant bridegroom was fetched into a Catholic sanctuary, which tones things down a bit.

Both were lovely and memorable ceremonies for the principal participants, with receptions thereafter. The Methodists stuck to fruit punch without music while in the other case the father of the bride popped for some Old Slippery Elm and a string band.

Well . . .

. . . there are probably 40 different ways to get married, as the fellow said, with the form of the ceremony meaning a good deal less in the long run than the significance of the vows.

If you want to push this a bit farther, you might observe that some of the fanciest of weddings have wound up in the juiciest of divorces, while some who started out with a $2 license, a $5 ring and a justice-of-the-peace office with mottled wallpaper went all the way, loving, honoring and cherishing. You never can tell . . .

But let us not delve into the joys or the pitfalls of matrimony. Instead, let us lament the fact that you don't see or hear any "bellings" these days. They throw a little rice as the young couple depart on honeymoon, then the guests return to sampling the reception. Heavens, dearie, I can remember when they threw everything the could get their hands on, including the bridegroom into the horse trough if he was not fast afoot.

The last belling of this recollection occurred about 30 years ago in Ohio, and honesty demands that it be called a mild affair by stern standards.

Our printer was finally hitched after having eluded nuptial bliss, ha, ha, until he was well into his thirties, and all they did to him was haul him around town for about a half-hour in a cattle truck. When the bride took to sniffling, they put her in the truck, too, and then they stood there in a warm embrace, lurching and counterbalancing, as the driver zoomed up and down the main drag, claxon sounding. Very touching, but it was a low-grade belling, really.

Much better ones had occurred some years earlier when there were threshing machines to be borrowed. If you got up a head of steam in a threshing machine and then tied the whistle down, everybody within 20 miles knew that something important had happened and they came to town posthaste.

A big circular saw, suspended from the limb of a tree and struck vigorously with a sledge hammer, also shattered the calm of the countryside and chased away any evil spirits which might be lurking in the bushes. Noise was essential at a belling, being as complimentary to the young couple as applause is to an actor, but there was an unwritten rule that no one would show up with a shotgun, ha, ha.

When the news got around that two of our citizens had agreed to honor and obey, through sickness and health and all the rest of that rigamorole, a concensus would be reached on the appropriate evening for the belling.

First Off...

... all the kids in town would assemble in front of the house where the newlyweds were staying and they would raise such a din and clatter as to frighten the birds and set the dogs to howling and the cows to mooing.

After a while the bridegroom would come out on the porch, a silly grin on his face, and he would either pass out the treats which had been stashed away for this occasion, or he would send everybody down to the drug store for an ice cream sody.

With the kids out of the way, the older folks took over the belling, and some times it got pretty rough. There were bridegrooms who didn't want to ride in the cattle truck, but they always did, prone or upright, their choice. This done, there would be something to eat and maybe a dollop of Old Slippery Elm, and everybody would live happily ever afterwards.

Breaking Big Bread

Dear Boss...

Your memo—"What did you do with the two hundred bucks?"— was on my desk, big as life and twice as sassy, when I returned from Canada Monday morning, so this will be an account of what happened the night we broke bread at Cobo Hall with Dear Ol' Lyndon.

As you doubtless remember, the tickets were $100 per single copy, cash on the barrelhead, so in reality we blew the whole bankroll before we even got into where the orchestra was playing. I had hoped to share an intimate cocktail with the President, for sometimes you get to know a man better under those relaxed circumstances, but I couldn't get near him.

The reason why I couldn't get near him, Boss, was because they were having the cocktail party in a different place—at $1,000 a snort, also cash on the barrelhead. Did you know that before you told me to go mingle with Lyndon? Something tells me you did.

You will note, Boss, that there have already been two references to "cash on the Barrelhead." Man, those Democrats weren't giving the time of night away while the President was in town.

It got so I was afraid to look at Lady Bird, for fear a precinct committeeman would come around and charge me extra. The Democrats may give a lot of money away when they control the Congress, but when they are trying to fatten up their campaign kitty, they can wring blood out of a turnip.

We had never eaten at a $100 per plate spread before, so all day long we stayed in training for it, subsisting on water and soda crackers. By seven o'clock, when the waitresses began to show slight signs of life, I could have eaten an 800 pound steer, single handed.

You Know How . . .

. . . you build yourself up for big deals, Boss? Well, sir, on the way down that evening I reached an agreement with the Girl Friend. I would give her my Baked Alaska if she would give me her Shrimp cocktail. We decided, too, that we would take the left-over steak—we couldn't possibly eat it all!—home to Toby, the Welch Terrier. Oh, boy: bring on the victuals!

So what happened? Boss, you won 't believe it, but those chintzy Democrats opened with a fruit cocktail. No fooling. A common, plain, ordinary, straight-up-and-down fruit cocktail.

No wonder the President came in late. And then they gave us what you expect when you get a fruit cocktail first—roast beef with string beans, the regular Blue Plate Special. Poor old Toby ate dog-food late that night.

But I am getting a little ahead of the story. Before the Blue Plate Special, the Democrats staged the Grand Entrance for their stalwarts. This was quite a production. Gus Scholle, the labor tycoon, would come stomping up this special aisle, see, looking as modest as a man possibly could under the circumstances, and all the Democrats would leap to their feet, yelling hooray and clapping their hands. You would have thought they hadn't seen Gus since the Spanish-American War.

They Kept . . .

. . . repeating this, for Walter Reuther, Soapy WIlliams, Neil Stabler, John Swainson, Jim Hare, John Mackie, one after another, until the fruit cocktail got warm. One thing about the Democrats, they aren't going to spring any new faces on an unsuspecting public this fall. They have the Old Team ready for the scrimmage.

That's about the way it went all evening, Boss, which isn't much for your 200 clams, so maybe I'd better itemize it out for you:

For Blue Plate Specials, $6.00; for hearing the music, $1.60; for seeing Gus Scholle, Walter Reuther, Jim Hare and John Mackei, $4.00 (total); for seeing and hearing John Swainson, $2.40; for seeing and hearing Neil Staebler, $3.00; for seeing and hearing Soapy Williams, $5.00; for seeing and hearing Lady Bird, $29.50; and for seeing and hearing Dear Ol' Lyndon, $148.50.

We thank you, Boss.

American Birthrights

If a young friend can keep it all together through the weekend he will pass his final examinations and receive his driver's license. Thereafter, the thrill of the open road. O to be young again, and in love with the Ramrod Eight!

I have been trying to remember how we learned to drive back in those dear, dim days before the schools took over such instruction. Mostly by observing the Old Man, as I recall, and by being permitted to slip behind the wheel when we came to a long stretch of country road. He sat beside you, nervous as a cat in a bird sanctuary, ready to grab the steering wheel in the slightest emergency, offering constant commentary on the pitfalls of wool-gathering and speed. Pay attention to what you are doing, he would say, and don't go so dadblasted fast.

What was fast? Well, once I came down a gentle grade at 20 miles an hour, and he like to had a fit with a bell on it. That lecture lasted for at least three miles, hill and dale, and it must have made an impression because I still remember it.

The neat trick in those days—the real test of dexterity—was to shift gears without clashing. We had an Overland touring car approximately the length and heft of today's White House limousine, powered by a four-cylinder engine that might have weighed 800 pounds. Man, they don't hardly build them like that anymore.

Anyhow, to get through the cycle—from first, to second and into high—without causing a nerve-shattering racket worthy of a small train wreck was an accomplishment of some consequence. We had a lady in Our Town who could clash her gears with the best of them. We could be playing baseball, for example, and tell when Mrs. Hatcher, as we shall call her, was starting out for a drive. It was a sound of shattering and tearing, of ripping and sundering I cannot put into words, but the memory of it shreds my fibers to this very moment. Holy Toledo!

The Overland at about 12 (my age) presented another problem in that when you settled into the hand-tooled leather seat behind the massive steering wheel, you had trouble seeing the road. You sort of sat on the end of your spine, back and neck as stiff as a board, and felt your way along, hoping for a paucity of on-coming traffic. What would have happened on a modern expressway is too ghastly to contemplate, which is probably the principal reason the schools are now featuring driver's training.

Learning to drive, cold-turkey, under today's conditions is difficult for an adult, as a family experience indicates. About two years ago a sister in Kentucky who had never owned or driven a car won one in a raffle and determined to keep it, advice to the contrary notwithstanding. It took her 18 months to win clearance from the Highway Patrol, which displayed admirable patience throughout the ordeal. Backing was her weak point. She would pass the early test up to the place where she had to reverse between a couple of barrels, then chaos would result. But she stuck with it and now she tools around Greenup County with elan, as the French put it, enjoying the flora and the fauna in all seasons.

———

Today you could not get that car away from Sis without a court order, which makes her typical of Americans at large. I alternate between laughing and shuddering whenever someone says we must reduce car ownership for one reason or another. The laugh is because I don't think people would put up with it; and the shudder is because even if you forced them into it, what would happen to our economy?

Take automobiles off the highways in any large percentage and you would bring on such a recession as to knock the whole system galley-west. What would happen to the motels, service stations, restaurants, tourist attractions and car washes, just to mention a few of the enterprises dependent on the passenger car? We need cleaner, safer and perhaps smaller autos, but anyone who has it in mind to de-wheel America had better make an early appointment with his shrink. Further, if you think the Nixon administration is in trouble because of Watergate, just wait and see what happens if we blunder into an acute gasoline shortage. Hoo, boy.

Meanwhile, happy motoring to one and all, young and old. And bring 'em back alive.

Beating the Dates Rap

A friend came hurtling into this cubicle a few days ago, pursued by the devil Forgetfulness, his happiness hanging by a thread, his Home Sweet Home about to dissolve around his ears, chaos but an hour away.

It was his 15th wedding anniversary and he had just remembered it, the Great Truth coming like a flash of light in the midst of a busy day, nearly blinding him, almost paralyzing him, leaving him with the quivers and shakes as though he had come within an inch of falling off Mt. Everest. There were 60 minutes of shopping time left at the store where he has a charge account.

"What shall I give her?," he demanded, throwing the entire burden of his predicament on my innocent shoulders.

"What does she want?," I asked.

"Don't be silly," he yelled. "She wants a mink stole. But what can I give her and have a legitimate excuse for it? What's traditional?"

I had no idea, so we looked it up. It turned out he could get away with crystal, so he tore over to the business district and bought her a bowl of sorts. Later, he reported it went off pretty well.

Since Then . . .

. . . it has occurred to me that other husbands, being but mere mortals, may also face a similar dilemma; so as an extra, added feature, at no increase in cost, as another way of keeping you on top of the world in the morning, not to mention the afternoons and evenings, I have decided to print the accepted list of traditional wedding anniversary gifts, as follows:

First, paper; second, cotton; third, leather; fourth, fruit; fifth, wood; sixth, candy; seventh, wool; eighth, pottery; ninth, willow; 10th, tin; 11th, steel; 12th, silk; 13th, lace; 14th, ivory; 15th, crystal; 20th, china; 25th, silver; 30th, pearl; 35th, coral; 40th, ruby; 45th, sapphire; 50th, golden; 75th, diamond.

The book also offers this sterling advice: "All wedding anniversaries are 'flower' anniversaries in that thoughtful husbands are more or less expected to send a dozen roses on the occasion of each anniversary until the accumulation of years makes a single rose for each year a respectable floral offering. All wedding anniversaries are important to all wives; and husbands who unfailingly remember them are deemed 'more precious than rubies—yea than fine rubies' . . . "

Well, that business about how you will come off looking better than a 'fine ruby' is something that has happened to mighty few of us, believe me, but I am a great believer in the absolute necessity of remembering all important dates, like birthdays and such. How you remember them is something else again.

The Wisest Man . . .

. . . I ever knew was my Uncle John, who spent 60 years "in the harness," as they used to call being married, and one day I asked him, Uncle John, how do you remember all the dates, like birthdays and such?

And he said to me, Son, that's impossible, no man occupied with making a living for his wife and kids can possibly remember all those dates, so I'll tell you what I do. If I go home and things seem cooler than usual, meaning if it is like someone had left the door of a mausoleum open in the dead of winter—you ever been in a mausoleum in February, Son?—why right off I know I have forgotten again.

So I go back downtown, Son, and I buy a present, it doesn't make much difference what, and I take it home, acting as though I was just arriving for the first time, and I hand it to her and I say. Happy Anniversary, Sweetheart. Nine tenths of the time it works, Son, and that's about as good as you can do in this vale of tears, Son, he said.

Frederick X. Hustle

A Fable of Sorts . . .

The fiscal year of the Amalgamated Post Hole Co. having ended early in August 1979, the board of directors convened in Owosso to cut the melon. They also faced the responsibility of naming a chairman and chief executive officer to replace Julius K. Slant, who was retired after 42 years at the helm.

"I am pleased to tell you," Mr. Slant said in his final report to the board, "that we have the competition on the run. As the result of the development of our triple-headed diggers, we can now drill more post holes in an hour than any other company in the country. We are known far and wide for our efficiency and fair dealing, and we haven't had a strike since 1972, when we finally convinced the union that the use of power equipment instead of manual diggers would be good for all concerned."

He also told the board that the company had earned $2.27 a share during the year; that the stock was holding firm at $14 on the New York exchange; that advance orders for 1980 were promising and that company assets, including cash on hand, amounted to $31,762,456.84.

Whereupon Mr. Slant took his departure, leaving the meeting in the charge of Frederick X. Hustle, his assistant and obvious successor.

———•••——— ———•••———

A few words about Mr. Hustle are in order.

He had joined Amalgamated Post Hole in 1975 after receiving a law degree from Yale, a master's in public relations from Pennsylvania and a doctorate in psychology from Wisconsin. He had served the Department of Health, Education and Welfare as an assistant secretary, but had resigned when his superiors refused to finance a program to provide every Eskimo family with a butane refrigerator. Under Julius K. Slant he had readily mastered the rudiments of the post hole industry and had successfully hidden the fact that deep inside he burned to set the business world ablaze. Now that he had the ball, he meant to run with it, pell mell.

"Gentlemen," he told the board after he had been elected chairman and chief executive officer, "it is time we hauled this company out of the horse-and-buggy age and put it on the expressway, varrooomm. Here we are with $31,762,456.84 in assets, and what are we going to do with it? Dig more post holes! What's the future in that? . . . "

A board member interrupted. "What do you have in mind?"

———•••——— ———•••———

Mr. Hustle was ready for him. "I think," he said, "that we ought to follow the national trend and become a conglomerate. Spread our wings—diversify, get into mass marketing through TV, sell something that the common man wants. And as a starter, gentlemen, I am recommending deodorants."

Deodorants? The board was stunned.

"Deodorants," Mr. Hustle repeated. "Look, everybody in this country wants to smell like something other than a human being.

They want to smell like leather, or old tennis shoes, or withered wisteria, or algae on the creek, or something. Obviously, the trend is back to nature because of all the kooky environmentalists, so let's go all the way. I know of a deodorant company we can buy for $20 million, and a bartender friend of mine has developed a scent we can call Muskrat Ramble. Think about it for a minute: come on home to Muskrat Ramble! It will knock 'em stiff . . . "

Yesterday, the board of directors of Amalgamated Post Hole held its 1980 meeting in Owosso. The directors brought sack lunches.

The company, Mr. Hustle told them, had lost $11 million during the fiscal year. There would be no dividend; the stock had fallen to $3.25 a share, and if you subtracted the $20 million spent for the deodorant company, the assets weren't worth a lawyer's time.

What happened, he explained, was that a competitor had come out with a scent called Foolish Foxes, "and it ate Muskrat Ramble alive."

But he had an answer. "We will borrow $100 million from the government." he said, "and save Amalgamated Post Hole." Cheers. He plans on running for president in 1984, for obviously the country needs a businessman in the White House.

It's Tonic Time

"Hiram," she would announce in those dear, dead days of yesteryear, "it is time for your spring tonic. Open your mouth."

"Aw, gee, Mom!"

"Open your mouth, mind you!"

So you would open your mouth, twisting your features into what you hoped was a look of absolute repugnance touched by terror, while standing on one foot, your hands clinched, your head turned and tilted—and in such a position, under such circumstances, you got your spring tonic.

Did it do any good? Heaven and the medical society know. However, despite your distaste for sulphur and molasses, or whatever the concoction consisted of, you believed it would be helpful, probably because she was unalterably convinced of it. In this life, confidence is at least 50 per cent of the battle.

Well, times have changed. Today, Junior is inoculated against everything but the jungle rot. Home remedies are frowned upon; there probably hasn't been a decent cup of sassafras tea brewed hereabouts in 30 years.

Why bother, when there is a commercial remedy for everything from housemaid's knee to tired blood? Sulphur and molasses, indeed.

Still, there is a tendency here to be old-fashioned. So without further ado, suffering constituents, you are going to receive a dose of Ol' Doc Arn's Spring Tonic For What's Wrong With Detroit and Michigan.

Open up!

For Just Once . . .

. . . let's stop worrying about the "poor downtrodden" long enough to do something worthwhile for the average citizen.

We have spent so much time and energy the past few years do-gooding and slavering over the have-nots that the whole State is getting a poor-mouth complex. We need a brightener, an uplifter, an act dedicated solely to the premise that Michigan is a grand place to live, only we are going to make it better.

What shall we do? Take a snort of Ol' Doc Arn's Spring Tonic— and lift the tolls on the Mackinac Bridge. Not because it "would be good for the Upper Peninsula." Not because it is wrong to have an economic barrier at the Straits of Mackinac.

But just because Michigan is better than any other State in the whole danged country and this is the way we show it!

We think big, we walk tall, we breath lung-straining blasts of the free, pure air—Michigan, my Michigan!

Open up!

In Detroit . . .

. . . there should be some sort of a program to hide the scars of the scorched earth urban renewal blast. Parts of this town look worse than Hamburg after a major R.A.F. raid.

A year ago, Mayor Jerry Cavanagh encouraged his Parks and Recreation people to plant rye, or some such, and there were scatterings of green stuff hither and yon. Can't this undertaking be expanded?

A few acres of corn in the Downtown area would be an improvement over the raw and tortured earth which presently meets the eye. Plant International Village to clover: do something!

It is a pity, too, the way the River Front goes to waste. Put John Patrick Casey on this project; perhaps he could do an encore of the wonderful work he accomplished when the Christmas Carnival was tossed in his lap. At least, it would keep him out of trouble with the press. Do something!

Paint up; clean up; plow and plant; beautify; stir up the State; galvanize the City; agitate the natives; titillate the tourists; walk tall; act big; get out of the rut; do something!

Have a gulp of Ol' Doc Arn's Spring Tonic. It rotates the eyeballs. It pivots the hormones. It electrifies the hair. It satisfies the ego. It makes you Think Big.

Open up!

It Stuck to the Ribs

All in a Lifetime . . .

As "escape literature"—or perhaps just for the pure joy of it!—I have been re-reading "Arundel," by Kenneth Roberts, first published in 1929 and received then with hurrahs by the critics. It deals with Indians, and the French, and the Tories, and Benedict Arnold and the march into Canada—and it is the sort of thing this hack would give his right arm, elbow and all, to be able to write.

Anyhow, in "Arundel" you come early to the description of a supper served in a back-country inn, and Mr. Roberts wrote of it in this manner:

"The fire was made bright, the floor swept smooth and re-sanded; and Malary set on the table two pots of beans with a relish of chopped cucumbers steeped in brine and flavored with onions, and two haunches of venison, and brown bread hot from the oven, and butter fresh from the churn.

"Close beside the table, on wooden scissors, was a barrel of my mother's small beer, though I know not why they call it small, for scarce a man can drink a gallon of it without thickening in his speech. Also there were six mince pies laced with rum, and a bowl of creamy cheese made from sour milk. If I had been a rich man in those days I would have traveled far to enjoy such a meal as that; for good provender was hard to come by; and our inns were rightly called ordinaries, especially in the matter of their food, which was so coarse and grease-laden as to bring on heartburn or even apoplexy . . . "

Reading that late at night, I was suddenly seized amidships by the pangs of hunger, so I crawled out of bed and went down and raided the ice box; and upon returning I was struck by the thought that while our "ordinaries" haven't changed too much since Revolutionary times, our eating habits have. A gallon of small beer, indeed!

Or, for that matter, a breakfast such as we used to eat, indeed. Let us consider this for a moment . . .

My Aunt Em . . .

. . . who was Southern born and reared, made biscuits every morning of her married life, which extended beyond the Golden Anniversary. These (the biscuits) were so light and fluffy that you had to put your knife across them to keep them from floating off your plate, and if you ate less than eight, buttered and jammed, she would consider you ill and force a draught of herb juice down your gullet.

Simultaneously, my dear Aunt Flora, Southern born but Northern indoctrinated, looked upon breakfast as man's first confrontation with the trepidations of a long and difficult day, and she prepared you accordingly.

On the other hand, my Aunt May was known within a radius of 40 miles (this was before the telephone, in general use, and the

REA) for her pancakes, which were accompanied by syrup of her own tender concoction.

I can remember one morning when Cousin Ortis, possibly wishing to make conversation, said, "I have et 18," and Uncle Grant, hearing him, responded, "You have et enough." Thereafter, it became an unwritten rule of the house that you would not reveal how many you had et.

And Now . . .

. . . we come to my mother. God bless her, name of Claudia, who was famous for her rolled oats. These she cooked in the late of the evening, in what I recollect as a "double-boiler," and the process required several hours.

They would be served at breakfast, piping hot, with fresh milk, and it was true what she claimed for them: They stuck to your ribs.

How did we get into all of this? Oh, yes: Mr. Roberts, "Arundel," and the changes in eating habits. Too, I think I have written it because I am slowly starving to death. All I had for breakfast— "This is all I have time for, Baby"—was a cup of coffee. Methinks I have the vapors.

Up with Green People

Under my government, dear constituents, we would bring to a grinding halt all of the nonsense research that has been going on in outer space and under water, and concentrate on something really worth while.

What we would do on a crash basis is invent a pill that would turn everybody in the whole crazy world the same color, and then a good many of our troubles would be over.

Under this Universal Color Project, it wouldn't make any difference whether a young 'un was born white, black, red or yellow. As soon as the child was old enough to take nourishment in any form, which is mighty quick in most instances, we would simply pop a pill into its mouth.

And, presto, it would be the accepted shade for the rest of its natural born days, guaranteed not to fade or run in rain, sleet or snow.
For a dollar extra we would also include a guarantee against deterioration in the sauna bath, an offer which practically no one else
could make under any circumstances.

For the older folks, Universal Color Project would work in the
following manner.

There would be an International Pill Taking Time with clocks
and watches synchronized in every town, village, hamlet and city.
At the stroke of 0900 hours Greenwich, the mayor would shout
into a microphone—"Bottoms Up!" Instantly, everybody would
pop a pill into the old kisser and gulp. If anyone, such as Cassius
Clay, tried to resist the movement, we would sic the defensive line
of the Purdue Boilermakers on them. This project would be for
everybody at the same time—one man, one color, so to speak.

All right—what color? Now we come to the moment of heavy
thinking. What color, indeed?

The obvious colors, or the standards, as you might call them, are
out. It couldn't be black because that would make George Wallace
sore as a boil. It couldn't be white or Rap Brown would want to
burn something. It coundn't be red because then everybody would
start chasing the cowboys. It couldn't be yellow because if you said
to a chap in an offhand way, "Gee, you're sure yellow today," he
might revert to his old instincts and start a fight.

Just to be on the safe side, we would also outlaw all shades of
the standard colors. A good many diehard Republicans, for example, would be infuriated by pink. This is very tricky, a matter for
deep consideration, as you can readily see.

Wait a minute! Ol' Arn may have it. Yes, sir, this may be the
answer . . .

The other evening some friends who are rich, invited us over to
see their new color television set in action. As with most beginners,
they shunned the operating manual and staged the performance
freelance. I haven't seen so many colors on human beings since the

explosion in the sauerkraut, pickle and relish factory down in Liberty Center. Hoo, boy.

Once we even had four-colored people, which must be the world's record. When we went home, my eyes looked like the insides of one of those penny jawbreakers we used to buy at the Bee Hive.

Anyhow, at one point they got the set tuned in just right and then we had green people. Lovely. Just lovely. For it wasn't a desk blotter green, or a how-your-mouth-feels-in-the-morning green, but sort of a young apple green. I liked it very much.

So that is what we are going to use in the Universal Color Project—young apple green. It will be unique, it will be in tune with Mother Nature, it will give this tired old world a new and restful look.

And it will make us brothers. Not white brothers or black brothers, but young apple green brothers. If you live out in Dearborn, for example, and you want to invite Federal Judge Wade McCree for dinner, he will be able to arrive before dark and Orvie Hubbard won't know the difference.

He can even go for a swim in the pool if he likes.

Nothing will be too nice for good ol' Wade, or taboo, or frowned upon as white folks' fun, because he will be just as equal as all of the other young apple greens.

You will have to admit that this is one of the greatest projects ever conceived by the human mind. The Universal Color Project is total in design and effect. It will do away with the Urban League, the NAACP, the Ku Klux Klan and the White Citizens' Council.

Ladies and gentlemen, even the Pope will be in favor of this pill!

Break Out the Abacus

A friend will inherit $15,000 after taxes (or so he hopes!) from a dear aunt who is on the ragged edge of departing this vale of tears, and of late he has been playing that wonderful game known as "What Shall I Do With The Dough?"

For a while he leaned toward using it to pay off the mortgage on his split-level, but presently he is a victim of the old adage to the effect that a little knowledge is a dangerous thing. He can do just enough arithmetic to create the nagging fear that if he retires the loan he may wind up losing money.

"You have to look at it this way," he said the other day as we awaited lunch. "I am paying six per cent interest on my mortgage, which is approximately $15,000. In round figures it is costing me $900 a year. Right?"

Now, I'm a Wizard . . .

. . . at figures, as I will show you. The way to do a problem like this is to take 15, representing the mortgage of $15,000, and multiply it by six, which is the interest. Six times five is aught and you carry three: and six times one is six and you add three and that makes 90. Obviously, six times 15,000 has to be more than 90, so you add a zero and it comes out at 900, which is what the man said.

(Ed. note: Is this the new math, Arn?)

"Right," I told my friend. "She comes out at nine hundred bucks on the nose. I checked her."

"All right," he said, "so in the raw, it is costing me $900 to finance $15,000. Only you can't really figure it in the raw."

"Why can't you?" I demanded. "What's wrong with figuring it in the raw, for crying out loud?"

"Because the $900 is deductible," he answered. "When you pay interest you can take it off on your dad-blasted income tax. The more deductions you have, the less tax you pay. There's a blank space on the tax form where I can write in, "Interest, $900." They never squawk about it because I can prove it."

"Oh," I said.

"But what I can't figure out," he continued, "is how much of that $900 isn't in the raw. In other words, and this is where she gets tricky, if I wasn't paying that $900 in interest, how much more tax money would I be paying the Government because I didn't have a deduction? You get the problem?"

"I get it," I replied, "but I can't handle it. This sounds like why they invented computers."

"Well," he went on, "we have only covered half the bases. Let's suppose I take that $15,000 from dear Aunt Matilda and put it out at four per cent interest, which any bank in town will pay. How much money will she bring in?"

(Want to try the system again? Four times five is aught and you carry two; four times one is four and you add two which makes 60. About one more zero ought to do her.)

"Six hundred dollars?" I ventured.

"That's how I figure it," he agreed. "So under this setup I am making $600 and I am paying out $900, only the $900 isn't in the raw. There's the matter of the deduction, which we have already discussed.

"So the way it looks to me," he continued, "is that if I bring her in at four per cent and pay her out at six per cent. I will be breaking just about even. And that's all a patriotic American ought to try to do in these parlous times."

"What's patriotism got to do with your problem?" I asked.

He Was Shocked . . .

. . . speechless, but not for long. "Have you ever considered what would happen in this country if everybody paid off their mortgages and debts?" he demanded. "Overnight, the banks and loan companies would have money running out of their windows.

"No sir," he concluded, "we have a society funded on debt and I'm not going to disturb it. Maybe I should take Aunt Matilda's money and make a grand tour of Europe."

And that, I agreed, Would by true-blue patriotism.

The Newest Profession

Within this span of years a new profession has snuck into being, either infiltrating into a void, or first creating the void and then filling it, I'm not sure which; but today, anyhow, you have the Public Relations Man, and he's the guy who is having all the fun.

When I started chasing news for a living, and if I wanted to know something about, let us say, the Amalgamated Posthole Co.... maybe why it was moving its main plant from Three Fingers, Mich., to Gurgle, Neb.... why, you called up the works manager, or the president, and you asked him, hey, Elmer, what in the world's going on? And he either gave it to you straight or told you to mind your own danged business, depending on whether his breakfast was sitting level or had shifted to a downhill lie.

In Those Days, Too . . .

. . . the politicians dealt directly with the press, lying in their teeth as often as possible, it is true; but when you caught a chap with his hand in the public coffers you walked up to him and asked, Joe, why did you steal it?, and then it was just the two of you for it, with no mimeograph machine in between.

Well, as was noted in the beginning, all of this has now been changed, thanks to the advent of the Public Relations Man, who is everywhere; meaning that not just one of them is everywhere, but that there are hundreds of them everywhere, sleek and purring, in government, in business, in entertainment, like I said, everywhere.

It has reached the point where you can tell how important a fellow is by the number of Public Relations Men he has attached to him. If he has less than three, you can bet he isn't making the Vital Decisions. Heavens, in a big company the Top Executive won't even say good morning to the parking lot attendant without first clearing it with the Public Relations Department.

Besides being everywhere, what does the Public Relations Man do to earn his bed and board?

Well again, his duties are myriad. There is much more to it than just drinking eight dollar whisky and inking the mimeograph machine. There is more to it, even, than keeping reporters off the Old Man's back. A good Public Relations Man is artful in a number of directions, as well as foxy at all points of the compass, and when you think about what he does, and how, you wonder that the universe didn't collapse before he came along.

Let us go back to Elmer, the president of the Amalgamated Posthole Co., and presume that he was invited to make a speech before a combined meeting of the Optimist—Kiwanis—Rotary—Lions clubs at the American Legion Hall.

Twenty years ago, Elmer would have been pretty dull, to put it mildly. He would have stood up there and put everybody to sleep with a detailed account of how you dig a posthole. No imagination; no pizazz; no sense of history; no soft sell with overtones of sincerity.

In Contrast . . .

. . . when Elmer goes out to make a speech these days he is armed with a document prepared by his Public Relations Department. It touches on the history of postholing dating back to the pyramids; it relates the struggle postholers have had against federal intervention; it deals with the future of the business, which is bright, especially in the Midwest.

In addition to writing speeches, a Public Relations Man arranges things for a company, ranging from a plant tour by the Ladies Sewing Circle to a golf tournament at Warwick Hills. He supplies answers; he handles ticklish mail; he worries about The Image, and polishes it.

And he is taking over the world.

A Different, Softer Time

Diary of a Country Correspondent . . .

Uppen atem on a frizzly morning with the thermometer standing at 18 degrees and to thinking kindly, albeit briefly, of Florida. Only when the mercury is below 20 does the land of alligators and real estate hustlers benefit from a benevolent recognition at this outpost. Otherwise, let 'em stew in their own swamps and pickle rattlesnakes for appetizers.

Schultz attends his master to the paper box and it is noted that he trots as straight as an arrow, fore and aft pointed due north. Book says a well-bred weimaraner should not travel slaunch-ways, looking as though its hind end was out of gear, and our hero is as forthright as a U.S. gyrene on full dress parade. It is noted, however, that he is getting a paunch even though he is technically on a strict diet. What he does is eat his full allotment and then bum, bum, bum when food is on the table. Master may take to eating his meals in the bathroom with the door locked.

Speaking of food, dear diary, had turkey sandwich for lunch yesterday, will have turkey sandwich today and turkey sandwich tomorrow, no doubt. Perhaps when Second Coming occurs, Jesus will feed multitudes on turkey. It ought to be easier.

Fortunately, have ample supply of vegetable soup in larder, crock-potted by Bonnie Nelson on this recipe: Two pounds stew meat: 28-ounce can tomatoes; two carrots, sliced; three stalks celery with tops, sliced; two medium onions, diced; three cups water; one teaspoon salt; four peppercorns; three beef bouillon cubes; 10-ounce package frozen mixed vegetables. Cooked high for six hours.

Very, very good. Perhaps the leading soup of the year. But, then, this has been the weather for it. To best of knowledge Schultz has never had soup, and he is not going to get "tried out" now.

Last night finished James Michener's "Poland." Excellent novel, never a dull segment. Usually it takes Mr. Michener a while to get loosened up, but not in this case. He throws a high hard one in the opening chapter and never eases off.

Admit to buying most novels belatedly in paperback for good reason. They are much easier to read in bed in that form, and when you get sleepy you can simply crimp a page, drop book on floor and turn out the lights. Zooonnnk.

Here is something else you should read: "Alex: The Life of a Child," in the December Reader's Digest. It is by Frank Deford, perhaps known best of all to subscribers of Sports Illustrated, a splendid writer, and his account of his daughter's struggle to overcome cystic fibrosis is a classic love story. It is prose that travels the razor's edge of heartbreak without ever losing its balance.

Read! Encourage your children to read! There is much available that is totally worthwhile if you stay away from the sleaze deliberately pandered for the soap opera and the mini-series.

We are into a difficult season, the time between Thanksgiving and Christmas, laden with sentiment and difficult for a writer, even for a lowly writer of columns, to handle. If there is going to be any beauty at all in a year's passing this is the time for it to occur, with Mary and Joseph drawn toward Bethlehem, with the Wise Men impelled by a force they did not understand, with giving, helping, sacrificing in the hearts of God's children everywhere.

One does not profess "religion." One only knows that we are caught in a different, a softer, time.

The U.P.'s Champion

Their is a new book on the market entitled "Laughing Whitefish" and on the dust jacket designed by the people at McGraw-Hill the author's name is listed in inch-high type as "Robert Traver."

This, of course, is the pen-name of John D. Voelker, who is best known in Michigan as the former State Supreme Court justice who quit the bench to devote his full time to writing and trout fishing, not necessarily in that order. As "Robert Traver," the Judge scored a literary, motion picture and financial triumph with "Anatomy of a Murder", and since then he has been akin to the fellow they couldn't keep down on the farm after he'd seen Broadway.

"Laughing Whitefish" I recommend to you for several reasons, one of them being that no one writes of our Upper Peninsula with the feel and affection of John Voelker.

In All Seasons . . .

. . . he loves that great admixture of howling wilderness and casual civilization, and he writes with such sensitive skill that he can make you see the splendid side of a 14-inch blizzard. After having been ice-bound in Marquette for a day last winter, I had about given up on the UP as a place to visit after the Fourth of July, but the Judge's prose has restored my flagging faith in the beauties of the rugged life.

This is a book about an Indian girl, a young attorney and the legal battle to gain recognition of a Red Man's claim against a mining company. In the end the good guys win, which is wholesome if not necessarily true to life, and in the process the Judge teaches you a bit about the intricacies of the law. No one writes a better court room scene than John Voelker, thus demonstrating, perhaps, that there is no substitute for experience.

However, "Laughing Whitefish" is intriguing to this observer for another reason. For a long time I have wondered why so many people obtain law degrees and then either not practice a lick or quit in the middle of promising careers. Offhand, I can think of four prominent Detroiters who never approach the bar, professionally speaking, and now comes the Judge to tell me why they have not taken advantage of their years of long and difficult preparation.

" . . . I had come to suspect," he has his hero muse, "that the law was the great catch-all of the professions. It was the alluring beacon that beckoned those bewildered and uncertain individuals who didn't know precisely what to do. In these days, I reflected, a young man of good family could not become an artist or poet. People would simply laugh at him, and moreover who was there to teach him these arts, where was he to learn these subtle crafts? Almost naturally, it seemed, many of them turned in desperation to the law. More and more I was becoming convinced that the law attracted and harbored more dissatisfied dreamers, yearning malcontents and outright misfits in its ranks than any other trade or profession under the sun . . . "

The Judge's . . .

. . . hero was doing his "reflecting" before the turn of the century, it should be noted, but this one suspects that what was true then is even more so now.

As long as we have come this far with "Laughing Whitefish," we might as well permit John Voelker to close out with seasonal reports on the glories of the Upper Peninsula.

Summer: "All about him he could hear the hot click of crickets and grasshoppers shrilling their ancient rivalry. And high above everything rode that ancient queen of the skies, the full moon, pouring its pale light upon the parched and dusty earth . . . "

And winter: " . . . The heavier snowfall had abated, and large lazy flakes, glistening like suspended jewels, floated slowly earthward, occasionally, when caught by the wind, flashing and banking like snowbirds . . . "

That is what the Upper Peninsula means to those who know it and love it, and in John Voelker they have a willing spokesman whose work now attracts a wide and enthusiastic audience.

FOUR
Reports from Clangville

And Then There Was Irish

"Get me to the church on time . . . "

That is, of course, a line from "My Fair Lady," warbled by a chap who wasn't at all sure he could weather "the night before" celebration planned by chums. In real life, meaning as of the here and now, it is the assignment loaded on the Hon. Ross Annatoyn, a pal with wide experience in the intricacies of matrimony who hails from Livingston County.

Brother Annatoyn has survived a wedding in which he was one of the principal characters. He has twice been the father of the bride and is in training for that role once more come late December. He has married off a son, which is not always as easy as it sounds. His youngest daughter, a freshman at Michigan State, is pretty enough to have garnered at least eight proposals by New Year's. He doesn't drink silver bullets, the code name for martinis, except on special occasions; and for more than 30 years he has warmed a Catholic pew as a neutral from a Protestant upbringing. Where, oh where, could you find a sturdier soul to serve as the best man at your wedding?

———————

Thus, that will be his role this morning when the lovely lady known as Irish gives her hand in marriage (that's a sweet old-fashioned phrase, isn't it?) to the curmudgeon, with the ceremony under the jurisdiction of the Rev. James Sam at St. Beatrice Church, Southfield.

The curmudgeon will not have slept late; he will not have had enough to guzzle the past six months to foment one decent hangover. But he will have the jitters; he won't remember where he put the ring or whether he picked up the marriage license; and every once in a while he may blurt out, "So long, loneliness!" Ah, Brother Annatoyn, you shall earn a silver bullet this day.

Perhaps the most widely clipped column to come out of this typewriter in 15 years was titled "Loneliness is a companion who follows everywhere," printed in the editions of Sept. 27, 1983. Hardly a week passes but someone says, "I re-read it again last night, and thought I would write and tell you . . . "

There was this line: "This society is full of the walking wounded, those left behind to fend off the devil loneliness as best they can." Then finally, thank God, along came Irish, and one of those who was stumbling in the ranks was rescued.

Already a number of readers (and several editors) have asked for more information about her, but we are dealing with a very private lady who has no desire for the limelight. You may be told, however, that she is a native Detroiter out of the Dolan connection. She is very pretty and so fair of complexion that in the summertime you can scarcely tell where one freckle ends and the other begins. She is a Democrat, may the saints preserve her. Mercy College is her alma mater, and early on she gave serious thought to teaching. We argue a lot; pick your own subject. Her great ambition as a cook is to match her mother's macaroni and cheese, may the saints have another preserving left in their systems. She has a dog called Tilly, which she considers the most marvelous four-legged critter to walk the earth since Gen. Robert E. Lee's horse, Traveller—Schultz begging to differ. There should be very few dull moments in the townhouse we have been readying. Goodbye, loneliness.

It was a laugh, almost, when we went to see Father Sam, and he wondered about the curmudgeon's baptismal certificate. Would he accept an honorable discharge from the U.S. Navy? There was not even a birth certificate recorded in Greenup County, Ky.; years later it took the influence of Soapy Williams to organize a passport. Irish had lost track of her baptismal document, too, but the archives of the church prevailed and that wiped the smile off the devil's face.

So here we go. Stand strong and tall, Brother Annatoyn; remember that the ring is in your right coat pocket, may the saints preserve us one more time.

Add a Bit of Zest

Home on the Range . . .

The lady known as Irish goes to work each weekday, arising at the hideous hour of 6:30 and floundering about in such a piteous state that the curmudgeon also abandons his nest and fixes her breakfast. No greater love, etc.

She is content with prunes (previously prepared), whole wheat toast and weakened coffee. Thus fortified, she tackles the 18 miles of clink, clank and clunk that will lead to her downtown office, where on a fair day by craning her neck she can see a slice of the Detroit River through a corner window.

One would feel even sorrier for her except that she was born in the city, has always lived in the city and has come to believe that this is the way the world is supposed to run. She would not have appreciated the heated emotion of Henry David Thoreau, who cursed in his own refined way when a single railroad track finally connected Concord to Boston. Well, it is said that it takes all kinds to make the world, and that is no doubt a good thing.

———

As for the man of the house, left to his own devices, he writes these pieces, hauls them to the office, keeps an eye on the dogs, answers mail (he is about 150 cards and letters behind), does most of the grocery shopping, and is back to Crockpotting, even though he feels that he has lost his touch.

Somehow, what he cooks does not seem to have the old zing, the old smackeroo, even though his dear wife praises his efforts and says she would not trade him for a dozen shares of Al Neuharth. Perhaps he needs to do more freewheeling with ingredients, and less sticking to the ritual of recipes, which are usually on the side of blandville.

Such was the case, at least, with his one recent success, which started out to be 50 percent of the makings called for in shrimp creole.

———————

Here is how it went:

Chopped onions, three-quarters cup; chopped celery, one-quarter cup; diced green pepper, one-half cup; whole tomatoes, 14-ounce can; half-teaspoons of salt, pepper, sugar; three drops of Tabasco sauce; one-half pound of fresh shrimp.

Then for the innovating. Instead of four ounces of tomato sauce, I used eight. I added uncooked mushrooms, sliced; a fistful of bean sprouts, and six ounces of V8 juice. I cooked it on low for about eight hours, stirring occasionally and withholding shrimp until the last hour. By golly—had verve and bounce, it did, thanks in part to the V8, which is one of the great culinary inventions of our times. I have never tried it on ice cream or bananas but may do it one of these days.

———————

Readers have inquired of the curmudgeon: How do you like suburban life after nine years in the country? His reply is that it is just about a standoff.

The traffic you have been told about—it makes a dirt road mutilated by washouts and permanently in-grown chuckholes seem rather attractive in retrospect. This may surprise you: Undertaking commerce, meaning banking and most shopping in general, was easier and friendlier out there than here. This may change as one becomes better known in the institutions he frequents, but there is an abruptness, even a harshness, here that was unknown in the hinterlands.

Example: A few weeks ago a check for $416, drawn on a highly reputable firm, was submitted for handling. Please deposit $400, return the $16 in cash. Let me see your driver's license. For heaven's sake, why? Because you are receiving cash. That frosted the curmudgeon, especially since he has been trying for two months to get the same institution to handle all of his monthly income, but they can't seem to get the blasted computer programmed right.

The plus side is the availability of culture, or at least what passes for it in these strange and peculiar times. There are plays to be seen and movies to attend; the Art Institute is a solid attraction. There are more restaurants than your gizzard can handle, although few are as good all the way through the menu as Gus' in Howell.

City living has changed, and so has country living. It has become a question of what you can stand with the least strain over a period of time.

Out with the Old

New Year's Eve

Father Time won't stop for cheer
As he starts another year.
Not a break is ever felt
In his great conveyor belt
Where he adds the nuts and bolts
Giving life its joys and jolts.
We who ride this seamless way
Like to think we pause today . . .
This, the marker made by men,
Letting them begin again.

—Margaret Rorke

Once More from Clangville . . .

Each holiday season a torrent of greetings reaches this desk from around the state and many parts of the nation. Invariably there is at least one with a message bordering on priceless.

Sometimes it doesn't have a thing to do with Christmas except in the general sense of how to make it from January to December in this disjointed society we have created. That was the case this year.

The card arrived after Christmas from Tom Stewart, the golfer-politician who is back in Harbor Springs after an extended visit to

Russia. On the cover is reprinted W.H. Channing's creed, "My Symphony." Listen:

"To live content with small means; to seek elegance rather than luxury, and refinement rather than fashion; to be worthy, not respectable, and wealthy, not rich; to study hard, think quietly, talk gently, act frankly; to listen to stars and birds, to babes and sages with open heart: to bear all cheerfully, do all bravely, await occasions, hurry never. In other words, to let the spiritual, unbidden and unconscious, grow up through the common. This is to be my symphony . . . "

Play it again, Sam, especially that line about how you should "listen to stars and birds."

———

No tears will moisten these cheeks when midnight comes. Good riddance, I shall say, perhaps nailing the sentiment down with a martini, especially if neither wife nor doctor is watching. Deep in this much-abused bosom lurks the suspicion that 1986 was the year of the phony statistic, implanted with malice aforethought by the nefarious hirelings of a federal government bent on hiding the truth.

Do you believe the figures on unemployment, as an example? I don't because I am convinced that the "employed" include the underemployed, the half-employed and those who are so weary of the fruitless search for work that they no longer make the rounds of factories and offices.

Among the employed, how many are now flipping hamburgers or patting pizzas who once had well-paying employment in industries that have either merged or simply faded away? We have had an absolutely murderous violation of the anti-trust laws in recent years, leading to the point where industries no longer grow by expanding facilities—building new plants—but by conglomerating and consolidating, in the process reducing competition and lowering employment. Teddy Roosevelt was not quite the trust-buster the schoolbooks made him out to be, but at the very least we need someone at the head of government who will say, "Now wait a minute."

———

Do you believe the statistics on inflation? I don't. These have to be among the most expensive times in the nation's history for the common man on the basis of money earned and money spent, and the inflation figures are lower only because they are based on late-Carter, early-Reagan, when the cost of borrowed money zoomed out of sight. To buy a suit, a coat, an armload of groceries, a car, treatment for yourself or a pet, education, utilities, rent—remember what they say: "Figures don't lie, but liars figure."

More and more as this year has progressed, I have become convinced that we should elect presidents for one six-year term and then turn them loose on the verge of burnout. Senators should be limited to two terms and representatives to four. This government was not designed as a place of permanent employment on the elective side, yet that is what we have made of it in too many instances. Politicians and baseball players have this much in common: They want to make lifelong ease and comfort out of pursuits that were designed for short bursts of high energy and quick accomplishments. Jack Morris wants to be able to coast after he quits pitching, and so do most of the holdovers in Washington.

Wanted: A Massive Overhaul

Notes from Clangville . . .

Nature is merciful and marvelous. Warm weather and gentle winds have combined to blossom and fatten the trees that shield the view from this watchtower. As a result, there are only flashes of the endless traffic that bangs and clatters up and down Southfield Road, bound for God only knows where.

Noise has also been abated by the foliage, so one finds himself growing rather fond of this form of cliff dwelling, which he detested only a few months ago. Perhaps it is true: You can learn to like hanging if you hang long enough.

Anyhow, we plan improvements in our courtyard, which is approximately the size of one of J.P. McCarthy's overcoats (see below); and we intend to stay put, at least until the real estate market recovers from the hysteria that is causing it to shake, rattle and roll.

Holy mackerel, chicken coops with patios are going these days for a hundred grand, whilst the moneylenders and the real estate brokers wax portly. Two years ago they couldn't have sold the Taj Mahal on a land contract. Now homes are changing hands in this area before the first advertisement appears. It is like what we used to say about production line workers in Flint: feathers today, chicken tomorrow.

But don't get the idea that everything is perfect out here in Clangville. The streets in some of the fancier suburbs have potholes large enough to bust the axles of an armored vehicle; the community in which this outpost is situated has open storm sewers; and the Birmingham-Bloomfield Eccentric began its lead editorial in a recent edition in this manner: "Last year, a local couple went for a stroll along the Rouge River. The man accidentally fell in, swallowed some water and days later died . . . "

Almost every community in America, it seems, has some form of difficulty, so perhaps we had better not heave too many more rocks at Coleman Young's People Mover. He might get the silly thing moving, and then all he would have to do is find some people.

Seriously, what this country needs is a massive overhaul of what the bureaucrats call the infrastructure—streets, highways, bridges, public buildings, parks, waterways, the whole gamut of life-giving arteries upon which we depend for survival.

Bring back the old Public Works Administration or something akin to it. Offer jobs to able-bodied citizens at decent wages and with a sense of dignity—after all, they would be stopping the Republic's slide toward mediocrity. Let the unions howl, if that is all the sense they have.

Many of the Republic's facilities are in a state of near collapse, but we don't seem able to elect public servants who will recognize the emergency and do something about it. Oh, well; it is said that the streets of heaven are paved with gold, and that's where we're all headed, aren't we?

Reference having been made in the third paragraph to J.P. McCarthy's overcoat, a modicum of substantiating evidence may be in order.

You are pointed, therefore, toward the cover of the June issue of "Detroit Monthly," in which he is posed in what seems to be a racing car. The moral of the photograph is that no one so well-padded should ever sit for public exposure in such a small machine. He appears to have swallowed at least four pumpkin seeds.

He is a splendid fellow, nonetheless, for he has saved the curmudgeon from going pantless. J.P. and his lovely Judy will soon celebrate their 20th wedding anniversary, a black-tie affair.

This one could find his tuxedo coat dating from Savannah, Ga., in the 1950s, but not the pants. Inquiry caused the lady known as Irish to look startled. Then she went to the basement, fished around in a large sack and fetched them forth. They were intended for Most Holy Trinity's easement of the poor, but instead they have gone through the nimble fingers of Ed Tamburrini, a noted Birmingham tailor, who has removed about a square yard from the seat. Thus the curmudgeon shall meet the requirements for admission to a gala affair.

Let us dance, dear Irish, but not too actively, for you can't tell about 30-year-old threads.

Break It Up!

The Clangville Clarion . . .

When baseball teams become too inept, (and start losing public support) or become too adroit (and the cost of operation soars), there is a tendency among management to "break them up." Fading stars are traded or sold; rookies are brought up from the minors; the manager is sacked; the ballpark is painted in new colors; the whole tone of the operation is altered, for better or worse.

Well, maybe that's what we ought to do with Washington. Break it up; disperse it as the principal city of the federal bureaucracy. God knows it hasn't had a winning season in the memory of a middle-aged taxpayer. It has become ingrown, isolated, snooty, stuck on itself, and full of cliques trained in the art of hiding scandals under rugs.

More than that, Washington, D.C., has become a one-industry town, perhaps even more so than Flint, Mich. Washington has attracted to its corporate limits thousands of individuals, many of them from Harvard, Yale, Vassar and Columbia, whose only driving force in life is to produce edicts, regulations, rules, findings and laws that cause the average citizen to stare in wonder, as though introduced to a foreign language.

This has been going on for decades as noted. There is probably a sufficient backlog of Washington production to run the country for at least 50 years. It just sits there, gathering dust, except on those occasions when lawyers or accountants dig through it, hunting for some appalling administrative order that will save a scoundrel from paying his taxes or serving a term in the cooler.

You can't say anything nearly as harsh about the one-product psychology of Flint. When they do something up there, it eventually moves out of town. It is either sold or General Motors unloads it on the dealers. Contrary to what some critics contend, it isn't the same old stuff, year after year, ground out by graduates of Harvard, Yale, Vassar and Columbia.

Flint is in a bit of the doldrums right now, but you just wait. Some sharp, young engineer from Purdue, Massachusetts Institute of Technology, U-M, MSU or Alma College will come up with an engine that will run on bottled hot air from political conventions and state legislatures. Customers will be lined up eight abreast, bank drafts in hand.

Besides, we don't have to worry about breaking up Flint. It has broken itself up at least a half-dozen times, but it has always come roaring back with a new concept for putting chuckholes in the nation's freeway system.

So let's concentrate on breaking up Washington, which has become both inept and overpriced. How are we going to do it?

Well, we probably ought to leave Congress and the president there, primarily because they deserve one another. There is also a tendency among voters to want the president to be a member of one political party and Congress controlled by the opposition. As long as that persists, neither of them will be able to agree on much of anything that hasn't already given the nation a permanent gall-bladder infection.

———————————

For crying out loud, though, move the State Department, maybe to New Mexico, although that is awfully close to Texas.

The reason why we must move the State Department is because it deals in foreign affairs, and whenever presidents get bored, or can't balance the budget, they stick their mitts into some other country's business.

The next thing you know some idiot is playing a fife or banging a drum, and the munitions industry is working three shifts. America would be heaven on earth if the State Department had an unlisted telephone number and no air conditioning in New Mexico. That would be a good location for the CIA, too, come to think of it.

Move Agriculture to Iowa, Kansas or one of the Dakotas, whichever has cost the least per capita since 1946; bring Labor to Michigan, where there would be plenty of clinical work; send the Pentagon to wherever in Pennsylvania there are the most Quakers; transfer Education to California, which needs it the most. Put all other departments up for bid, with the proviso that no two go to the same state.

Was God Extra Kind?

All in a Lifetime . . .

The Republic seems to be having a heap of trouble with its offspring these days. Leastwise, that's what you read in the papers or see on the telly.

There are a scattered few of us who don't have children, or grandchildren, or even nephews or nieces in jail, or on parole, or living in sin, or toting firearms, or expelled from school, or pregnant at 16. So we have to depend on outside sources for our information. It sure looks and sounds like a mess, and there are times when you think maybe God was being extra kind to you when He said, in effect: "Don't give that poor sucker any kids to worry about."

———————— ————————

Still, there are youngsters all over this area of Clangsville, and they seem perfectly normal by recognizable standards. They are out in the streets playing ball, or in the driveways shooting baskets, or fiddling with electronically controlled miniature cars, or going, "Blam! Blam!" in what passes these days for cowboys and Indians; and once in a while you spot one or two, usually little girls, with schoolbooks under their arms.

They do not seem to be overly friendly, or even polite, but that went out of metro culture a long time ago. Over the last 25 years, I must have nodded, spoken or waved at 2,000 strangers who gave me neither sign nor sound in return.

If the gift of communication is ever lost or declines to grunting, whence it came, the initial blight will begin in the cities, where people are too busy, or too suspicious, or too self-centered, or too snooty to exchange common pleasantries. Tom Jefferson hated the baleful eyes-straight-ahead of city-ites, and I guess that's one of the reasons I have always called myself a Jeffersonian Democrat; although such a commitment hasn't left many Democrats to vote for, come to think of it.

———————— ————————

Where were we? Oh yes, the children—or the damned kids, as they are called on off days. What's happened to them?

Well, someone once said that if you don't have youngsters of your own, that qualifies you as an expert, so I will hazard a few guesses—nothing scientific, mind you, just a couple of notions collected from a seat in the bleachers.

There is the opinion that if there was one point in time when things started going wacko, it was right after World War II and the discharge of about 15 million of us who came home determined to make the world better for everyone, especially for ourselves and our offspring.

Before the war—before she was declared ineligible because she had dared to get married—Fern taught school, and she kept a paddle atop the blackboard that would have scared an ox. She was a gentle soul, apt to turn all mushy inside at the sight of a head of curls or a wistful smile, but she had been taught discipline, and she believed in it, and she would whack a mischief maker if it came down to it. If that didn't put an end to the trouble, off the kid would go to the principal's office, and that was hell on the Wabash, no holds barred.

———————

Later, one of Fern's half-sisters took up the teaching trade. When she was hired away from Ohio by the California system, she suddenly learned that she needed insurance to protect herself from irate parents who were outraged at the mere thought of their Susy or their Johnny being reprimanded. All teachers carried insurance.

After she had come out of Mercy College, Irish took up teaching for a spell in the Detroit system, and the word came down to her that she was not to punish a child, and she was not to fail a child, and she was not to send a child to the principal's office. Horrors.

A few years after the war it got so a kid couldn't even play baseball without being organized, supervised and lionized. Since I had no kids and was therefore immune to partisanship. I was elected president of two Little Leagues, Ohio and Illinois. The parents had most of the fun and did all of the caterwauling.

Kids were going to have it better, that's all there was to it. What was better than growing up under a decent set of rules? Childhood was not busted, really, but we were determined to fix it. Now we are trying to conduct parenthood in the papers and on TV. Tough going.

Some Thankfuls

Join Hands

Let's join hands across the table,
Thanking God that we are able
To be present at His board;

Feeling grateful for His blessing
On the turkey and the dressing,
And the harvest we have stored . . .

Firmly press the touching fingers
'Til you feel the warmth that lingers,
The sensation sweetly odd.
That's transmitting pure affection
And a moment's introspection
With our loved ones and our God.

—Margaret Rorke

Now that Ms. Rorke has reminded us again whence all good things come; and now that Jerry Rideout has said once more, "Arn, it's better than the alternative!"; I will add a quota of "thankfuls" and "ungratefuls."

I am thankful to Irish, who has helped me reclimb the mountain after too many long and lonely years in the valley; I feel sheltered by her family, and I am slowly becoming pals with her dog, Tilly, who was born in England and would probably snarl at the Queen if Her Highness got too friendly, too soon.

I am pleased with such health as I have, although I am bored stiff with regimented exercise and detest taking at least 14 pills every day. I don't think I have lost any friends over the year and may have added a few, which is a pleasant thought.

It is either a miracle supported by heaven or a commentary on the low grade of alternative housing available that I have come to appreciate our place in Clangville and no longer harbor the urge to cause such a ruckus on Southfield Road that traffic would have to be re-routed for 12 years.

Having said all of this, having been thankful for an outlet in which to let off steam twice a week, and having attended at least a dozen masses during which he scarcely understood a single word or maneuver, the backslid curmudgeon rides again, as follows:

———◆———   ———◆———

Anyone who can be thankful for the performance of this Legislature and this governor since the last general election had better stop eating oyster dressing and gravy, else he come down with cholera morbus ere dusk settles on Thanksgiving Day. Someone recently said that thus far the bunch in Lansing has passed a 65 m.p.h. speed limit and erected a 75-foot Christmas tree, and that's it, brother. An exaggeration, maybe, but not by much.

Everywhere you look—education, the drug scene, the need for highway expansion, the attraction of new industry, the retention of old industry—Michigan has been coasting. True, travel has increased, to the point that as of Nov. 10, there had been more crossings of the Mackinac Bridge than in all of last year, which meant, of course, that mainly we were visiting one another. Yet I have no sense that Michigan has been "with it" in the real uppen atem style, and if you could have concentrated all the wheel-spinning in Lansing, there would be a gulch as deep as the Grand Canyon.

As for Detroit, I'll have some horseradish on my turkey, please. I have never believed in the trickle-down theory of economics, and as for the use of it in the rebuilding of a city—malarkey.

There have been cosmetic improvements downtown, of which the already underridden People Mover is a sterling example, but many once-fine neighborhoods have become full of wrack, ruin, unemployment, drugs, terror. It doesn't do any good that Coleman Young and some of his super-scouts go around blaming it all on the white folks. Let's face it—if Detroit is bailed out, the whites are going to have to do it, at least with their money.

That's another thing I don't like about this state government, incidentally. There hasn't been enough attention paid to the terrible problems of Detroit, which remains the key to a booming Michigan.

As for the Washington bunch, as we admire "the harvest we have stored," make sure it includes plenty of antacid pills. I have personal recollection of many—too many!—federal administrations, and this is the worst of the lot. Shoot, bring back Richard Nixon by comparison! I agree with the Columbia Journalism Review that it is the fault of the media, meaning print.

It began early in 1980 when we really didn't check Ronald Reagan out in California. He lied about his "accomplishments" out there and got away with it, and its' been downhill ever since. Thanksgiving Eve, and already the curmudgeon has a bellyache!

The Hang of Clangville

Notes from Clangville . . .

This is being undertaken on a beautiful early summer day, with Michigan, my Michigan on its very best behavior and, therefore, worthy to be compared with any slice of territory on the planet Earth. There is a sweet and gentle breeze; the sun shines; the humidity is probably about 40; the blooming foliage at the side of the townhouse deadens the sound of traffic; Schultz sleeps and snores on the office couch; Tilly is sacked out in her favorite hidey-hole, and Irish is at her office helping to make a living. A man would have to border on sainthood to have it any better.

———◆◆——— ———◆◆———

It was on a day similar to this just a week short of a decade ago that the curmudgeon moved his beloveds and his chattels to the country, settling between Howell and Brighton after 17 years in Detroit. Fern was earthbound then, as was Old Yeller, and together we conquered vast sproutings and hangings of poison ivy, planted more than an acre of grass and a slew of flowers and shrubs. Gradually, we learned how to cut back on the steam and adjust to the rural pace.

At night it was so quiet and so dark as to be the next thing to scary; sometimes we would walk to the head of the driveway and search the eastward sky for the faint glow of the city's lights. Some of the friends who came to visit had difficulty hiding their reactions—"You're crazy!" One friend, for example, was always overcome by twitchings and jerkings, as though he expected a bear to come out of the woods and eat the front tires off his Ramrod 8.

But we learned to love the country, even though we understood that the newspapers out there were doing a marvelous job of covering up the crime rate. Very little of America is completely safe, and that certainly applies to Livingston County. It is perhaps a commentary on the resilience of latter-day Americans that we have learned to live on the edge of larceny, reacting to it mainly when it happens to us.

We returned to the country a few days ago—Dr. Phil Schmitt is still in charge of the maintenance of this hulk—and stopped in front of the old place. Schultz did not show much interest; perhaps it is true that dogs are content away from ancient haunts as long as they are with their so-called owners. Within the Innerman, however, there stirred memories of both the golden days and the painful days. Those 10 years were neither wasted nor lost. It was simply time to go, to move on to whatever else life had to offer. Ah, Clangville . . .

———————

Gradually, one is piecing together the Birmingham area. It is deceiving. On the surface it has the appearance of perhaps 50 other Midwestern suburbs, but underneath it is different.

Birmingham proper has sort of a cutesy shopping area that is remindful of a high-class tourist center, but the city itself is caught in the crossfire of growth vs. containment. Presently, a fever runs against high rises, and there is a considerable restoration of old homes as well as an obvious pride of ownership.

Still, there is more of Clangville to it than the various Grosse Pointes seem to demonstrate, and one would think that it comes closer to representing at least the middle-management of the automobile industry and its satellites. For those who consider such things important, it is a sought-after mailing address, and its public school system receives high marks.

———————

The curmudgeon and his crew live within a short block of the Birmingham border, share its postal facilities and would send a child to school there if God hauled off and performed a miracle, but geographically we are within the confines of Beverly Hills. It, too, is different, with residential areas, generally speaking, of considerable tone, whereas the business section is on the slim side.

Clangville is a region where corporation limits overlap with startling swiftness, and it takes a while for the newcomer to become oriented. One can now find Royal Oak on a clear day, and knows the difference (colorwise) between the street signs in Beverly Hills and those in Southfield, but he still gets lost on occasion and swears prettily.

Irish does most of the driving and fears not. Schultz and Tilly fear not. Only the curmudgeon fears.

The Best Is Yet to Be

Common Chatter

When folks get together,
They talk of the weather
For that is a subject we share.
What pundits are saying,
What taxes we're paying
Are topics that go on from there.
What children are doing,
What battles are brewing
Abroad or in some local sphere;
The dullards and sages
Down all the ages
"Have tried to make perfectly clear."

—Margaret Rorke

Lady of Leisure . . .

When Irish came downstairs this morning, there seemed to be a special gleam in her eyes and bounce in her steps. Before she left the house, she scrootched around in her skirt to make sure all of the pleats were aligned, and then with the promise of "a light supper" she was gone—down the chute toward retirement, which occurs Friday.

She will be jumping the gun by more than—well, I had better not tell you how much for that would reveal her age, about which there is a sensitivity of fistfighting fervor among many of her gender. She has spent a goodly number of years answering the bell with her dukes up, though, and now she wants to take up some of the slack, bless her heart.

The other evening I asked her to summarize her career as briefly as possible, and it turned out that she has worked in 14 places, holding more than one position in several of them, with a high of three in the Secretary of State's Office, which she will be departing as the director of the driver training division under the bureau of driver improvement. Betimes she has also been a schoolteacher, a librarian and a member of the Detroit jury commission as an appointee of dear old Soapy Williams. She has been with the city's commission on children and youth after recruitment by our dazzling boy mayor, Jerry Cavanagh; with the opportunity program sponsored by the Archdiocese of Detroit; with the housing commission; with the University of Detroit; with Marygrove College; with Wayne State University; and with alumnae relations at Mercy College, where she received three degrees—English, speech and education. This is not quite the whole itinerary of the one we know as Irish, but, obviously, she has done a lot of prancing around in her day. It is no wonder her feet hurt.

———◦•◦——— ———◦•◦———

I stayed out of all of the preliminaries leading up to this cataclysmic decision for several reasons. It should be a personal decision as to the spending of an individual's leisure years. We are told by the savants that there are some men and women for whom retirement is a short form of hell. I did not want my anticipated pleasure at having her home to weigh in the final decision. It may turn out that we will wrangle like a couple of irritable foofs, but the morning has never passed when I did not regret her departure; and the evening has not occurred when I did not welcome her return. Besides, I have been semi-retired for nearly 12 years, and I am getting pretty good at it, if I do say so myself.

We have talked about what we might do "with the rest of our lives," but we have not pushed the topic too fiercely because we recognize that we come from different upbringings and backgrounds. She is a city girl, nurtured by the culture of Detroit and environs, and she clings by instinct to Clangville. In contrast, I am a country boy, son of a father who pioneered in railroading, and was always full of wonder at the size and shape and variety of America. Quite often, I yearn to see what is going on out yonder. I have now been in Michigan nearly 29 years, but what do you suppose is happening in Montana or Vermont?

Oh, Irish, we shall see, shan't we?

———

The other day we were talking of her forthcoming drop in income and how it might temper our life-style, and she laughed and said, "You stick with me, kiddo, and you will have a rhinestone in your navel!" Where do you suppose she heard that? Women are a constant source of surprise, mostly on the side of delight.

Sometimes I think I am more worried about her retirement than she is, probably because of what the experts have said. I do want her to be happy, and I have resolved that I will not rant and rave if she winds up campaigning for some damfool politician. She didn't list that among her 14 career experiences, but she could have.

Loping Towards Christmas

It Is Well

It is well we yearly travel
To the cave behind the inn
Where our tensions can unravel,
And the world of lose and win—
And of lack and limitation
Can be left outside a while
As we kneel in adoration
To absorb a baby's smile.

—Margaret Rorke

Take It Easy . . .

We are loping into the Christmas season, a time for politicians to button their lips, columnists to sheath their swords, and haters to go hide in the closet. Take it easy; let there be at least nine days of peace and tranquility.

With the exception of Irish, who is as subject to change as one of Sonny Eliot's weather forecasts, my shopping list is in order. Thus far she has presented four suggestions, only to withdraw them the next day.

Once she said, "Don't give me anything. After all, I have you, and our home, and Tilly and Schultz, so what more could I want?" How sweet of her. But if you think that would stand the gaff on Christmas morning, you're a better man that I am, Gunga Din.

We went "Christmas looking"—which is sort of a warm-up for "Christmas shopping," I have learned—at one of the malls on Sunday. Many of the stores were busy in the sense that merchandise was being eyed, unracked, held either at arm's length or up close for examination, then reracked. The hour of decision had not arrived.

Irish tried on numerous long coats, belted in back, circa maybe 1928, while I silently prayed for an early spring. Later I joined numerous husbands—I presumed they were husbands—who were sitting in the hallways, tuckered out from the long march to Christmas Day, although it had scarcely begun. patience, chums. This, too, shall pass.

———

We are also in the process of decorating the townhouse, although it is obvious that we will be outshone by many neighbors. This section of Clangville pays a heavy premium to Detroit Edison during Yuletide, with enough lights on some of the houses to illuminate a runway at Metro Airport.

Nonetheless, we shall have one unique feature—a lighted tree in a corner of the deck. Only two human beings and two dogs, not counting airplane passengers at 8,000 feet, or guests, shall be able to see it, for the area is snug by high walls. But that is what Irish wants, and you fellows know how that goes. It ought to be quite a sight, especially if it rains, freezes and then snows.

In that event we may run an advertisement in the Eccentric and invite viewers at 25 cents per head, children for free, to peek through an opened gate.

Anyhow, it is shaping up as a Christmas season relatively free of uncontrollable stress and turmoil. After all, there is nothing we can do about the uproar in Washington until the congressional committees and special investigators have reported their findings; and surely Roger Smith of General Motors will remain calm, cool and collected until after the 25th instant. So relax. Stop fuming. Be nonchalant, have a glass of soda pop and be kind to one another.

Meanwhile, should hunger transcend the cookies and other sweets of the season, here is a recipe for you, in response to the recent yelp for help from Judge David F. Breck of the Sixth Judicial Circuit.

More than a year ago, while browsing in a health food store in Brighton, I came upon a 12-ounce box of "substitute elbows" by De Boles, featuring American (Jerusalem) artichoke flour. Included was the recipe for "Macaroni and Cheese Surprise," which I made in the Crockpot instead of a casserole dish. I think you could use standard elbows off your grocer's rack as well. Anyhow:

Put one-third cup of butter or margarine; four tbsp. of flour; one tsp. salt; one-half tsp. celery salt; one quarter tsp. pepper; three cups milk; one pound medium sharp cheese, shredded or cubed, in Crockpot on high for one hour, stirring frequently; then add cooked macaroni and one cup pimento-stuffed olives, sliced, and cook all together, on low, for about four hours. If this doesn't get you an A, you are living with ingrates.

Live It Up

We come now to National Secretaries Week, a pleasant interlude during which a modicum of praise will be lavished on those who keep business and industry glued together. Speaking commercially, back of every successful man there is at least one woman—his secretary—and this is her chance to preen and prance, prettily.

In Detroit, the festivities will reach a crescendo of sorts on Wednesday evening when the local chapter of the National Secretaries Association stages its annual gala at the Sheraton-Cadillac Hotel. Miss Marguerite Glandomenico, a City employee, will be recognized as "secretary of the year," an honor so high and doubt-less so deserved that Common Council ought to name a street or park after her.

The advent of this occasion has led to a brief excursion into the realm of women at work, with rather surprising results.

From the Department of Labor, for instance, comes the intelli-gence that in 1960, the last year for which statistics are available, there were 893,091 female wage earners in Michigan alone—39 per cent more than in 1950 and 95 per cent more than in 1940. The increases, eye-bugging as they seem to me, roughly parallel the na-tional averages.

Further, we learn that one out of every three women in the whole nation is now involved in the "labor force," with approximately 30 per cent listed as "clerical workers," meaning secretaries of as-sorted types. The information on pay scales is too ancient to be truly significant, with Labor reporting that "in 1959, women workers in Michigan earned an average of $2,438. Sixty per cent earned less than $3,000 and only ten per cent $5,000 or more . . . " Salaries have increased since then, no doubt, but it might be diffi-cult to find a secretary who is totally happy with her weekly stipend.

One more statistic, by your leave: three out of five women work-ers are married, indicating that in the beginning years of what we used to call "nuptial bliss," it now takes two to make a living, es-pecially if you want a few of the "luxuries."

The Department provides this final note: "About half of today's young women are married by age 20 and have their last child at age 26; by the time the youngest is in school, the mother may have 40 or more years of life before her."

What will she do when Susie and Junior are safely tucked into kindergarten? Go back to work, in many instances. There is a growing indication that more and more women are becoming bored stiff with the routine of house-tending, accounting in part for the upsurge in the sales of tranquilizers, sleeping pills, hard liquor and psychiatric treatments. Today's "way of life" is tough on Momma, too. Especially Young Momma, whose upbringing gave her no preparation for the bleak side of domesticity. As the fellow said, everybody has problems . . .

Where were we? Oh, yes—secretaries. What do they want out of the 9 to 5 in addition to good pay and fringe benefits?

This may be presumptuous of me, but the suspicion exists that they would appreciate a bit more recognition.

Not banquets-and-flowers-recognition once a year, mind you, but the simple, day-in and day-out unspoken recognition that they, too, are capable, dedicated and competent members of "the team," willing and qualified to share responsibility and shoulder a portion of the total burden of management.

Too many chaps treat their secretaries as though they were dealing with semi-idiots, saying—"Do this, or do that, Miss Smathers"—whereas Miss Smathers has already been doing this or doing that for five years, without hitch or flaw, on the numbers. She could probably assume 25 per cent of her boss' administrative duties without becoming ruffled or over-taxed, but it has never occurred to him that she craves this type of recognition, of sharing in the company's success story. We think of women as being sensitive, but too often in business we treat them shallowly.

So, hurrah for National Secretaries Week. Live it up.

Sweet Corn

Monday's Mulligans . . .

Ah, dear friends, we are in the full blush of the sweet corn and tomato season, and if there is better eating than this anywhere, the name of the place must be Heaven.

One is especially exuberant because he has finally mastered the art of masticating a roasting ear with his China Clipper uppers. This has taken the better part of two seasons of hard practice, and at times the spirit weakened and the corn was cut from the cob with a knife. But something was lost, both in savor and in the sense of accomplishment, so new tactics were employed.

Now, by emulating the chipmunk, the succulent rows of buttered and well-seasoned grain are nipped off with dispatch, and new strength is thus added to one's vital juices. There will be no public demonstration of this technique, but in the privacy of the kitchen the system works, hallelujah.

There is no substitute known to man for freshly plucked, boiled, buttered, salted and peppered sweet corn. This is one treat for the taste buds the laboratory technicians have not been able to imitate. Thus, you eat it with a salute to the pioneers, sharing an untarnished joy intimately related to the goodness of Mother Nature. They, too, had a short season and struck while the butter was hot. And so must you. Science can not prolong this ecstacy. It is now or never. Full speed ahead and the devil take the hindmost. We will separate the men from the boys after the fourth ear.

Something must also be said for the tomato in its natural, freshly ripened state. When canned they are excellent but when raw they are superb. Fantastic. To think that civilization was retarded by the early notion that they were poisonous. What an Age of Darkness that was! But now they come to the market in a tumultuous flow, the weather permitting, and mankind is blessed and upgraded. When winter falls upon us we will rescue them from tins and have them in assorted sauces. But now, thank you Lord, in slices. Add a sprinkling of chopped onions and peppers (fresh) and the sublimity of life will nearly overwhelm you.

This is the prime time of the year. The sun warms our muscles and lengthens our backswing. The politicians are between uproars. Children are bearable—they will soon be socked back into school. The mornings are bright and cheerful; the evenings long and tranquil. And the bounty of the land floods upon us. Ah, these are the days.

Two Roads

About 25 miles west of downtown Detroit you come to a fork in the road, to borrow a phrase from yesterday, whereupon you are faced with the choice of competing worlds.

If you angle to the left and follow the freeway (I-696), you eventually pass through commercial developments which in most respects are a tribute to the progressiveness of today's society. There is some gimcrackery along the way, unfortunately, but in the main this is how a modern urban area should look and function, and you are left with the impression that there is plenty of octane left in the "imperialist camp," as Lenin once referred to us.

Conversely, if you meander to the right at the fork in the road you are astride Grand River, and in due course this will lead you into a once-prosperous complex of stores and shops which has since fallen into the most dismal state of wrack and ruin. This is the bleak side of "decadent capitalism"—Lenin once more—and the sight of it inspires the bolting of the car doors and leaves the after-chill of an unpleasant dream.

By the simple turning of the steering wheel, then, you have the choice of two Americas, one opulent and attractive, the other neglected and ugly, and sometimes you wonder how this came about and you question the sagacity of a system which either caused it or permitted it to happen.

———————

Between the summers of 1959 and 1976 your commentator traversed sections of Grand River five days each week, mornings and evenings, and witnessed the month-by-month spread of desolation. It was a rare month when there was not at least one boarding-up of a sizable place of business, and these mournful occurrences were sometimes recorded in this column.

The leaders of the city, state and nation were aware of what was going on, at least in the broad sense, and there were countless declarations against creeping decay and promises of rectification. One president, Lyndon Johnson, used the campus of the University of Michigan as the launching pad for a war against poverty, and millions of dollars were spent in Detroit alone in an effort to revitalize the inner city.

Another war—Vietnam—undercut the federal programs, yet even when they were functioning it took an optimist with rose-colored glasses to spot physical improvements. There was enough money to give a comparative handful of citizens decent jobs, and to institute such undertakings as Head Start, but we never really got into the vital business of replanning and rebuilding the stricken commercial and residential areas. One remembers his daily travels through those burgeoning wastelands and counts them as partial atonement for his sins.

———

Meanwhile, the westward trek of progress began and there is no end in sight. Beginning in about 1960 the extension of the Lodge Freeway which is Business I-96 started to blossom with office buildings, light industrial centers and various other types of enterprise, creating a tax base and employment opportunities without parallel between Chicago and New York.

Metropolitan Detroit has prospered beyond all forecasts over these years, and is one of the richest settlements in all of America. It is only the city itself, the corporation core, you might say, which has languished. We have surrounded yesterday with today, and that is tragic because yesterday in this instance is tired, and bleeding, and worn out.

Again, what caused this to happen? Even at this late date there is no pat answer, but one continues to sift through the debris in an effort to appease his own conscience.

It seems now that Detroit and all other major cities were struck all most simultaneously with major problems, or challenges, for which they were totally unprepared. As an illustration, the freeways revolutionized urban mobility—not only into the city, but out of the city. This made the flight to the suburbs easy when the civil rights movement grew in intensity, and of course it encouraged shopping in centers away from the traditional neighborhood stores.

———

One has to believe, too, that city planning was woefully short in foresight and force. The portents of decay were not met with bright, swift-counter-strokes. Early on, many corporations large and small left the city because room was not made for them in the midst of growing ruin. City Hall rarely found an alternative to hand-wringing.

Now we have the westward fork in the road, with the other elsewhere. One way to progress, the other to decay. If you are uneasy about the future of our system, this adds to it.

The Drill Instructor!

We have arrived at still another anniversary of what Franklin D. Roosevelt called "The day of infamy," so be careful of those who would tell you where they were when the Japs assaulted Pearl Harbor, and what they did thereafter.

It was Douglas MacArthur who reminded us that old soldiers do not die, they just fade away, but what he forgot to add was that they go out yakking. The only critter more loquacious than a World War II veteran is a World War I doughboy, especially if he spent a little time with the female French.

Even now, at 80 or thereabouts, the fire comes into his eyes and if it weren't for his blasted arthritis, or his lumbago, or his rheumatism, or maybe a touch of all three, why he would cock his overseas cap over his right eye and set forth on an errand of mercy, for surely the women still need him. What do today's 19- or 20-year-old whippersnappers know about luff, as Charles Boyer whispered it. I luff you, cherie. O, come back, Big Daddy. Why doesn't God reserve arthritis, lumbago and rheumatism for the kids? If a constitutional convention is ever called in Heaven, that is one of the things they should consider.

Where were we? Oh, yes—the day the Japs started losing the war and winning the peace. We are flooded with nostalgia, the rank and file of us, and it is amazing—and alarming!—that a good deal of it is pleasant. The farther we get away from the war, the more romantic it seems.

How did William Tecumseh Sherman feel 10 years after he had said, "War is Hell"? We do not know, precisely. He kept showing up at the annual encampments of the Grand Army of the Republic, so something must have attracted him. However, there is no evidence that he mellowed sufficiently to speak kindly of his Drill Instructor, if he ever had one, and that is the acid test.

———••———   ———••———

If the time ever comes, ol' buddy, when you are thinking fondly of your Drill Instructor, turn yourself in before you become a menace to international peace and goodwill. Tojo you can forgive, and Hitler and Mussolini, but your Drill Instructor, never. Never, never, never. Just remember that your first instincts were right: When they sang about "the Halls of Montezuma," that's where you hoped they would lock him up, forever. That was a good, clean, positive thought and you should never abandon it.

One is a bit foggy as to what the Army called those entrusted with making life miserable for recruits. Perhaps they just used plain old sergeants who were so mean the mules couldn't stand them. In the Marines and the Navy, however, these characters were called Drill Instructors, and they were so ornery rattlesnakes would hide from them and alligators would flee for their lives.

We fell into the clutches of an Irishman from Holy Cross University who was so downright beastly that he made everything you had ever heard about the potato famine sound reasonable. Hurrah for the bloody English. He was the sort of jock-o who would stand in front of a mirror and practice outrages. Old Yeller would have chewed him up one side and down the other, just out of instinct. But we would have called him off because no dog could have stood contact with such bile. If it had been brought to a vote of the company—"Shall we hang the Drill Instructor or Tojo?"—the DI would have carried every precinct.

———••———   ———••———

Thereafter, we never met a Blue Jacket or a Gyrene who had a kind word to say about his Drill Instructor. Later, Leon Uris wrote a great book about the Marines, "Battle Cry," and he devoted thousands of words to Boot Camp and a sadist named Whitlock. Listen:

"There were many aggravating tricks that Whitlock constantly pulled from his grab-bag. A favorite was to march the platoon back and forth before a water fountain at Port Arms. As the sun blistered down, he would take a sip of the cool stuff and march them in rear marches until they were dizzy, their tongues hanging out, and their arms falling off from the weight of their rifles. When they were at the point of collapse he would give them three minutes rest, then double time them through the ankle deep sand of the boondocks. Then, carrying their pieces at an arm-breaking Trail Arms he would run them clear back to the barracks . . . "

Young Arn, who had come out of a newspaper office to enlist in the Navy, ran until his tongue looked like a necktie, and then ran some more, the Drill Instructor snapping at his heels. Oh, he was a jewel, that one, and whenever we get to thinking that there was a pleasant side to the war, we remember him. That does it. Peace!

Oh, Canada!

War, Whiskey and Loyalty . . .

Every centralized government, whether old or new, large or small, insists on exercising its authority. The odds are eight to one that this is what will happen in China when the old men in power weary of kids clogging the main squares of the principal cities. In the United States, power, as a tool of authority, has been used since 1791.

That was the year that our infant Congress, afflicted with a money fever it has never overcome, passed legislation to collect excise taxes. This was done at the urging of Alexander Hamilton, the secretary of the treasury, who was not only anxious to raise money for the national debt, but also was panting to assert the power of the federal government.

Anyhow, by 1794, it became apparent that a good place to raise money and assert authority was in western Pennsylvania, where farmers were distilling whiskey. Farmers distilled whiskey for two reasons: It tasted good and it was much easier to transport to market than the grain from which it was fermented. And they didn't pay taxes on it. Farmers have always been stubborn about taxes, and they have always been against overloading a good horse. That's why it has taken corporations so long to run them off all of our land.

———————————

Well, in 1794, George Washington finally got sick and tired of listening to Alexander Hamilton bleating about those damn farmers violating the law, so he sent 13,000 troops into western Pennsylvania to assert authority and collect the tax. There were only about 500 farmers involved, so it wasn't much of a melee. Two farmers were arrested and convicted of treason, but were pardoned by the president. The events, however, went down in history as the Whiskey Rebellion.

The Sons of the Whiskey Rebellion is a Detroit-area organization that has a simple rule: If one of your ancestors was present at the original rebellion, or had known of it but maybe his wife wouldn't let him go, you are eligible for membership.

Thus, at a recent noontime, members gathered in Windsor at an unusual site, the armory of the Essex and Scottish Regiment, one of Canada's proudest and finest units. At the proper moment the company commander and president of the officer's mess, Michael Robinson, raised his glass and said: "To the queen!" This Yank had no glass, so he simply raised his hand. For the first time— "To the queen!"

It came as a surprise, a gesture as unexpected as the handshake of a president, and yet it symbolized a red running thread of courage, loyalty and fidelity then and tomorrow—if the occasion should arise—symbolized by the surroundings and their meaning. The Essex and Scottish Regiment is part of the war and remembrance of Canada and empire, and on one wall of the drill room there has been painted a huge Union Jack. Beneath it are these words:

"What if the best of our wages be an empty sleeve and a stiff knee a crutch for the rest of life who cares so long as the one flag floats and dares . . . "

That was the old empire, you say, and things have changed. Well, perhaps. But somehow there was the feeling that Michael Robinson was speaking for others beyond his command when he said that there is more Canadian and commonwealth loyalty than meets the eye. What he meant was that the declaration, "To the queen!" remains more than a polite formality, which is a surprise to a Yank who went to war with Franklin D. Roosevelt without having a second thought, but might have gone out of the country as a youngster under President Lyndon Johnson. There is a tradition there, a solidarity, and sort of a recently-kicked-around pride that may well transcend what the average American understands.

After all, the Essex and Kent Scottish Regiment was formed in 1793, and it fought in the War of 1812, slipping across the river and taking poorly defended Detroit. To this day, a portion of the plat of our city—our city, damn it!—is framed on a wall. There are many other trophies, memorials and memories.

Do you remember the raid on Dieppe, France, Aug. 18, 1942, which was a cross-channel "feeling out" of German positions? The Canadians were there in vast majority, including the Essex Scottish, and it was disaster that played on the nerves and haunted the thinking of Allied commanders until D-Day. Only two officers and 23 others out of a force of nearly 600 got off the beach at Dieppe.

And when D-Day finally came during that uncertain June of 1944, the Essex and Scottish Regiment was there, and its commanding officer, Maj. Fred A. Tilston was to be awarded the Victoria Cross. He remains one of five living Canadians to hold the highest honor of the empire; there have been 94 in all.

The battalion suffered 552 killed and 2,150 casualties in all during World War II, the highest in the Canadian Army. And now: "To the queen!" And to Canada, a neighbor of great worth.

FIVE
Country Living

Loneliness

The way the calendar falls, your narrator has been a widower eight months to this day. "Outsiders" will no doubt think it strange that such a date should be remembered. "Insiders" will understand, and they are no small minority. This society is full of the walking wounded, those left behind to fend off the devil loneliness as best they can.

Sometimes, or so it seems to this observer, they are joined by those who have been sent to the sidelines by divorce. One does not stand for or against divorce as a legal or moral concept. One only knows that it quite often creates its own particular type of walking wounded, its own brand of loneliness. Ah, you should read the mail that frequently comes to this address!

So? So the question becomes, how do you learn to live alone and like it? And the answer is . . .

———

Sometimes you think, well, by Jupiter, I will duck out on loneliness. So you buy yourself a ticket to New Orleans, let us say, and you stomp up and down Canal Street, renewing the sights, and then you go over to the French Quarter and have a fine dinner, with Oysters Rockefeller and a bottle of wine covered with cobwebs old enough to vote, and you go to your hotel, and take off your jacket, and look in the mirror, and there you are, a lonely old haykicker from Michigan, My Michigan!

There is no freeloader in all of the civilized world of the persistence and durability of loneliness. If you have a ticket to the ball-

127

game—it has a ticket to the ballgame. It eats with you, drinks with you, reads with you, sits under the trees with you, sleeps with you, counts your money, drives your car, pets your dog, wears your clothes, haunts your haunts, your shadow at noontime and midnight. There are moments when you get so sore at loneliness you would be willing to emulate the character in literature and give it 40 licks with a hatchet, but it is much too sly and illusive for that.

———

Loneliness makes you uncertain of yourself and of others. There is a new-found friendship, perhaps, but you are unsure of it. Is it a friendship founded on common interests and needs, or is it based on the quicksand of "I feel sorry for him?" One grows leery of commitment, fearing that he may make an ass of himself and fall into the bass drum while the band is playing "All of Me."

It has been said that one should wait at least a year before making major decisions, including changes in life-style, after loneliness first sets in, but that is probably another of those ancient "truisms" uttered by an individual who lacked experience.

There is this much to it. Regardless of age, no one has a year in which to "coast," to fritter, to dilly-dally, to play Scarlett O'Hara and say, "Oh, I'll worry about that tomorrow."

One is intimately connected with a fellow who will soon be 72. He will tell you, if invited, that yesterday—just yesterday—he was 27. That's how fast it all went down the chute. And he will also tell you, if encouraged, that the older you get the swifter time flies. It took eight years to travel from 19 to 21—and it took 45 days to reach 65 from 60. So if you were to say to him, "Take a year before making any decisions," he might reply: "I am sorry, dear friend, but years are in very short supply at the moment. Could you use a month instead?"

———

It now occurs that years ago someone wrote a book entitled "How To Live Alone And Like It," or pretty close to that. We recall much more of the title than the theme, but the secret to it, no doubt, was that the individual involved put his head down, and said to hell with what happened yesterday, and plowed off-tackle in one of those "student body right" maneuvers you sometimes see in football.

And you know something? That still might be the only way to whip loneliness. It will eat you alive if you pamper it; it will dog you to your grave if you try to compromise with it. Eat, drink, be merry, and fall through the bass drum. Does anyone have a better cure?

On Leaving the City

Very shortly we shall start "burning the embassy papers," as they say in diplomatic circles when the enemy is beating at the gate and it is time to fall back to a less exposed position.

Henceforth, activity will be transferred to the house in Livingston County, where columns will be cobbled together for display on Tuesdays, Thursdays and Sundays. The rest of the space will belong to that refugee from Lapeer, the Hon. J. Fitzgerald, and let us wish him all of the luck there is to spare.

A few minutes ago the first desk drawer was explored in an effort to separate keepables from throwables, and what do you know?—there was a lapel button bearing the inscription: "I Love Detroit." How long it had been there was beyond remembrance, but the thought occurred that it was a nice and appropriate discovery on the eve of departure.

Over the years of this tenure, Detroit has been a haven for rich and poor alike. There being some possibility that the rich would have thrived most anywhere, we will concentrate the bulk of what follows on the poor.

If you believe in divine guidance even up to a point, you may be willing to accept the premise that God helped design places such as Detroit in order that the poor might have a place to concentrate and catch their wind. Someday the real and earnest history of sanctuaries such as this will be written, and then it will be recorded that democracy for the dispossessed and the disenfranchised found at least part of its footing in these precincts, and flowered despite shaky beginnings.

America is in the process of change, dear friends, and when it is finally reformed part of it will bear the imprimatur—"Made in

Detroit." Those without hope, learning or prospects came here and found at least a bit of each in most instances, and this is now being passed on in line of succession to others, and still others to come, and eventually the process will transform the Republic and bring it a bit nearer to the perfection so long sought.

The prediction is, then, that out of the trauma of these times, the chaos, the crime, the heartbreak and the uncertainty, will come a better breed of Americans than would have been possible had these doors been closed to them. In a very real sense, Detroit has been the Ellis Island of decades four, through seven of the 20th Century, and out of this cauldron will come a citizenry eminently qualified to take its place in the middle ground of our society.

Every day Detroit educates some needy children, provides a few new jobs, upgrades a house or an apartment or two, contributes slowly but surely to hope, learning and prospects. That is the unwritten story of this city, as of other cities, and too few outlanders appreciate the tortured grinding of the wheels of progress. But if there is any honor in history the truth will out in due time, and there will be belated thanks for those who stood fast during the hard and lonely years.

There have been numerous periods during which Detroit was a very special place to live. Before the automobile this was one of the loveliest cities in all of North America. After the automobile, the excitement of the industrial breakthrough made our place-name famous around the globe. During the Second World War, we became the arsenal of democracy. And there have been other times when Detroit was foremost in the minds and hearts of residents and onlookers alike.

But in this moment of transition, your commentator clings to the notion that he may have lived and worked here during one of the most important periods of all. For these have been the years when the very soul of a great city was tested, when it was necessary to make do with less than was needed, when despair and slander were the daily lot, when the poor came in torrents in search of their share of the dream, and some found it and passed it along to the eager hands of their children.

Ah, yes. Detroit shall overcome!

The Party Continues

Next to girl watching, a highly competitive sport in which your correspondent holds four varsity letters, nothing is more fun than to sit in the shadows and look upon guys and dolls in the 50-to-60 age bracket at play. Wow!

This particular afternoon and evening there has been a party at the home of a friend, with 20 couples involved. They have much in common: members of the same country club; kids mostly through school; either well-settled in jobs or beyond the grasp of their creditors as businessmen; kind people, jovial people, nice people.

Parties . . .

. . . follow a pattern, and this one was no exception. In the beginning, there was the usual mass reserve punctuated by small talk . . . "My goodness, Jim, I haven't seen you in several months . . . Hey, baby, you've been wintering well . . . We went to Biloxi in November and had a good time" . . . That sort of thing.

Then the bar was opened, a football pool was organized—and the thaw set in. By halftime you couldn't hear the television announcer's voice above the rattle and clangor of social exchange. Those who had selected low numbers in the pool were calling "hold 'em!", while those with high numbers were yelling "score!" A lady kept asking, "who's playing?" and somebody finally told her, "Baltimore's in the black suits." That seemed to satisfy her: she never did ask who was in the white. I kept watch during a commercial; not a soul paid the slightest attention. The guy on the screen shaved himself in absolute privacy . . .

The chap who won the pool found a Confederate dollar "in the loot," as he kept calling it, and he yelled, "Why, John, you old --- -- - -----!" Delighted, John refreshed the loot with a Yankee dollar, and the party roared on.

The host went to the record cabinet, sorted through the discs, rejected several and then selected an obvious favorite. He gave the volume dial a twist, set the needle and it was "Mack The Knife" and Katy bar the door. "Everybody circle," he called, and from then on it was troop and stomp, with a beat and a throb.

What kids are doing today just ain't dancin', believe me. Why, there was one fellow who did the Charleston, the Black Bottom, the Two-Step, the Twist and the Watusi, practically all at the same time. When his partner didn't know what else to do, she shimmied. Another chap, who only last fall had a seige of the President's disease, gall bladderitis, was at least 18 inches off the floor a good two-thirds of the time. There was Bunny Huggin' and cheek-and-jowlin 'all over the place.

We must have done "Mack the Knife" at least six times, with a couple of rounds of "Yes, Sir, That's My Baby" tossed in for good measure. It was dancin', man, tribal and pristine, with the beast turned loose.

Almost as suddenly as it had started, the dancing ended. Somebody remembered that the final four holes of the Los Angeles Open were being shown, so it was back to the television sets. Come on, Arnold Palmer—Arney, baby!

For some reason, he identifies with the 50-to-60 set. Is it because we admire success? Perhaps. But he is ours. Gary Player is ours, too, but not quite so much as Arney.

Youth . . .

. . . has exuberance, yes, and vitality and strength and suppleness and easy grace and instant willingness and all of those other things we spent so freely before the frost settled back of our ears. What do we have left at party time?

A fierceness, you might call it, the overwhelming urge to throw what is left of low blood pressure into the pot and the devil take the hindmost. Frank Sinatra, who is not particularly ours, has captured some of this in a song in which he tells how it was at 17 as compared with how it is now. Now it is the autumn; now time is of the essence; now let us be fierce in our love for life this once more.

Dear Santa!

Merry Christmas

The sparkle from a pair of eyes
Lit up by Santa's sweet surprise,
A hearty laugh from one himself
Who acts a bit like that old elf,
A healthy home with spicy smells
That blend with pine, a few church bells,
Some cards, a visit from a friend,
A moment that you'll have to spend
Rereading Luke, some carols sung:
All this and more you'll find among
The wishes that I wish your way
To merry-up your Christmas Day.

—Margaret Rorke

Perhaps it is the "lace" left in the trees by last night's heavy fog and subsequent freeze, or it could be Margaret Rorke's poem, which has touched all of the happy chords of Christmas, but for whatever reason your commentator is in no mood this particular morning to wrestle with the problems of the world. With the permission of Scarlett O'Hara, we will worry about OPEC, unemployment, the Carter cabinet, salary increases for politicians, crime in the streets and various other unpleasantries tomorrow. Or the day after. By now, life should have taught us there is always time for fretting. We might be better off, as individuals and Americans, if we found more reasons to count our blessings.

———————

This will be our first Christmas in the woods and your commentator, who is sorely in need of a chain saw, is apprehensive lest

Santa Claus may not have been advised of our change of address. This concern was heightened a few minutes ago when an important piece of mail arrived from the personnel office of the Free Press—after it had been initially delivered to the house on Grandmont we departed in July. Holy Toledo, if communications aren't any better between here and the North Pole, it is going to be a long, hard winter.

Under what might be loosely termed the division of labor, the man of this house has been assigned the chore of providing fuel for the fireplace, a cavernous arrangement of bricks and mortar which dominates the family room. The builder evidently had in mind the possibility of roasting a whole steer at one fell swoop, which would have been a splendid idea had he sold the place to a woodsman.

Instead, he peddled the property to a candy ankle who had never swung an ax in all of his born days, and was restrained from doing so after giving a brief demonstration of his lack of prowess. The friend who brought the ax, and witnessed its handling, turned as white as the driven snow after two or three prelimary licks and reclaimed his property. "I will not be responsible for your loss of limbs and other vital parts," he said. "Go buy a hatchet."

So a hatchet was purchased and it has sufficed to this point due to the prevalence of small timbers from trees which were felled near the house. Many hours have been spent hacking and slashing away and in this laborious manner the maw of the fireplace has been satiated.

When we lived in the city we touched off the fireplace perhaps 10 times a year, drawing upon a cord of wood which was purchased in about 1970 and seemed ample for the rest of this decade. In short, we utilized the fireplace only on "occasions," usually when guests were gathering, looking upon it as sort of an ornate way of adding a special touch to the surroundings.

Out here, however, we cannot honor the sun for going over the yardarm unless that danged fireplace is snapping and cracking. Already this has led, alas, to the depletion of the easy pickings, the small timbers and bits and pieces which would respond to the fevered swinging of the hatchet. Now we are down to the sawlogs and other nitty-gritty, and that is why your commentator simply has to have that chain saw. He has already had a lesson in the use of such a lethal device from Jess Spalding, who departed with his equipment after a prediction which would have pleasured Jimmy the Greek. "The odds," Jess said, "are that you can get away with it. But you'd better keep plenty of tourniquets on hand." Hoo, boy.

———————————

Many years ago a cyclone went through this area and leveled vast stands of timber. Our woods are full of such residue, plus the natural fallings and topplings of subsequent times. Your commentator is confident he can keep ahead of that blasted fireplace if only he gets a chain saw for Christmas. Yoooo hoooo, Santa Claus. Out this way, please!

High Prices, Hard Times

What's wrong with the country, dear friends, is very simple: The age-old law of supply and demand has stripped its gears.

Here we are in either the onset or the middle of a recession (the economists can't make up their minds), yet even though we have more of practically everything we can use, prices in many instances continue to increase. This applies to oil.

An example. A few days ago the gentleman who keeps an eye on our fuel tank provided a refill. Wow; 95.4 cents per gallon, going on a dollar as sure as an Irishman heading for green beer on St. Patrick's Day.

Being somewhat old-fashioned, we presumed aloud that this had something to do with scarcity of the product—the law of supply and demand. But no. The driver said that the company for which he works has oil running out of its gaskets. All of its holding tanks are topped-off and, moreover, an additional allotment of 100,000 gallons has been canceled. It has been a mild winter, remember.

Well, there is probably no way we can induce OPEC to observe the laws of supply and demand, but you have to wonder about other circumstances within the economy, for when hard times do not bring about lower prices, our people are subjected to double-trouble.

———◆◇◆—— ——◆◇◆———

Real estate taxes keep going up, as you may have heard, and it is difficult to relate all of the increase to the rapacity of the Sheikhs of Araby, who get blamed for most everything these days. Once more Detroit seems to be aflame with indignation over the arithmetic of its assessors, and it is noted that the Hon. Coleman Young has brushed aside these objections, saying that property owners should be delighted their holdings have increased in value. Think of the profits in the event of resale!

This is pishposh of the highest order for several reasons. Regardless of how much property may have increased in the tax assessor's estimation, the average homeowner is no better off than when he first signed the mortgage unless he can talk his family into living in a tent or moving in with relatives. For if he sells he must re-enter a crazily inflated market and pay much more for both money and property than he did originally; while if he rents, he falls into the orbit of landlords, who have also learned a thing or two about pricing.

It should be noted, incidentally, that Detroiters are not alone in their displeasure with assessors. Out here in the wilderness we have had steadily increasing valuations and we have been warned to expect another 20 percent boost this year.

———◆◇◆—— ——◆◇◆———

What has been happening, of course, is that there has been no serious effort to trim services to meet the supply of tax money. When Detroit started running out of revenue, it appealed to Lansing and Washington for succor, and outlying provinces have followed the same policy. At many levels the bureaucracy is still functioning as though the golden goose had all of its feathers, and when elected officials, including legislators, make halfhearted moves to trim outlays by reducing the ranks or limiting wage increases, they are confronted by the hard facts that they have lost control over government and that the law of supply and demand is an ancient joke.

———◆◇◆—— ——◆◇◆———

In the private sector the automakers are offering temporary rebates on hard-to-sell models, and Chrysler employees have taken a wage cut to save their jobs; but throughout commerce and industry we are witnessing few of the reactions once associated with the law of supply and demand. And there is more to it than "the cost of energy."

What it comes down to is that we have lost the art of responding to economic adversity, and this is one of the worst of all times to be unemployed in America.

Back Yard Friends

Splendid afternoon this, with shimmering patches of sunlight penetrating heavy foliage provided by elm trees. Can't grow flowers in back yard because of shade, but it sure beats Los Angeles, where temperature is 109, according to a telephone call from perspiring relatives. To heck with that noise, as fellow said.

Have been sitting here thinking pure and pristine thoughts while watching Feathered Follies in vicinity of bird feeder. Have come to conclusion that birds have more fun than anyone, as fellow also said.

Papa Cardinal came zooming in a few minutes ago, a flame of red against the green of lawn, ferns and overhanging leaves. Made perfect two-point landing with flaps up atop feeder, nervously cased joint to make sure Blue Jay was not lurking in shadows, then sampled a sunflower seed.

Ate another one, constantly shifting head in all directions, then stiffened as small sound—"cheep, cheep"—came from base of feeder. Well, what do you know?—the Old Boy was baby sitting. For on the ground, about as big as a sparrow, was Junior Cardinal, clamoring for a share of loot.

Old Man put choice seed in beak, fluttered to ground, stuffed the seed into Junior's kisser. Kid acted as though he had just sampled first hot dog at ball park. Jumped up and down and said "cheep, cheep" again. Papa returned to feeder, found another morsel, came back down, dropped it into yawning chasm—junior has mouth like late Joe E. Brown.

Could make book on Old Man getting sick and tired of that routine in short order. Sure enough, as soon as pigeon came lumbering into yard, as awkward as cargo carrier. Papa Cardinal sounded alarm, took off, with Junior tagging behind, barely clearing fence.

Strange pigeon we have here. Albino, mostly, almost pure white, with splotches of black. Looks like he is wearing sports coat. Unusual chap, but lives harried life for Lady of House has low opinion of pigeons in general.

Shooshes them off, she does, whereupon they roost on garage and watch proceedings from safe distance, sneaking back to bird feeder when she is not looking. Quite a flock of them, really, and very persistent. Takes lots of shooshing to preserve law and order.

Personally, consider sparrows a bigger problem. They come by dozens and decimate supply of bird seed. Very smart operators. Two or three will get on feeder and sweep goodies onto ground with short side strokes of bills, like golfer hacking away in sand trap. In 15 or 20 minutes, will unload feeder while relatives gather at base and have a ball. Brave lads, though. Not afraid of other birds and even give Blue Jay the cold shoulder when he comes storming in.

Sparrows will eat you out of house and home and come back for mortgage. But they are attractive in a way, quick, alert and sassy, and have oodles of enterprise. Can hold own with Thomas The Squirrel Jr., who hasn't been around much this summer. Think he has been making love, for notice small tads in yard. That's just what we need—two or three more squirrels. Holy Toledo.

It's All A Pipe Dream

All in a Lifetime . . .

A "health magazine," noting that I kicked the cigaret habit about nine months ago in favor of the pipe, has offered a small fee for a piece recounting the ardors and agonies of the experience.

There is just one catch: The essay must end on an approving note, with a peroration, so to speak in absolute support of will power, strength of character and high morality. In other words, the good guys have to win.

Urged on by the prospect of a windfall, I have taken several swipes at the assignment, but it is no go: I just can't bring it off. Invariably, the wheels stop turning when I reach the moment of truth, which can not be averted: "Arney, do you really, truly, honestly feel better now that you have shucked the weed?"

There Are Moments

. . . when I can say: "A little." But mostly, the answer is "nah." Not a bit; feel just the same; feel my age. Lousy.

It used to be that during the course of burning up two packs of cigarets a day, I would have "chest seizures." Sudden, sharp little pains starting about the belly-button and shooting upward. Hooboy. Enough to make you look forward to the next payment on your life insurance.

Well, I still have sudden, sharp little pains starting about the belly-button and shooting upward. In fact, about the only time I don't have sudden, sharp little pains starting about the belly-button and shooting upward is when I am playing golf, lying on a sofa or just sitting and staring.

In other words, chums, if you will fix it so I can escape the pressure of work, at full pay. I will smoke rope and live to be 94. Otherwise, it doesn't make any difference what I smoke, I am going to have sudden, sharp little pains starting about the belly-button and shooting upward.

Oh, I Used to Be

. . . a slave to the cigaret, sometimes having two of them fired up at the same time. Without a cigaret, I was subject to the heebie-jeebies and the whim-whams. Growled at the dog and kicked the wife, or vice versa. Silly way to live. So I quit the darned things . . .

And now I am a slave to the pipe, although it is practically impossible to keep two of them going at once. One is enough, heaven knows. But whereas my "equipment" was formerly a small package and a book of matches, now there are seven or eight pipes, cleaners, a reamer, a digger outer, a pouch and at least four books of matches.

When you see a fellow walking down the street with a list, either to port or to starboard, the odds are that he is a pipe smoker. He is a victim, therefore, of daily chores and nightly rituals, of cleaning, reaming, storing away and lugging the day's dottle to the trash can.

As for a pipe "hurting you less than cigarets," I am not at all sure about the truth of this. Have you ever seen what comes out of a pipe when you ram a cleaner up the stem? Ugh. Some of it gets through; I have swallowed dollops that knocked my knees, crossed my eyes and turned me green. You betcha some of it gets through . . .

You Hear It Said . . .

. . . "Pipe smokers don't inhale." Malarkey, Baloney. Pish-tosh. Horse feathers. Of course they inhale. If they didn't inhale they would be just like cigaret smokers fresh out of ammunition: They would get the heebie-jeebies and the whim-whams.

A pipe isn't a "pacifier." It is how you get your kicks, bub. It is that old nicotine, a-percolatin' through the system, a-soothin' the frazzled nerves.

So I will tell you something; If you are going to quit cigarets, quit 'em cold—fight it out to the bitter end, either you are a man or a mouse. There are no half-way measures.

Especially not a pipe. It is just as habit-forming as marijuana.

Nothing Equals Efficiency

Diary of a Country Correspondent . . .

Flower beds in front of house need weeding, so Old Man licks fingers, hitches up britches, and enters the fray. Hot and humid day stirs memories of New Orleans, circa 1942, when first heat rash was experienced, so decide to wage campaign on efficient, no-wasted-moves basis. Nothing like American planning and know-how for getting a job done without spinning extra wheels.

Select hoe and leaf rake as basic tools, with gleanings to be stowed in paper bag salvaged from trip to supermarket. A little thrift, a little thinking ahead—that's what made the country great. Cal Coolidge and Henry Ford knew what they were talking about.

Approach first section of flower beds feeling sorry for weeds. What a thrashing they are going to get! Wield hoe with gusto and make marvelous progress until run into root which has snuggled up against foundation. Cannot reach it in such a cowardly position so go get large pruning shears and cut it off after considerable exertion. Have yearning for glass of lemonade, but stifle it for sake of efficiency. Must hang in there and finish undertaking without shilly-shallying. Uppen atem, Old Man.

Start clearing away debris but discover that leaf rake is gathering more dirt into pile than want to lose, so decide to switch to garden rake. Go get it. Works better. Right tool for right job, as fellow said. That's American way. Japanese way, too, come to think of it. Original planning now slightly out of kilter, but you have to adapt to circumstances. Have sudden vision of lemonade in tall frosted glass, but eschew it.

Sweep all debris from first section into pile, and obviously it is too big to pick up by hand. Take a month of Sundays, that way. So walk to garage and get snow shovel, which, when used in conjunction with leaf rake, is very efficient piece of gear.

Load snow shovel with debris and try to pour it into paper bag, which collapses and tears apart. Must be putting cruddy material in paper bags these days. Will use wheelbarrow. Find it is in back of garage and have to move car to get it out. Complete maneuver, then submit to desire for lemonade. Have two glasses.

Push wheelbarrow into yard, eye pile of debris, contemplate work still to be done, conclude that wagon and tractor would be more efficient. Put wheelbarrow back in garage, straddle tractor and drive to shed, unload wagon which is full of flower pots and so forth, hook it to tractor and steam to scene of project. Finish job in workmanlike manner, hauling debris into woods, where two million mosquitoes are lurking. Holy Toledo.

Put hoe, leaf rake, garden rake, pruning shears, snow shovel, and busted bag into wagon, throw bag in trash can, hang tools on wall, take wagon to shed, reload it with flower pots and so forth, put tractor in garage, ditto car which had been left in driveway, wipe sweat off brow, go into house and switch from lemonade to Old Slippery Elm.

Review events of past two hours and raise glass in salute to memory of pioneers, who had very few tools to contend with, and may have been the last efficient Americans, all claims to the contrary notwithstanding.

One of great galloping myths prevalent across nation is that use of machinery has done away with manual labor. To understand extent of this pishtosh, just get yourself involved in construction project. Sure, workmen will operate mechanical monsters twice as large as what they are setting out to build, and in process they will scarcely touch a common tool. But after they are gone, who has to man the rake, the shovel, the hoe, the seeder? One guess to a customer.

A long time ago the Old Man came to the conclusion that the more equipment a corporation has, the less efficient it is apt to be. "We get more work done" is a common claim, but efficiency must also include the quality of the work done and the state of the environment after it is finished. Instead of paying people we are paying machines, and one wonders about the long-range wisdom of this.

Ah, the Country Life

Seven long years ago there were friends who thought your narrator was addled in the noggin when he moved to the country, and that opinion seems to be holding fast. We have made fewer converts than a missionary promising salvation to savages if only they would stop drinking fermented pineapple juice.

Hard-core city dwellers are beyond redemption. They testify that they are overcrowded, overtaxed, overmugged, overstressed and over-the-barrel, and yet when dusk approaches in the hinterlands, they readily crank up the engines in their Ramrod Fours and head back to the concrete jungle. One stands in the driveway and waves a fond farewell, praying they reach the bright lights before something untoward happens to them, such as an attack by a mosquito, a horsefly or a no-see-um. They can deal, more or less, with footpads armed with butcher knives or snub-nosed revolvers, but the prospect of confronting things that go whooooo in the night leaves them limp.

It is lonely in the country, they sometimes observe, and this is true if you have been brought up on din and clatter. After the sun goes down, about the only noises we hear are caused by the forces of nature, leading to the rustling of trees and the scratching of small limbs against roofs or sidings. Betimes there may be the muted rumble and clumping of a car in the road, probably steered by a young swain en route to one of the hellholes in Howell or Brighton, where beer is served by the pitcher and Willie Nelson sings by the yard on the juke box.

In seven years there is the recollection of three sirens, two of them sounded when a certain party had to be ambulanced to the hospital. We have had but one fire engine in the neighborhood, and a deputy sheriff shows the flag every three or four weeks. Oh, it is quiet out here, or lonely if you insist, and it is not for everyone.

Of a summer's late afternoon, the sun having gone over the yardarm—meaning that it is 5 p.m. and high time to brace the innerman—he will concoct a martini, whistle up his dog, and they will go into the backyard, where a lawn chair sits under a shade tree.

They have a working agreement that is never violated. The master sips the drink, the dog eats the ice cubes, and they are at peace with one another. Sometimes the dog will snap and devour a fly, or even a bumblebee, demonstrating that heaven provides all things, including hors d'oeuvres, if you remain uppen atem.

In years past there were too many trees in the yard, and in their search for sunlight, some grew as straight and tall as the masts on Captain Bligh's ill-fated packet. Some would call the survivors unsightly, but they serve useful purposes, for they give some shade to the house; and moreover they give the illusion of performing a dance as they weave and thrash in the lightest of breezes. It is nature's floor show without a cover charge, and one does not tire of it.

So they sit there, the man and his dog, and while one cannot be sure of what the latter is thinking, he is positive of his own processes. He does not complain to himself of taxes; he does not cuss the government or those hired to tend it; he does not lament having fetched in so few sheaves when younger; he does not covet his neighbor's pole barn or his convertible; he does not rue the necessity of soon having to bestir himself and get supper. He is content in the country.

Friends will come from the city again, he knows, and say, "Why don't you return to where you belong?" And they will list some of the delights of their surroundings, which are many.

He has learned not to argue with them. He assumes they are as happy as they can be under their circumstances, and he believes he is as happy as he can be under his circumstances.

God made city folks, and country folks, which was very smart of him. Otherwise, either the dancing trees or the dancing girls would be without patrons.

Somebody Else Was There

A friend has returned from a vacation in Ireland where she was subjected to so much Gaelic bamboozle that her eyes have turned from blue to green. Four other friends departed a fortnight ago for San Francisco, there to board a Norwegian luxury liner for an invasion of Alaska. Still another friend took off Monday for Europe, with stopovers in West Germany, Austria, Switzerland and one other country that escapes memory. And before this month is finished two other friends will pull stakes on a journey around the world, covering vast sections of Russia and China by train.

Meanwhile, the Old Curmudgeon tends the store, toiling at the typewriter and hoping to get to Owosso before the snow flies. Fortunately, there is not an ounce of jealously in his entire carcass, thanks to a Spartan upbringing. He was a child of that portion of this century during which you learned to benefit from the travels of others and be thankful for small favors.

In northwestern Ohio in the 1920s, let us say, a citizen who made his way to Cleveland was looked upon with respect. A villager who got all the way to Washington was held in awe. And anyone who dared brave the rigors of a journey to New York City was automatically invited to address the public at an oyster supper.

Aside from the doughboys who had been shipped to France to make the world safe for democracy, there is no recollection of anyone venturing to Europe. As for the Orient, forget it. There were those who thought it started somewhere beyond Denver, but that was just a guess. They had never been to Des Moines, let alone Denver.

———————

In truth, one of the most sought-after citizens of our town was a fellow who crawled out of bed the morning of July 4, 1919, took the train to Toledo, saw the Willard-Dempsey fight for the heavyweight championship of the world, and came back that evening on the westbound Wabash. He was met by a delegation of townspeople and gave such a graphic demonstration of what had occurred, including feints, grunts and fallings-down, that the memory of it sticks to this moment. Two years after, people were still saying to him, "Frank, tell us about the fight," and he would comply, the performance getting better with each presentation. He should have won the Oscar but it hadn't been invented. Shoot, Hollywood was just then being invented.

Now, as noted, people are traveling every which way to the point where bragging rights are hard to come by. If you are at a party, for instance, and you say, "Hey, I was in Jerusalem last weekend," someone is apt to reply, "Yeah? Well, I was there a month ago." Golfers invade Scotland, fisherman seek out the illusive char in the Arctic Circle, and hunters will go most anywhere for a shot at most anything. One used to boast about having been in Ouagadougou with Soapy and Nancy Williams, but even that is getting treacherous. As for a once-obscure object such as the Blarney Stone, it has been kissed by so many Americans that it is starting to taste like Spearmint gum.

One hopes all of this traveling has been broadening, for Americans as well as those upon whom they have descended. One of the drawbacks of such visitations is that they are ordinarily made as guided tours, which is akin to trying to figure out what is happening in the Republic by listening to a presidential press conference. If you were really interested in what an Irishman thinks about an Englishman, you would probably have to get into a peat bog and thrash it out with him. Still, it is no doubt better to have a filtered view of other people than no view at all. Americans still have a somewhat limited perspective of the rest of the world, but we aren't as dumb as we used to be.

As for your narrator, he has been just about every place he ever wanted to go except Russia and China. He would have made that upcoming trip around the world with friends except they won't take singles on the train in question—and there was no relief in sight.

Fern Was an Artist

Martin F. Kohn of our staff wrote a lovely obituary detailing the highlights of the life and times of Fern Haver Arnett, and there is gratitude to him and to the editors who assigned the task.

There was, however, a slight discrepancy in one paragraph, which read, "She was also an artist and an avid golfer."

Well, now. She was indeed an artist of considerable talent, taking to painting much like those who skillfully play the piano without knowing the precise location of middle C. With little instruction, she set up an easel while we were living in the house on Grandmont and thereafter produced a number of paintings which grace the walls of this wilderness manse. A few others are in the possession of close friends and relatives.

James Ross, a true professional who is earning a national reputation from his gallery near Howell, has said of her that she would have made a splendid student, with perhaps the chance of widespread recognition, but she didn't have that in mind. She painted because it was a way of expressing the sense of beauty in all things which dwelt within her, and the results are among the priceless keepsakes which mark our years together.

———

Now, about that phrase "an avid golfer." Hoo, boy. In truth, she was a "golf widow," a gentle and understanding stay-at-home while her old man spent Saturdays and Sundays pretending he was Ben Hogan. Infrequently she would play with friends or in mixed foursomes, but she was much more interested in her surroundings, the trees, the wild flowers, the birds, than in walloping the ball with any semblance of precision. She never really "took to the game," as the saying goes, and therein lies an admission of guilt . . .

To use an old-fashioned phrase, "we went together" for four years prior to marriage, and once in a while in the bliss of summertime we would go to a country course near Liberty Center and strut our stuff. Those fairways and greens, casualties of World War II, have long since been returned to rolling pastureland, but they remain retraceable in memory.

The ninth tee was situated on a hill, then there was a valley bisected by a creek, and beyond it were trees in multitude rooted into a sharp embankment. If you carried those obstacles, it was a par four of medium difficulty, but if you didn't . . .

She hit the ball into the valley; and then into the creek; and back into the creek a time or two; then into the woods; and there followed a fusillade of ricochets, as though several woodpeckers were working overtime; and all the while her dumb boyfriend was hooting and hollering and counting the strokes, which finally reached 27. He should have been hit on the head with a mashie-niblick, and surely he demonstrated characteristics which indicated he would not make a sound partner in holy wedlock, but she kept a fixed little smile on her face and forgave him his idiocy.

Thereafter, however, her enthusiasm for golf as a participant was somewhat less than intense, and half a century later he blames this incident for it and considers himself a fool.

No one believed him a few weeks ago when he wrote a column saying that he was giving up golf, but he had resolved not to extend her tenure as the "widow" of a hobby. Too little, too late, you might say.

———

What that paragraph should have said was that she was an "avid gardener." She considered flowers one of nature's supreme gifts and was never happier than when an arrangement of cuttings brightened the house. She may have been too ill to fully appreciate the flower garden Mark Lemak and her husband fashioned for her last spring, but it was a tribute to her, nonetheless, even though the designers scarcely knew the difference between a petunia and a dahlia.

Now time has marched on and one must trust the judgment of God, who selects those to be called and those to stay. He recalls the opening line of the 23d Psalm: "The Lord is my shepherd, I shall not want . . . " It's no less than the promise of a miracle.

The Only Philosophy

All in a Lifetime . . .

A young fellow knocked at the door a few mornings ago and asked for the job of chopping down a large maple tree that leans over the front yard, clinging for dear life by only a portion of its root system.

The answer was no. The tree, a real beauty, has been caterwampussed since we moved here eight years ago, yet every summer it has produced excellent shade, and every fall it has released a torrent of leaves. It might hang on for another eight years, or another 20. Who knows? Let it stand in peace. . . .

If anything has been learned from life, it is approximately this: It is next to impossible within the realm of nature or the order of man to tell what is going to happen next. No one knows what "The

Plan" is, if indeed there is one. The individual who lives "one day at a time," taking in stride whatever occurs, may not be as dumb or as careless as he or she sounds. You hear it said, "Don't give me any surprises!" but in truth life is full of them. Survivors rise above surprises.

———

Who will live and who will die is beyond the ken of the casual observer. Vivid is the memory of a friend who looked as though he would live forever. He was robust, and lusty, and eager for the day's challenges, and full of plans for the future. What he didn't plan on was dying within a month of the inception of an illness. Another friend comes to mind—frail, constantly at pain from one ailment or another, she won't make it to Christmas was the annual prognosis. She is now 82, still functioning on at least one cylinder.

Most of the great changes that have moved society in one direction or another have come as surprises.

The automobile was a rich man's toy, or so it was said; Robert Fulton gave up on the steamboat because he ran out of money and incentive; Abraham Lincoln wasn't the least bit certain his Gettysburg Address would live beyond the next day's editions of a largely hostile press; Henry David Thoreau thought the railroad was an abomination; only a handful of dreamers saw a future in mass transportation for the airplane; there were economists in 1929 who were convinced that the perfect society, free of financial panics, had finally been created in America; and Woodrow Wilson was truly of the opinion that he could make the world safe for democracy.

The wheels go around, and once in a while general conditions are altered by a millimeter or two, but who or what is in charge of locomotion? It is not mortal planner or schemer. Tolstoy wrote that society had not changed for the better over the course of his lifetime. The Durants, Will and Ariel, searched all of their remarkable lives for the lessons of history—and came up with a book one-half inch thick. How whatever happens happens, and why, remain the mystery of the ages. Ah, there is much to be said for "one day at a time. . . . "

———

Man has become very agile where technology is involved, and that is where the conditions of life are being altered. The computer reaches into outer space; if doctors can match your ailment to the right machine, your span of years will probably be increased; no doubt we have not yet crossed the threshold of scientific wonders.

But even though we alter some of the conditions of life, we do not run it, we do not know what "The Plan" is, and we are not immune to surprises, some of them bordering on catastrophes. We are not as smart as we think we are.

Live one day at a time; roll with the punches; and keep the ax-man away from the maple tree. In a nutshell, that is the only "philosophy" the Curmudgeon has for you at the moment.

Harvest of Adventure

The garden had no sooner been roto-tilled than Miss Fern took to her hands and knees and planted two rows of peas. In the nearly 50 years of our association (going on 44 married) she has never relinquished the notion that fresh creamed peas and new small potatoes make one of the finest dishes this side of New Orleans gumbo. How bedrock Midwestern can you get?

Since moving to the country we have learned there is a good deal of adventure connected with gardening in Michigan. This adds spice to the investment of time and seed and makes us happy we do not live in Rhode Island, let us say, where nothing untoward ever happens.

The weather is perhaps the least of the uncertainties confronted by the gardener in our neck of the woods. As a matter of fact, there is no record of a season so sparse in sunshine that peas did not mature. If you have enough patience, your efforts will be rewarded with something.

The reputation of our climate suffers from the inability of the weather bureau to forecast it. We probably get more punk information than the citizens of any other region, including Alaska. This keeps us on tenterhooks and causes us to wallow in skepticism and ill-humor, like the folks who heard the little boy holler "wolf!" too often. In short, our weather is better than what we expect from it or say about it. We are the exact opposite of Floridians, who have been brainwashed into bragging about how good their weather is. If you could get them to tell you the truth about May through September, you wouldn't shiver just thinking about January.

Where were we? The adventures of gardening. Never a dull moment.

Out our way, it is a battle of wits between the two-leggeds and the four-leggeds, and ties don't count. The gardener has to keep in mind that in addition to himself and his heirs and assigns, he also has to figure on feeding the rabbits, the squirrels, the chipmunks, the raccoons, the possums, the deer, and other critters too numerous to mention. It takes a heap of planting to fill all of those tummies.

And there are times when the two-leggeds are left holding the sack in the snipe hunt. More than one gardener can make you cry, almost, with a tale of how the raccoons wiped out the sweet corn the night before it was to be served to deprived friends and relatives from the city. We have rabbits as big as cocker spaniels, fat and sassy from bellying up to the lettuce bed at midnight. For that matter, our crows, conditioned on 39-cents-a-package seeds, would make marvelous fighting cocks—if you could catch them.

However, the most exciting of all adventures comes when you garden new soil, especially if it has been rescued from woodlot. What will the harvest be?

Last year, Miss Fern produced one of the gol-dangest crops of stalks, vines and shoots the realm of horticulture has ever experienced. She had one tomato plant that grew so big and mean looking Old Yeller got afraid to lift his leg on it, and you could have hit flies to the outfield with the roots on her radishes. The harvest was amazing in a weird sort of way.

Patently the nutrients, or whatever you call them, in the soil were out of sync, so during the winter we took a can of it to the Livingston Count Co-operative Extension Service for analysis. Pour on the limestone and the 6-24-24 fertilizer, they recommended, and this done we are now awaiting the miracles. Last year vines, this year tomatoes! Yes indeedy.

The Way of Friendship

On a recent Sabbath, having anticipated four guests for dinner, the Lady of the House nearly suffered an attack of the vapors when 10 showed up. "Holy Toledo," she whispered as they kept streaming through the front door, "how am I going to stretch that casserole to feed all of this crowd?"

I was about to remind her of the miracle of the loaves and the fishes when one of the guests, noting the alarm on her face, said: "Don't worry. We have brought plenty of food." And so they had—so much, in fact, that her casserole went untouched and I have been eating it all week. There is something to be said for a casserole after one meal. There is a bit less to be said after two meals. But when you are eating for six, the darned thing becomes unspeakable.

Anyhow, the guest list for this auspicious occasion embraced Jim and Barbara Jones of Bloomfield Hills; and John and Helen Turi, Method and Irene Gavura, Ken and Ruth MacGillwray, and Jerry and Marj Rideout of Flint and environs.

Mr. Rideout, a golfing partner known far and wide as being short off the tee but long on confidence, handled the logistics of the Flint expedition and they arrived in the motor home owned by the MacGillwrays.

———

The sight of this equipage steaming up his driveway left Old Yeller on the verge of the vapors, too, but after he had smelled the food he rallied and shook hands all around and otherwise ingratiated himself. One suspects the Goths could invade our place without risk of fang or claw if they arrived with something bubbling in a pot. It is a terrible thing to say of him, but to this point one must admit that Old Yeller has displayed the defense of the New York Jets and the offense of the Detroit Lions. A lover and an eater, this one.

It was a splendid evening. We laughed, and talked, and remember-whened, and praised one another, and ate, and excluded the troubles of the world from our midst, and when they left Mr. Gavura and Mr. Rideout were in the back end of the motor home, locked in the intensity of a gin rummy game which has been running for about 27 years.

The house seemed deserted, abandoned, but after a while we were warmed by old memories. This, we told one another, was the way friendship had flourished during our younger years, and we resolved to be less formal in our social arrangements in the days to come.

<hr />

It has been said that the best things in life are free, and to this you might add that most of them are spontaneous, too. The firmest friendships are based on the loosest of formalities. People are near and dear when you can telephone and say, "What are you doing?" And if the answer is "Nothing," and your reply is, "We'll be right over!" and they say "Fine!" and mean it—then you have something going that is worthy of that good, solid word—"friendship." It sure beats the heck out of making a note in your social calendar that you are to see them two weeks from Tuesday at 8 p.m.

We had the best times of our lives when we were young, and very poor, and eagerly responsive to those around us. In the company of those for whom there was affection we ate enough popcorn to fill Cobo Hall, we played cards—bridge occasionally, but usually some spirited game such as euchre or horse n' pepper—we listened to the radio if it was worth it, and we went to the movies if Hollywood had produced a spectacular beyond resistance.

There is the recollection that we paid 75 cents each—wow!—to see "Gone with the Wind," first run, and I wrote a piece for the sheet then paying me $25 a week saying that Leslie Howard sure had a strange Southern accent. The rerun on television a few nights ago left the impression that for once in my life I was right.

———⊷⊶——— ———⊷⊶———

From a safe distance comes the notion that today's young people feel about one another much as we did long ago. Oh, sure, these kids have much more money than we did, and cars to boot, but there is a lack of formality to their relationships, a casual openness and sense of caring, which is remindful of an era now gone. Some critics may say they have substituted pot for popcorn, but that could be a blanket indictment which is not only unfair but misleading. Previously, no generation had been all good or all bad, and one suspects the record is still intact.

Gelett Burgess wrote that "Love is only chatter, Friends are all that matter." A bit strong, perhaps, but you can't dispute the fact that without friends, life would be empty, indeed.

PTCA—Quite an Experience

All in a Lifetime . . .

Well, sir, things sure move at a full gallop these days. This includes health service, where there is a contest to see which hospital can throw you into the street with the least hanging out, the soonest.

The Curmudgeon kids, of course, but not by much, as the following may demonstrate . . .

On a recent Tuesday morning he was out in his yard, thumping away at a clutch of weeds and old leaves which were beneath the dignity of budding spring. All at once he was seized by a sharp pain in the chest, and he stood up and swore prettily as it spread to his shoulders and down his back.

Indigestion, no doubt. So he went into the house and unbottled three Tums, which are one of the two products he would not be without, the other being Noxema. He munched the pellets, which have cured monumental upheavels over the years, then sat for a spell in a chair.

Shortly he was cured. Heaven bless Tums. So it was back to raking, and later to riding the tractor and mower, and in the evening to taking friends to dinner, and at about 10:30 in the pitch of night—Holy Toledo, but it gets dark out here—to being seized again, only this time by bands of steel, fore and aft, so powerful that a whole clutch of Tums did no good. The Curmudgeon was in a fix and the sweat poured from his furrowed brow as he paced the floor whilst attempting to settle the concern of his faithful dog, Schultz.

At Wednesday mid-morning that great internist and marvelous friend, Dr. Phil Schmitt, took one quick look at an EKG and said, "We are going to St. Joe's." And that was where we went, St. Joe's in Ann Arbor, the good doctor at the wheel of his Ramrod 8, scattering chickens and causing on-coming motorists to raise their eyebrows until their hats fell off. (A ride with Doc Schmitt under ordinary circumstances will clear your nasal passages, out-set your eyeballs by a quarter of an inch and wear rings around your rosary, if you carry one.)

And there awaiting us was Dr. John Fischer, cardiologist, a mentor of two previous visits to St. Joe's. Strange: A fellow lives donkey's years and never sets foot in a hospital as a patient, then all at once he shows up at the same one three times in two years, pleading for succor. It was forthcoming on a fast track.

Within an hour they had the Curmudgeon stretched out like 170 pounds of prime blubber, and John Fischer and his cohort, Dr. Frank Smith, flanked by nurses and technicians, were administering Percutaneous Transluminal Coronary Angioplasty. Dr. Lincoln Innes, uncle by marriage, fighter of the 1919 influenza epidemic with a bottle of aspirin, would not have believed it.

PTCA, let us call it, involves a hat-pin-like tube with a tiny balloon at the tip. Now we quote from the manual: "When the doctor inflates the balloon inside your blocked artery, the pressure forces the blockage against the artery walls. This allows more oxygen-filled blood to flow through the artery to feed your heart." Think of a mouse gnawing its way through a slab of Swiss cheese. That brings it down to a working man's level.

St. Joe's is one of the few Michigan hospitals that can do PTCA, and it is rarer yet in that it can do more than one artery at the same time. That was exceedingly helpful inasmuch as the Curmudgeon had trouble in two—90 percent blockage in one, 99 percent in the other. Incidentally, he saw pictures of his artery system leading to the heart, and it looked like a handful of snakes. Goodness gracious.

PTCA is an ingenious procedure of late design and it will doubtless do away with a good deal of open heart surgery. It also speeds you out of the hospital, in this case on Sunday. One is a bit woozy as he puts an end to this, but he is extremely grateful for having ducked what would surely have developed into a major heart attack.

SIX
Man's Best Friends

The Invasion of Thomas

Being weary of hoof and otherwise debilitated by the rigors of vacation, your commentator sought the solace of the parlor davenport shortly after arriving home Sunday afternoon.

Snuggled under the afghan, recalling with favor the one resounding tee shot he had struck during four outings on an Arizona golf course, he was on the verge of sleepy-bye when suddenly there was a strange noise.

"Chitter-chatter-crunch-crackle-kazambo!," was the way it sounded, and the first inclination was to charge it off to ear strain from high altitude flying. The pressurized cabin has not been invented which will protect these shell-like lobes from unusual poppings and snappings, sometimes for days after travel's end.

But then there was an encore of the noise—"Chitter-chatter-crunch-crackle-kazambo!!"—so I sat up and peered toward the front window. Hark!—hear also the sound of rustling.

Well, you probably won't believe this, but so help me Hannah and keep me steadfast, there—perched atop the rod upon which the draperies slide—was Thomas The Squirrel Jr. Think of it, mates: Cold sober and I see Thomas The Squirrel Jr. in my own parlor. Let me tell you, it was enough to drive a temperate man to instant drink.

Anyhow, Thomas The Squirrel Jr. was sitting there, hunkered in an alert position, eyes glistening, and he was giving me what for.

"Chitter-chatter-crunch-crackle-kazambol!," he said again, and I read him loud and clear, "Corn," I thought, "he ran out of corn while we were gone, so he decided to invade the base of supply." Smart little critters, squirrels.

I rolled off the davenport and walked toward the window, talking to him all the while.

"Thomas," I said, "you had better come down off those draperies or you are going to get into more trouble than you can handle. The lady of this house will crown you with a two-gallon stew pot if you snag those draperies. So come down off there, right now. You hear me?"

"Chitter-chatter-crunch-crackle-kazambo!," he replied, sitting up on his haunches. You could tell he was nervous but defiant, determined to fight it out on that line if it took until Memorial Day.

"I'll give you some corn," I said, "if you'll come down off those draperies and behave yourself. But you're not going to eat it in the parlor. Heaven's man, nobody eats in the parlor around here."

"Chitter-chatter-crunch-crackle-kazambo!," he responded, and it was obvious we had reached an impasse, as they say in labor-management circles on the eve of a six-months' strike.

———————

Attracted by this conversation, which was a bit unusual even for our place; the lady of house came into the parlor. "What's going on around here?" she demanded. I pointed to where he was sitting.

"Thomas The Squirrel Jr.," she yelled, matching him eye for eye and glitter for glitter, "you get down off those draperies before you snag them. You ought to be ashamed of yourself, that's what you ought to be!"

"I warned you," I told him, and then I went and got the stepladder.

Well, sir, when I put the stepladder at one end of the draperies, Thomas The Squirrel Jr. ran to the other end, chittering and chattering, and I was not over-anxious, if the truth be known, to reach any distance and snatch him, what with us being buddies and all—and not to mention his angry little teeth. The thought occurred to throw something over him, but when she brought a sweater he suddenly dropped to the floor and cut across the parlor toward another window.

"Don't you dare snag those draperies!" she called after him. so he veered into the kitchen and we closed the door behind him. Then we shut off the parlor hallway and the doors to the den and bathroom, and I opened the door to the back porch and propped the snow shovel against the screen door, and after a while he found his way out, protesting to high heaven, determined to have the last word.

He had come down the chimney, we later discovered, slipping past a protective device which was not secured, and had evidently been in the house for at least a day. He was no doubt hungry and thirsty when he spotted me on the davenport, and had we not returned he would have gone foraging in earnest. But we had our conversation before he snagged the draperies, thank goodness.

She Called Him Old Yeller

Old Yeller, as Fern immediately called him, showed up at our house Friday afternoon. What we may have here is the four-legged version of "The Man Who Came to Dinner."

"There is a dog in the shrubbery near the front door," she reported as soon as I arrived home. "I think he is very sick, so maybe we had better call someone."

Who? The police? They were busy hassling one another that particular day. So we went out and had a firsthand look.

Sure enough, there was Old Yeller, deep in the bushes. He was all stretched out, with his nose on his front paws, and there seemed to be about two yards of him. Holy Toledo, what a critter. You had to shift your eyeballs to see all of him, fore to aft. Only a fool would have gone in after him without the assistance of a couple of beaters and a gun bearer.

We gave him some sweet talk, larded with "poor old fellas" and "nice guys like you," and finally he thumped his tail a time or two, sighed and rolled his head to one side. You could see that his left ear had either been chewed on or caught in something and his legs were caked with mud, as though he had travelled a far piece under trying circumstances. Gradually, it became evident that he was burdened with exhaustion. Not sick, just tuckered out.

Well, sir, Fern brought a pan of water and I poked it through the underbrush to within a foot of his muzzle, and he scrouched forward and lapped it with a tongue as big as a T-bone steak. He did the same thing to an offering of milk. After we sweet-talked him some more, we parted the shrubbery and he came staggering out.

He was limping on his left rear paw and gave the general impression of being a senior citizen very much down on his luck. In the sunlight, though, there were flashes of red in his short, wiry coat and there was something about him, decrepit as he seemed, which spoke of class.

At one time, this was a handsome, swashbuckling dude, with a long, strong jaw, sad brown eyes and a carriage indicating well-controlled strength. As he followed us into the backyard he stood well above my knees at his front shoulder. Although he was gaunt in the fanks, I estimated him at 75 pounds, minimum. His ancestry was not easy to define. Some Golden Retriever, possibly, and perhaps a touch of Airedale. A big reddish-yellow fellow, of the type sought by farmers or families with numerous children. No collar, no license, an old, set-upon chap a long way from home.

He took on another pan of milk fortified with bread and then he collapsed in the grass, stretching to catch the last warmth of the evening sun. We watched him and talked of his "incredible journey," as we envisioned it, and wondered what in the world we were going to do with him. He might rest a while and then go on to whatever he was searching for, we agreed. We would put him up for the night on the back porch and then the next day leave the gate open, with no hard feelings on either side when he decided to say so long.

He was still there this morning, getting younger by the minute. Most of the limp is gone, his ear is responding to treatment, he is alert and full of head-on-knee affection and already he has upset the balance of power in the neighborhood. Yesterday afternoon he casually sent a cat up a telephone pole and an uneasy truce, at best, prevails where Thomas The Squirrel Jr. is concerned.

It is against Old Yeller's instincts, and maybe even his religion, to permit squirrels to invade his turf, but he is so well-mannered that upon command he will just sit quivering from head to tail and glare at Thomas. He is obedient, a light eater for his size and condition, fastidious in personal habits and full of the desire to please.

He is also a victim of the recession, in all likelihood. Ron Blauet, manager of the Humane Society, tells us that unemployment plus curtailed activities by the Dog Pound have put more strays than ever before on the streets. They are adrift, homeless, unclaimed, unattended, unloved. What is to become of them? For that matter, what is to become of Old Yeller, who is more chum than we anticipated?

Down-in-the-Country Dog

A number of constituents have requested an additional progress report on the life and times of Old Yeller, the stray dog that came to our house a month ago, wobbly of knee and very much down in the mouth. Inasmuch as there is firm belief in this quarter that public demand should be recognized, this will bring you up to date.

Dear friends, Old Yeller is—or at least was—a complete fraud, a real snake oil salesman. At first glance we assumed he was in his dotage, over the hill and just one short jump ahead of the funeral director. You may recall how we coaxed him out of the shrubbery and how he limped into the back yard, creaking in every joint and dragging his left rear paw. He was a spectacle to bring a lump to your throat and tears to your eyes. If you had not been guilty of a kind and gentle thought in 42 years, the sight of him would have squeezed one out of you. No character in all of literature would have been able to deny him, including Scrooge.

Well, sir, I have since come to the conclusion that what happened to Old Yeller was that he had been out drinkin' white lightnin' and chasin' the girls. Since he has been living a clean and decent life he has undergone an amazing transformation. He is now first in war, last in peace and somewhere near the bottom in the hearts of his four-legged countrymen. He has a running battle going with every squirrel in the neighborhood and he detests cats and dogs. This got him into a heap of trouble a few days ago.

———

The back porch was recently re-screened at considerable expense and we left him out there one evening while we went to dinner. When we returned he was in the yard, dancing around in pursuit of a bumble bee.

"How did Old Yeller get in the yard?" Fern wanted to know as we put the car in the garage.

Oh, my. Sinking feeling. "Just look at the screen in that panel near the door," I said.

He had plowed through it, ker-wham, no doubt in pursuit of one of his mortal enemies. A cat, most likely. A terrible half hour followed, full of viewings with alarm and lectures on loyalty, the state of the budget and good behavior in return for love and affection. He was so far in the doghouse that it took him two transfers just to reach the exit.

But he wiggled out of it, primarily because he is an irresistible character. That plus the fact that he has known hard times. One evening when we started out for a walk there was a small tree limb on the sidewalk and I reached down and picked it up, intending to throw it on the scrap pile. Immediately, Old Yeller dropped to his side, pulled up his feet and started cowering and whimpering, no doubt in anticipation of a thrashing. That did something to me. No longer do we pay attention to sticks or other debris when we are strolling. The voice—"No!"—is restraint and punishment enough. He is beautifully mannered if you insist on it, being in that respect akin to his two-legged contemporaries.

———

We have exhausted our imaginations in an effort to learn his former name, calling him everything from "Butch" to "Snoopy," but nothing has registered. He is really too young to be known as Old Yeller, but a suitable substitute has not come to mind. He is an old-fashioned, all-American, down-in-the-country dog, the type you used to see around farmhouses and in small towns. The American Kennel Club would not permit him within 400 yards of a dog show, but he could probably out-fight and out-womanize any recent champion. What he lacks in pedigree he makes up in smarts. In a curious way, he reminds me of Abe Lincoln.

"Hey, Old Yeller," we will say to him when it is time for some ear scratching or back rubbing, and he will come ambling over, eyes bright with anticipation, tongue lolling, body twitching and turning. Just a big, fraudulent lollygagger.

He isn't worth much—but he is priceless. Surely you have known dogs like that.

He Didn't Believe in Overtime

Old Yeller tore into the woods the other day in hot pursuit of something—it could have been a rabbit, a raccoon, a squirrel, a skunk (oh, no!) or just a figment of his imagination—and when he emerged about an hour later he had a bemused look on his face, like a relief pitcher who has lost the smoke on his fast ball, and he drank two quarts of water without coming up for air.

There are times when living out in the country seems almost more than Old Yeller can bear, what with the guarding he has to do and the wildlife he must boss around, but just before he has a nervous breakdown he will go to sleep in the shade for a couple of hours, and when he wakes up he is as fresh as a daisy and ready for love.

The front offices and board rooms of our commercial and industrial complexes are full of high-priced geniuses who could learn a thing or two from Old Yeller, who knows just how far he can stretch the rubber band in his gizzard before it will snap and leave him twirly. Dogs are subject to numerous strange and curious ailments, and have a short life span as a result of constitutional deficiencies and a medical science that isn't even written in their language, but their instinct tells them how and when to relax and you rarely meet one who believes in overtime.

Old Yeller has learned to live with modern conveniences and the gadgetry of our times. The other morning, as an illustration, the smoke alarm went off at five o'clock, making a terrible bbrrrrrrrrrr! sound and sending Miss Fern and yours truly galloping all over the premises, hollering at one another and looking for fire in the most remarkable places, including the inside of the refrigerator, but at the pitch of this hysteria, he merely wagged his tail a time or two and then plunked back down on his bed.

Somehow, he knew it was a false alarm, that the danged klaxon had gone off because of Murphy's Law or a visitation by a gremlin passing through en route to duty in the Carter administration, and he wasn't about to get excited by fire and smoke that weren't there.

Incidentally, just why the alarm did sound has been a matter of some discussion at our house, and Miss Fern has come up with a theory. It is her conviction that a moth or some other summer bug found its way into the element where the light burns, was in due course incinerated, causing sufficient smoke to touch off the system.

This seems a rather flimsy scenario upon which to base such a hellacious amount of racket, but it is the best notion we have at the moment unless you want to accept Murphy's Law or the stray gremlin.

Further, our puzzlement is compounded by the fact that the same thing happened shortly after we had moved here two years ago, with a similar lack of obvious reason. No smoke, no fire, no evidence of either. Just bbrrrrrrrrrr! Old Yeller joined in the tearing around and running into each other that time, at one-thirty in the morning it was, so maybe he figures this is what his folks do now that they are too ancient for whoopee. People are crazy, of that he is certain.

Mark Twain knew a great deal about dogs, and wrote of them with affection, but it was his belief that a cayote (or what we would now call a coyote) was more resourceful.

In fact, he wrote a short story called "The Cayote" and in it he had a city dog without any on-the-job training, such as Old Yeller, join a wagon train and head West. Well, the countryside was full of cayotes in those days, and eventually the pup got on the trail of one of them, which led him all over you-know-where's half-acre, and about ran his poor legs off and frazzled him, and finally the dog gave up and this was what he thought, according to Mark Twain:

"It makes his head swim. He stops and looks all around; climbs the nearest sand-mound and gazes into the distance; shakes his head reflectively, and then, without a word, he turns and jogs along back to his train, and takes up a humble position under the hindmost wagon, and feels unspeakably mean, and looks ashamed, and hangs his tail at half-mast for a week. And for as much as a year after that, whenever there is a great hue and cry after a cayote, that dog will merely glance in that direction without emotion, and apparently observe to himself: 'I believe I do not wish any of that pie.' "

One prefers to believe that Old Yeller is less confused by his chases through the woods, although it must be admitted that he has never returned with any evidence of the hunt. He simply disappears in an orange blur; we may hear him yelping in the distance; and then he will return as noted, energy at low ebb, yes, but not dismayed or ready for a psychiatrist. Shucks. Bring on a cayote!

There Went Arizona

Friend and compatriot George Puscas of our sporting department recently returned from a long weekend in the North Country. It is now his measured testimony that life in such a clime can be beautiful, if you give it half a chance.

He says this even though, during his last hour at the lodge, three skiers were carted off the premises with legs encased in those inflatible plastic bags which usually indicate fractures.

It could be, in fact, that his new assessment of the charms of February was influenced by his determination not to attempt anything violent. No careening down a precipitous slope on bed slats for him. Mr. Puscas stuck, instead, to cross-country mushing, the joys of a log fire and girl watching, and now we have another winter lover in our midst.

All of this is very interesting and instructive to your commentator and his heirs and assigns, simply because about 10 days ago we decided—oh, what a loose word!—that eventually we would move to Arizona. The Golden West in a Buckskin Vest—that was our slogan. We would go out there and rough it with Barry Goldwater and other strong but-not-so-silent types. High noon at the Longbranch Saloon. Yippeeee! Hand me my Stetson, Podner, and I will go out and bag a Gila monster for lunch.

———◆◇——— ———◇◆———

We had been influenced by the receipt of another brochure from a nationally known sales organization depicting the marvels of life in the desert.

Sunshine 310 days a year, practically guaranteed by the Chamber of Commerce. Seventy-two golf courses, more or less, within a niblick shot of your own Arizona Room. A recreation center just around the corner and a hospital only a block away. No kids. My, they seem to have thought of everything.

And with a degree of seriousness, this should be said about Arizona: Within this knowledge, there are no better housing buys in America. For $35,000, part down and the rest when they catch you, you can live in the lap of luxury, including central air conditioning. On today's market, in case you hadn't noticed, that is like finding money in an old pair of pants.

So we shook hands on it, telling each other that we had, By Grabbies, finally made a decision. Arizona or bust. Onward and outward and may your grandchildren never have the Michigan arthritis.

———◆◇——— ———◇◆———

Two early mornings later, give or take a few minutes of three o'clock, there was a rude interruption in the even tenor of this resolution. Bolt upright in the bed the question was confronted: "What is Old Yeller going to do if we move to Arizona?"

Why, he is going to go along, of course. Naturally. He is part of the family, isn't he? We are buddies, aren't we? What a silly question!

And then I tried to picture him in the backyard in Arizona, surrounded by rocks and cacti, the temperature edging toward 115 degrees and the sweat pouring off the end of his tongue, and not a tree or bush to hunker under.

And when, in mind's eye, I combed him his hair came out in great orange swatches and he had such a sad look on his face that I put my head under the covers and ignored him when he came to the side of the bed, which he will do if he hears the slightest stirring. Go back to sleep, Yeller, I willed him, and he did.

———————

You know, I had forgotten about trees. Elms and birches and pines and maples and cherry and apple and plum—only God, etc. That is true: Poets have a subtle way with the truth, don't they? And so does memory, especially at three o'clock in the morning.

Fantasy, now. Gradually the bedroom was filled with all of the trees I had ever known and loved, and a gentle wind in their branches kept whispering: "You will miss me, you rascal, if you go to Arizona . . . "

And then, as extra penance, memory fetched the vistas of the long, ocean-like swells of our countryside, green in the early spring, the summer and the autumn, and white in the winter. Best of all when speckled with "the teeth of the lion," as the French speak of the dandelion. But snow is all right, when we permit it to remain majestic. Or speckled with pretty girls.

A few evenings later we were doing the dishes when she said, I have been thinking some more about Arizona. And what about it, my pet? I have been thinking, she said, that I might prefer to stay in Michigan. Trees, I thought, and maybe a touch of Old Yeller, too.

The Final Tribute

Dr. Robert F. Willson, the head keeper of the Detroit Zoo during some of its more progressive years, was one of the hundreds who either wrote, called, or delivered their regrets in person during the immediate aftermath of Old Yeller's departure from this mortal coil. We remember what he said via telephone: "Animals have a way of walking through your heart."

How true, as several fetching stories since then have illustrated. Surely most of us rooted for the gentleman who lost his cat, offered $500 reward, received a look-alike in an early exchange, but was finally reunited with the right tabby. And then, of course, there is Benji, the alert and devilish-looking pup, rescued from a busy thoroughfare by a beautiful female bus driver, mended by $400 worth of medical treatment for which she went into hock, a public figure long enough to bring in cash to pay the debts, and now the center of attraction in a new home with a loving young mistress.

These are sometimes called "warm and cuddly stories" by hardened newsmen, and frequently there are debates as to how much space and preparation time they should receive. Little logic will be forthcoming from this quarter, for we are left with a heart walked through by a combination airedale and golden retriever, and a stack of unanswerable mail from those who developed affection for him as the years rolled by.

Old Yeller, who came to us during the hard recession year of 1975, when it was estimated that Detroit strays numbered at least 80,000, was a consumate actor from the very beginning. Fern first spotted him deep in the shrubbery at the House on Grandmont, and later when we coaxed him into limping to the backyard, a spectacle that would have squeezed tears out of a statue, she exclaimed, "He looks like Old Yeller in the movie." The name stuck although perhaps it would have been more appropriate to have called him "Dee-troit," for he turned out to have the courage and pride of the city badly shaken by adversity. In more ways than one, he, too, overcame.

He soon developed into something of a public trust. Early on, an uncounted number of readers wrote in to say, simply, "God sent him to you." While we never quite believed that, it became part of the responsibility of his care and upkeep.

Eventually, it was a rare day when we did not receive at least one letter urging tender, loving care upon him. Infrequently, of course, someone would complain that we ought to devote all of our time and space to saving the world, and to heck with God's creatures, including stray dogs, but less and less in late years have we agreed with that. There has been the growing feeling, instead, that until God's creatures are secure, there is little chance for what is loosely called "humanity," nor should there be. It is about time, in short, that man showed a little class and gave some thought to the claim that he deserves to be king of the hill.

How does it happen, this "walking through your heart" that Doc Willson mentioned? As with most falling in love, it is a subtle process, sometimes following on the heels of contention.

Do you remember how Old Yeller plowed through the screens of our back porch in Detroit, right after we had paid $160 to have them refurbished? He made four such banzai attacks against Thomas the Squirrel Jr., if memory is correct, and we spent a good part of that first summer making awkward repairs. Twice, when left alone in the house, he tore curtains off the windows and violated all of the rules of sanitation, and after a particularly devastating uprising, we opened the back gate and ordered him to beat it, to go back to Skid Row if that was the way he wanted to live, and be quick about it. He refused. He knew something.

What he knew was that mutual affection was flowering, and would lead to an accommodation—instead of leaving him alone, we would take him with us almost everywhere we went. Thereafter he was destined to spend hundreds of hours in the car, perfectly content as we visited friends, went to dinner or the movies, or shopped at market or mall. He saw much of man's world from the back seat of the Ramrod Eight and seemed to enjoy every minute of it.

Life became a series of small rituals—going for the paper, going for the mail, going to town—and to this moment it is impossible to pick up a small stick in the yard without anticipating his "attack," for he loved to grab and tug. And how we miss him at night, when it is time to stand at the head of the driveway and say goodnight to the universe.

Ah, yes—they "walk through your heart." This has been a promised final tribute to a dear friend, of whom we shall hear no more. It is time, in fact, to go on vacation, far, far away.

Saga at Breakfast

Now it is morning at the House on Grandmont and Thomas The Squirrel has come for his breakfast.

We are sitting in the breakfast nook, sharing the Morning Friendly. The coffee is hot, the toast is succulent (if that is possible!), it is a snug and reposed moment in advance of the ferment of the day.

Then the Girl Friend rustles her portion of the paper. "Oh, oh," she says.

A familiar warning. So I look out the window to the left and there is Thomas The Squirrel. He has come down an elm tree and he is about three feet from the ground, hanging head foremost.

"Here we go again," I say, and she smiles and cautions, "be quiet—and let's watch him." Perfectly still, we wait for the drama to unfold.

Thomas The Squirrel raises his head and cases the windows of the breakfast nook. Then he lashes his tail three times, left-right-left and back to neutral. His tail is as big as a feather duster and the rest of him is sleek and fat and his red coat sparkles in the sunlight. He has been livin' good, Ol' Thomas has, with free board and room and no alimony or mortgage payments.

He is very quiet, head up, eyes shifting, for about 20 seconds and then he decides that everything is kopasetic, as we used to say in the Navy. So he comes down the tree, daintily, and plants his paws in the fresh snow, making precise little indentations. He is still, again, and then he takes one hop toward the bird feeder which is located directly in front of the middle window of the breakfast nook.

What was that? (I had rattled cup and saucer, just slightly). Thomas The Squirrel is now up on his hind paws, alert, body poised, tail flat out, head turning, ears pointed. Shall I go back to the tree? You know he is asking himself, but he decides to play it cool. He waits. The noise is not repeated. Ten seconds pass. It is safe. He hops over to the bird feeder . . .

It is a store-bought bird feeder with the container, about two quarts in capacity, sitting atop a long metal rod, or shaft, which has been pushed into the earth. It is about four feet from the ground to the bottom of the container, and it is about six inches from where the rod joins the middle of the bottom to the edge of the container.

It looks a good deal like one of those lights the gas company will install in your lawn for a nominal fee (adv.), but it is much less stable. It sways in the wind, gently, and I suppose those who run the animal kingdom would call the installation rickety.

Well, sir. Thomas The Squirrel gets back up on his hind paws and eyes the rod, which towers above him like the Eiffel Tower. It has been snowing-raining-freezing and the rod is slippery. He evidently knows this for he sort of licks his fingers and hitches up his pants and then he leaps astraddle of it and starts pulling himself upward.

———◆———◆———

He uses the same motions, or maneuvers, as a fireman climbing a pole. He pulls with his arms and pushes with his legs, so to speak, and when he does the latter, his fanny sticks out. He is a sight to behold.

He gets about halfway up but then he loses traction and comes sliding down. Thomas hits the snow with a soft plop! and then he gathers himself together and starts all over again.

This time he makes it all the way to the bottom of the container. But now he really has a problem—how is he going to get from the rod to the edge of the container? He thinks about this for a while, catching his wind. Now . . .

Instead of hugging the rod he stands against it with all four paws, his body delicately balanced. He reaches out and back with a front paw and catches the edge of the container. He hangs there, precariously, for a second or two and then he grabs hold with his other front paw. He is like the hero in a movie hanging over a cliff.

Will he make it? Heavens, yes! He swings a hind leg over the lip of the container and then he just rolls himself upward and into the bird feeder.

Breakfast at Tiffany's. He sits there and eats sunflower seeds, Thomas does, until they come out of his ears.

Then Came Schultz

The wind had the rough, surly edge of a hacksaw blade early this morning when the side door was opened for the convenience of Schultz, the weimaraner, and you could tell he was aghast at what he saw and felt. Snow on the ground, nearly two inches' worth; small drifts being formed and reformed by swirling gusts straight out of Upper Canada; and a chill factor, the man on the radio was to say, of about 24 degrees below zero. Schultz wanted no part of it, thank you.

But the Old Curmudgeon prodded him forth, determined not to share his potty with him as he already shares his groceries and pad. There is just so much you can take off a danged dog, even a weimaraner.

This is a highly unusual breed, a fact which did not penetrate this reasoning despite early warnings. Shortly after Schultz moved in there were letters from constituents who said, almost in unison, "You've never had a dog like this one!" Shoot, now. A dog is a dog is a dog, to paraphrase the lady and her roses. You board them, you bed them, you pet them, you talk with them when no one else will listen to you, you give a little and you take a little and after a while you establish areas of mutual respect and authority and you live happily ever after. That's how it was with Pat, who was mostly collie; and Scoop, pure cocker spaniel; and Toby, sweetly Welsh terrier; and Old Yeller, who was east side, west sides and all-around Detroit. And that's how it would be with Schultz. Just wait and see.

———

Well, we should have paid more attention to the manual ("The Right Dog for You" by Arthur Liebers.) This in part is what it has to say about Schultz and his ancestors:

"For the first hundred years of their existence, ownership of a weimaraner was truly a sign of distinction. The breed was developed by the German nobility of Weimar as an all-around hunter and house dog and their ownership was rigidly restricted . . . Breeding was carried on under careful scrutiny of the weimaraner club and only the finest specimens were bred. At no time where there more than about 1,500 of these dogs in Germany. Prospective owners could be 'black-balled' and traveling club wardens passed on the merits of new litters; any puppies not coming up to standard were destroyed. In addition, there was a firm rule against allowing any outside of Germany. It was not until 1929 that the first weimaraners appeared in the United States when a pair were imported and later several others were brought in as a foundation stock . . . "

And so on. What it all adds up to is that Schultz looks upon himself as a Prussian Prince, or thereabouts, who has been relegated by fate to spend his remaining years (he will soon be five) with a middle-class American family. Obviously, they are a bit backward in their understanding of how royalty should be treated, a lack of social grace which he has been attempting to correct, with considerable success.

⸺ ⸺

For years there was a standing rule that no dog—repeat, NO dog—was allowed on Fern's davenport, and this regulation was the more severely enforced starting in mid-1978 when we bought a new one, a rather massive sink-out-of-sight-in-the-cushions-affair which takes up most of one wall of the family room. From this vantage point the Lady of the House read, played solitaire (she literally wears the spots off a deck before replacing it), watched television and reclined in independent splendor, above and beyond trespass. It was an area as restricted as an officers' club for admirals and generals only.

In the early autumn, then, Schultz was content to curl up not at his master's feet, but behind them. He would wait until the Old Curmudgeon was settled in his chair, then he would root himself a place behind his heels, wiggling and twisting until he was just so, comfy and toasty, whereupon he would fall asleep and snore. After about an hour of this, the Old Curmudgeon's legs would feel as though they had been cut off at the knees, but it is the lot of the commoner to suffer when in the presence of a Baron from Bavaria.

The advent of cold weather brought about the ultimate campaign for the rights of royalty—Schultz versus the davenport. He would leave his nest behind his master's feet and sidle over to that verboten haven, oozing charm and supplication. "No!" she would say as he stood beside her. "No!No!" Back to the drafty floor. Then over again. Another rejection. German perseverance against a bad treaty. Two weeks later she forgot to say "No!" and he was up there quicker than a cat going over a fence. Permanently.

That's where he is now. We just looked. He has his head on two pillows and his rump braced against a third. Snoring. That's a dog's life for you, Prussian Prince style.

The Birds Flocked In

Diary of a Country Correspondent . . .

The shank of the evening—now there's an old-timey expression for you—comes at our house about 9 o'clock, and with it the all's-well-that-ends-well ritual.

Schultz falls off the davenport one leg at a time and slouches to where his lord and master, ha, is reading. Failing immediate attention, he uses his nose like the scoop shovel on a backhoe and gives book or magazine an upward heave. This is the signal: The moment has come to give the premises a final check, and then it will be cheese time.

This dog, now in the 80-pound range, keeps the cheese industry solvent. He would rather have a slice of cheddar than a T-bone, and it is an unusual occasion when the shopping list does not include cheese, for to risk an exhausted supply would be to invite mutiny. When our nightly patrol is finished, he stands at the knees of his master, ha again, and stows away four or five slices of any popular brand, ranging from mild through sharp. Then, shown the largest slab of all, he prances into the bedroom, sits at the end of the bed and polishes it off as though he hadn't eaten in two weeks. Thereafter he is content to stretch out and snore until the windows rattle, unmindful of the night light that permits another hour or so of reading.

One does not know where dogs rank in intelligence among the so-called critters of the earth, although he has heard it said that pigs are smarter and horses dumber. There is the growing conviction, however, that we, the people, are surrounded by communications for which we have neither the ear nor the knowledge.

Yesterday morning, as an example, there was not a bird at the feeder or in sight when we decided on impulse to replenish the supply of sunflower seed. A light snow was falling, it was cold—Holy Toledo, it has been cold since October!—the hour had the feel of the frozen tundra, and there was small hope of inspiring any backyard activity.

Yet within a minute of returning to the house there was a chickadee at the freshly-stocked feeder, and then another—the chickadees are always the bravest and the foremost—and then the blue jays came roaring in, and the sparrows, and a dove or two, and a whole blessed family of cardinals, two males aflame with gorgeous self-importance and females less spectacular but lovely in their own right. It was akin to watching a session of the Democratic National Convention on a 10-inch TV screen, with much bobbing and flitting around, an occasional argument but no fist fights.

But the question is, how did all of those birds know that sunflower seed had been added to the feeder and strewn about its base? There simply had to be communication. In a way we do not comprehend, the word was spread, and they came out of their nests or off their perches as though they had simultaneously read an announcement—"The Old Curmudgeon will pop for all hands at 10:20 EST." And here they came, a whole squadron of them, as different in appearances as the Chinese and the English, yet all speaking the same language, or communicating on the same wave length, or whatever it is they do that "superior beings" are unable to grasp.

There are moments when Schultz will stand in the driveway and the hair will rise on his back as he listens to distant barking. Then quite suddenly his coat will return to normal, and he will trot on his merry way, as though he had been listening to neighborhood gossip that turned out to be old stuff. But he was listening to something, and understood it, and rejected it as unworthy of further investigation.

This is what amazes and frustrates those of us who are under the spell of nature. There is something—much!—going on "out there" that is completely over our heads. Birds, again, have navigational instincts that confound the imagination, and intelligence will never be equally shared and appreciated until all of nature's children understand one another.

Ah, it is a wonderful world. And the best part of it is that there is so much room for improvement.

Lord Byron—Dog's Pal

Except for when he was kidnapped and subjected to all manner of gross indecencies in the hospital, and except for when he has gone to town to replenish the larder, the Old Curmudgeon has been off this property but once in six weeks. On a recent evening, he accepted an invitation to dinner by Gretchen Sopcak, who is one of the greatest cooks this side of Australia, but he was home by nine.

This has given your narrator ample time in which to talk with his dog, Schultz, and they have become the boonest of companions, sharing everything including the incoming mail. Schultz has become very fond of greeting cards, especially if they feature dogs on the cover. Posies he can put up with, but cats leave him cold.

This unedited exchange of intelligence from the constituency recently led to a rather embarrassing situation, for there was a letter from L. F. (Lin) Bush of Milford, quoting Lord Byron. Now this is a very high-class audience we have here, friends, fully equipped and qualified to start a new and better world if put to it tomorrow. Still, in the 24 years we have been together, one does not recall ever having received a quotation from Lord Byron. Class, this was pure class, and Schultz was ordered to his top form, a position he adopts whenever he assumes someone is going to hand him a choice goody from the table.

This was what he heard:

> *"One who possesses beauty without vanity,*
> *Strength without insolence,*
> *Courage without ferocity,*
> *And all the virtues of man without his vices,*
> *This praise, which would be of unmeaning*
> *Flattery said of a human,*
> *Is but a just tribute to my dog."*

He sat there a while longer, as though expecting a handout from luncheon leftovers, but after he had been stroked a bit, and his ears rubbed, he went to the davenport and assumed the "at ease position"—flat on his back with all four paws in the air. Within minutes he was snoring and muttering in his sleep, as innocent of conceit as a newborn babe. It took more than Lord Byron to turn his head.

Of course, he has had a lot of practice with attention, for of the hundreds of letters and cards which have reached this manse lately, at least two-thirds have inquired about him, and many have shown more concern for his well-being than for the Old Curmudgeon's.

Moreover, he has been an admirable companion, alert to the smallest of alarms, and if there was just some way to teach him to answer the telephone, which quite often goes unheard by his master, his performance would be perfect. The telephone seems to puzzle him. Leastwise, when an outside number is dialed, he will sit there with his eyes shining, and as soon as conversation is joined, he will start barking. He can't stand the thought of people yakking at one another without him sharing in it.

———————

He hates water, yet he has not the slightest fear of storms. A heavy rain with thunder and lightning is beating around our ears at the moment, but he is stretched out on the bedroom floor, his nose pointed in this direction.

It was said of him that he was an excellent hunter when young, but he has never been under a gun since coming to us. Once in a while in the autumn, the call of the wild will get to him and he will disappear into the woods for awhile, but he likes his own sack too well to rough it out in the briars and brambles. Yesterday, he treed a squirrel about four inches long, and you would have thought he had brought a rhinoceros to bay. What a ferocious critter.

Well, this has been a piece about a dog—ol'Schultz—sort of the result of popular demand. If you are lucky, you have one you love just as much, so whistle it up and read it Lord Byron's tribute.

The Violence of Loneliness

Midway through the second evening the dog went to where the man was sitting and offered its massive head for stroking and its long pliable body for hugging. The man sighed and responded and then he offered a benediction of sorts: "Forgive us for the violence of our loneliness . . . "

For the better part of two days they had been aloof from one another, observing only the bare bones of friendship. The dog, wary and unsettled, had picked at its food. The man, angry and feeling out-of-pocket, had been ungracious and unforgiving. They were the victims of what shall be remembered as the Terror of the Utility Room.

The dog had been put there out of what the man considered kindness of heart. It had been raining and the only other place of confinement, the garage, was damp and cold. So the man fixed the dog a pad in the utility room, piling blanket upon blanket; he left water and the remnants of supper; he gave assurances of an early return; he departed for dinner with friends.

When the man returned a few hours later, he was appalled by the sight of the utility room. It reminded him of a scene out of World War II, after the Japanese had been driven out of Manila or the Russians had marched into Berlin. The dog had chewed vast strips out of two long pieces of woodwork, mingling splinters with its bed, its food, its water. It had scratched and clawed three doors, one of them so severely it will have to be replaced. It had upset a flower pot in the adjacent half-bath and had scattered the contents of a waste basket all over the place.

The man was outraged. He struck the dog, heavily, and called it a sonofab----, which was sort of funny when you think of it. He also accused it of being ungrateful and unworthy of a good home, and he stomped and fumed for an hour while clearing away the debris. And then he added insult to injury by giving the dog a sponge bath, which it hated, slopping water all over the garage and cussing a blue streak.

And that was the way things stood between them until the dog put its head in the man's lap and he said, "Forgive us the violence of our loneliness . . . "

The dog had been lonely and afraid of further loneliness. It, too, remembered when there had been conversation in the house, and laughter even during illness, and the sharing of the davenport with its mistress, and the affection of a soft voice and the tenderness of gentle hands. And then it, too, was alone, or at least half-alone, with only one another to turn to in those moments when loneliness settled like a stone in the pit of its stomach.

And then the man put the dog in the utility room, which is as narrow as a prison cell, and closed the doors and went away. And the dog was overcome by the terror and the violence of loneliness.

It ripped at the woodwork so powerfully it left stain marks on its muzzle, and snarled and slashed at the doors, and scattered that damned bed, and upset food and water, and caved and ranted in cold fury, and doubtless cried out to whatever gods it recognizes— "Why have you done this to me?"

How does the man know all of this? Because there is an affinity, an awareness, between people and animals, if only the people are intelligent enough to realize it, and because the man has suffered the terror and the violence of loneliness a time or two himself.

There have been moments in the deep of night when he has been scared stiff, as though she in her helplessness could have protected him. There have been times when he wanted to heave a paperweight at some silly ass on television. And there have been occasions when he had to repel the urge to climb into his Ramrod Four and drive, and drive, and drive, ending up in Alabama, perhaps, far, far from everything . . .

That is loneliness for you in the capsule form, and the dog reacted to it. But the man was too dumb to recognize it until the dog offered its massive head for stroking and its long pliable body for hugging. Now they are buddies again, but the man is still ashamed of himself. How blind could he get?

Auf Wiedersehen

A pal has departed this vale of tears and this will be a remembrance of him, shared, it is hoped, with the legions who have saluted him in cards, letters and conversations in years gone by.

The Michigan arthritis finally caught up with Schultz late last week, spreading along his spine from hips to forelegs, and this time there was no stemming the agonizing onslaught. So his friend at the Kelly Veterinary Hospital, Dr. Wayne Stockton, eased him out of his misery.

Three years earlier, almost to the week, Schultz fought off a similar attack through subjection to massive doses of cortisone, first through injections given by Dr. Renton in Howell, and then at home. Persistent readers may recall the incident of my cupping 14 pills in one hand, holding Schultz's mouth open with the other, then pouring the pills down his gullet like coal into a chute. That continued for two weeks, with the dosage reduced one pill a day. He was an exemplary patient, sighing sometimes but never resisting.

This time, alas, it was determined that his system would not have withstood the shock of such powerful treatment, so when lesser medication failed we had to give him up. He was 12 in February, a Weimaraner with enough credentials to high-nose his way into any dog show, but at our house he will be recalled as a people lover—all bark, no bite, boundless affection.

I do not have the answer to the question: "Is there an after-life for pets?" I have an opinion, though. If our four-legged friends don't share and brighten the Out Yonder, it is sadly in need of reform. A backslid Methodist would appreciate the pope's address-ing this subject as would thousands of others, one presumes.

I have been owned by five dogs; no truer, gentler, kinder, more generous friends ever crossed my path. Presently I am working on my sixth apprenticeship with the permission of Irish, who is al-ready willingly staked out by Tilly, a West Highland terrier now as-signed to holding down the office davenport all by her lonesome self, a forlorn little figure fitful in the slumber of her 15th year. She has spent much of her reserve of energy looking for her late buddy, who was four times her size but equal in all circumstances.

Does Tilly believe that the spirit of Schultz is "somewhere?" I wouldn't be surprised, but then I have quite often been accused of conceding animals more sensitivity than some of their two-legged masters are willing to concede.

Of the others who have owned me, perhaps Old Yeller, who came to us at the House on Grandmont from the streets of Detroit, was the strongest character. After we moved to the country, he was in seventh heaven, the absolute boss of all he surveyed, and once he just sort of meandered over and lifted his leg on a chap who had come uninvited into the driveway to dispute in surly tones a remark that had appeared in this space.

After he had been injured in a recreational vehicle due to the ne-cessity of a sudden stop, he never again would enter it. He would climb into the passenger car with or without invitation, but he would hide rather than ride in that damned Blazer. His somewhat likeness, cast in stone, sits on the front stoop of this outpost in Clangville.

Scoop, the cocker spaniel puppy I carried home in a jacket pocket, was destined to become our county-weekly's mascot in Ohio and Illinois; Pat, our first pup, dating to a St. Patrick's Day in late 1936, was the only one in a large squirming litter to nip Fern on the finger as though to say, "I'm the one, darlin.'" And he was; and Toby—oh, we must not neglect Toby—who was the lovely Welsh terrier, gift of John and Morley Driver when John was still well enough to serve as city editor of the Free Press, fearing no man and agitating the percales of the Old Gray Lady Down the Street.

That has been the crew, all different, all true-blue loyal, all intertwined into our affairs and, at times, dictators of the outcome.

I cannot begin to tell you how it hurts to have lost Schultz. I keep looking for him. I keep hoping he will come to me in at least one dream. And sometimes I say, "Arouse and beware, old Schultzer, wherever you are, and thanks for the memories . . . "

He came to us at the age of 4½ when neighbors, both working, were unable to give him the care he needed after a cruel attack of heartworm infection. I must admit to being guilty of some "rustling," for almost daily I would sneak over and bring him to our place, sending him home in the evening. Sometimes he would sit under our bedroom window and howl before continuing his journey.

Finally it was arranged for him to join us for better or for worse, and he saw me through personal crises and eventually took Clangville in stride. He was my pal.

Bless the Pets

First Overnight Snow

I woke up this morning,
And there it was.
My world was all covered
with fluffy fuzz—
A scene so enchanting
A fairy deed,
So taken for granted
As days proceed,

—Margaret Rorke

All in a Lifetime . . .

Irish usually attends mass on Saturday, and thus she returned home this past weekend to announce that her pastor, the Rev. Robert E. Burke of Holy Name Catholic Church in Birmingham, had declared that on the following afternoon, in the church parking lot, he would bless the pets of his parishioners.

There would be some limits, he indicated. No alligators or snakes or stuff like that, but otherwise the field was wide open and—you guessed it—would include the star of our household, Wild Poppy.

Dogs have a way of knowing when something beyond the ordinary has been planned for their well-being, even though they would just as soon get along without it, so Poppy was somewhat withdrawn—not actually uneasy but a trifle leery, you might say—during the evening. Then, on Sunday, when her brush and comb were hauled out and she was groomed fore and aft and athwartships, she collapsed in resignation and was as limber as a small sack of cornmeal as her thick coat was burnished.

———————————

At the parking lot there was a rather surprising array of pets (one cat included) and their owners. That's a misstatement, of course, for in truth pets own people, not vice versa. Anyhow, Burke was there, hanging on to the leash attached to his schnauzer, and while there was a moderate dissonance of yips, yelps and subdued barks, the total sound was no more than a group of bingo players might have produced.

Birmingham has a number of reputations, and one of them claims that it is a center for big canines. The gathering for the blessing largely sustained this notion, for there were labradors, golden retrievers, collies, and one fellow who might have been a sheepdog, only he had so much hair he could also have been a bear. There was also an honest-to-goodness bulldog, of the British battleship construction, and the sight of him smote the inner regions where memories of the late Hoover Jones are retained. Of the mediums and smaller types, a sheltie and a basset hound were spotted, and the terriers included either a full-grown Welsh or a sprouting Airedale—there was quite a milling around by this time, with Poppy clinging to the arms of Irish as Burke began.

"The animals of God's creation inhabit the skies, the earth and the seas," he said in part. "They share in the ways of human beings. They have a part in our lives. Francis of Assisi recognized this when he called the animals, wild and tame, his brothers and sisters.

Remembering Francis' love for these brothers and sisters of ours, we invoke God's blessing on these animals, and we thank God for letting us share the Earth with all the creatures . . . "

Dispersed, we thought of Schultz, Tillie, and Old Yeller, and the others who have graced a lifetime, and blessed them the best we could.

Here Comes Liberty Center

There was this lean, long-legged pacer by the name of Josedale Dazzler, and right away I could tell that he would win by two rods, or more, thus leaving the expert handicappers in their normal post-race posture—mouths agape.

Man, they had really goofed on this one! The Railbird and Trackman had agreed on Bonnie Zombelle; Sulky Joe and our own Andy Capper had plunked for Fleet Bay; Morning Clocker was positive that Topheel would take it all; while Doc Brown, the self-styled "Wizard of the Trotters," was high on Uncle Creed. Ha, ha, ha. Dunderheads!

For all you had to do was look at the program and you could tell that Josedale Dazzler was a mortal cinch, an absolute shoo-in. Heavens to Betsy, this hunk of horseflesh, straining for action, was born in Liberty Center, Ohio! Enough said . . .

So I Headed . . .

. . . for the $2 window with a semi-guilty conscience, like a big kid about to yank a stick of candy away from a little kid. It really wasn't fair to take advantage of the track in this fashion.

"Give me $2 worth of Josedale Dazzler on the nose," I said to the man behind the counter, adding: "It's Liberty Center against the world."

"That's all right with me, buddy," he replied, somewhat puzzled, "as long as you include the Russians in on the deal."

"Liberty Center isn't afraid of the Russians, either," I assured him, and then the man on the loudspeaker said: "Here they come . . . !"

(Our house was on Maple Street, just a hop, skip and a jump from the main drag, where on long, lazy afternoons the noble steeds of the farmers were tethered to the hitching rails. In the stores, as the heavy thinkers congregated, there was general agreement on one topic: Liberty Center had the best of everything. The best horses, the best food, the best dog fights, the best baseball team—you name it and we've got it, stranger. Hurrah for Liberty Center!)

Well, Sir . . .

. . . Josedale Dazzler slipped into fifth place as they whirled around the first turn, giving away, politely, to a pushy horse that was in a hurry to run himself bowlegged, and then they settled down, the seven of them.

They came around once, hooves flashing, dirt flying, drivers clucking, trappings jangling, and you could tell that a few of them were pretty well tuckered. But Josedale Dazzler, bless his money-in-the-bank-sweet-little-old-hide, was just a-pacing away, breathing easily, biding his time, holding himself in for the big, overpowering, Liberty Center-like surge.

They kept pumping away, closely bunched, until they reached the far turn, and then Josedale Dazzler, who is owned by my friend Cecil Strock, started to pour it on. He collared the fourth horse as they approached the stretch; he came wide to avoid a traffic jam as they straightened out and headed home; he was flying now, that $2 multiplied by the track odds coming to $17, which seemed like a swindle, but business is business, and hurrah for Liberty Center!

And Then . . .

. . . Well, I don't know how to explain this except to say that a gremlin from Napoleon, O., which is the arch rival of Liberty Center, flew onto the track and distracted Josedale Dazzler.

All at once he broke stride, raring a bit, his hooves dancing like he had slipped in the bathtub, and before he could get settled down all of the horses, including the tuckered-out ones, had zoomed past. Tragedy, tragedy, tragedy!

But that's the sort of nasty, underhanded stuff us Liberty Centerites have learned to expect from Napoleon gremlins, so I tore up the $2 ticket and upon restudy of the experts was amazed to learn that Doc Brown had picked the winner—Uncle Creed.

Pete

Having been brought to heel by a slight case of the miseries, I have for the past several days been writing these pieces from the sanctuary of the House On Grandmont.

A taxi driver seizes the completed drafts and speeds them Downtown to the printers, his Klaxon blaring, the fenders of his machine standing straight out in the wind, whereupon I fall back into my bed and suffer a recurring nightmare.

In this sweated dream, the Hon. Stewart Udall, armed with a knobheaded club, chases the Hon. Senator Phil Hart up and down the Sleeping Bear Dunes, the while shouting: "Don't you dare compromise!" He gets closer and closer: the club, brandished violently, becomes more and more menacing. Run, Phil! Oh, Lord . . . if this bout with the flu doesn't end soon, Udall may catch him.

But enough of this nightmare. There has been too much in this space lately about Stu The Terrible and Phil The Gentle. Today I wouldst write about sweet and gentle things, including my fine-feathered friend, Pete The Parakeet.

When I Came . . .

. . . to this table a few minutes ago, Pete stuck his lemon-colored noggin through the bars of his cage and said: "Hi, sweetie pie. How's my boy this morning?"

"Hello, buddy," I responded.

"The rain in Spain is mainly in the plain," he observed.

"Your darned tootin' it is," I answered.

"Pretty boy," he replied, and then he added: "I'm a pea picker."

"You sure are," I said, opening the typewriter, and he seemed to know that the conversation was ended. For he jumped up on his perch, rocked back and forth a few times, looked out the window to make certain that all was well, then tucked his head under his wing and went to sleep.

We bought Pete about five years ago in Florida, and after listening for three or four days to the noises he made, which were pure gibberish, I wrote a piece for the St. Petersburg Times in which I said, airily, that it was about time somebody exploded the nonsense to the effect that birds could talk. Rubbish!

Well, sir, the upshot was an invitation from a lady in Coldwater to come over and hear her parakeet, name of Rocky, guaranteed to be a spellbinder. And I'll be darned if he wasn't . . .

That little guy could sit on his perch and recite long tracts from the Constitution of the United States. He knew some poetry. He could sing "Dixie." And his vocabulary was replete with quotations, smart sayings, bon mots and cuties.

From then on I knew there was hope for Pete, and the first time he said, "Pretty Boy!" loud and clear, it was as though Junior had just come home with an A-plus in solid geometry.

I Am Convinced . . .

. . . Pete would have been an orator of the William Jennings Bryan school had it not been for the arrival in our household of Toby, the Welsh Terrier, who is a kissin' cousin of Charlie Kennedy.

She took one look at Pete, or rather she heard him just once, and then she leaped three feet straight up, yelping and whining, and since then they have been mortal enemies. She knows that danged bird can talk, and she is green with envy. We haven't been able to spend much time teaching Pete because of her interference.

Want to have some fun? Well, right now I happen to know that Toby is upstairs in my bed, curled up in the covers with her head on the pillow. A real sack hound. But if I just say something to Pete loud enough for her to hear, she will scramble out of there and come tearing downstairs, her eyes blazing, her hair on end, ready for war . . .

"GOOD MORNING, PETE!"

And here she comes!

SEVEN
The World Around Us

Hostages' Release

It has been said that the return of the former hostages—President Reagan has referred to them as "prisoners of war"—has glued the country back together again and given us new resolve to overcome old problems.

Let us hope so, for we need motivation as seldom before in this century. And, if it is true that the ordeal shouldered by 52 Americans over 444 days turns out to be sufficient catalyst to get the country moving again, then—to quote another president—they will not have suffered in vain and the rest of us will have paid a very small price for revival.

At the risk, however, of seeming small, mean, and cynical, the Old Curmudgeon will now offer odds—eight to one—that today's euphoria will not necessarily turn out to be tomorrow's driving force. One of the reasons that ancient settlers among us become such pains in the neck is that we collect memories, some of them having to do with other glue-ings together that did not withstand the rigors of usage. We remember, for instance, the landing of the first astronauts on the moon; the return of the POWs from Vietnam; the victory of the American hockey team in the Winter Olympics; the piercing of Red China's isolation by Richard Nixon, and so on and so forth. Each of these events in turn was supposed to pick us up by the bootstraps and hurtle us over our obstacles, but they fell short of the mark.

⸻

Why? One thinks of two reasons, closely related. The average American has little concept of the trouble we are in, and has been

189

conditioned by his peerless leaders to believe that a small miracle which might occur at any moment will get us out of our difficulties.

This was brought to mind a few days ago during a conversation with a fortyish citizen who has spent a number of years in the communications business and should know what is going on. He was depressed by the state of the state and the state of the union. But there was one plus in the present situation, he said: "Things can't get any worse!" God help us all, he was serious; he may even have assumed that he was being profound.

Well, on a things-can't-get-worse-scale-of-one-to-ten, we would guess that the Republic now stands at six, or maybe even seven. In other words, dear friends, there is plenty of room left for deterioration, and it is going to take some true blue buckling down to avoid it.

What could be worse, you ask? We will spare you the full litany, offering only this brief resume. There have been times when one couldn't get one's money out of the banks because the banks weren't there any more. There have been occasions when "blue chip stocks" became so worthless they were scarcely worth the fancy paper on which they were printed. There have been instances where deflation was more painful than inflation. There have been . . . but enough, you cry? All right, enough. We add only the reminder that these things, and many others happened in the United States of America during the past 50 years.

———◆◆——— ———◆◆———

We do not predict a re-run of these doleful events. The point is simply this: Anyone who thinks the hostages' return is the small miracle we have been waiting for still has his feet hanging over Cloud Nine and is in danger of a serious tumble.

Prices are scandalous and so are some wages. The runaway cost of government, at home and nationally, is devouring tax dollars faster than the work force can generate them without shortchanging family needs. We are spending hundreds of billions each year on "preparedness," yet if Cuba outraged diplomatic decency tomorrow, our only immediate recourse would be nuclear fission. And perhaps worst of all, high members of our business community are now whimpering that the way to offset foreign competition is to eliminate it.

These are a select few of our problems. Euphoria won't resolve them. Sorry about that, those of you still in dreamland.

Memories That Haunt

Home again . . . with some new memories.

Low comedy usually dogs the footsteps of high drama, and this was certainly the case in Mississippi. Not everything that happened down there was grim or tragic.

I am still chuckling, for example, over the story they were telling in Jackson about Willie, a colored gentleman who is considered something of a town character.

He was on the street a day or two before the rioting started at Oxford, and someone asked—"Willie, what do you think about all of this trouble between the white people and James Meredith?"

Willie thought a moment and then he replied: "I can't rightly say, 'cause I've got relatives on both sides!"

One of the . . .

. . . memories I have brought back is that of groups of Negroes standing in the public square on the day of the rioting in Oxford proper. They were there from beginning to end, from the first appearance of the ruffians to the dispersal action by the Federal troops.

No one approached them and they seemed to exchange a minimum of conversation among themselves. There was no outward animation: no expressions of anger when the punks yelled "nigger lovers!" at passing vehicles—and no laughter or applause when tear gas terminated the affray. They were just there: quiet shadows in the background of a testing of mob rule versus law and order . . .

I have since wondered what the Negroes thought as all of the arrogance, the braggadocio, the effrontery, the vulgarity, the obscenity, the fire-and-brimstone melted out of the rioters the instant they realized that the troops meant business.

Did any of them think: "What a poor lot of white men to have to look up to!"

Coming Home . . .

. . . on the plane late Wednesday night, I was plagued by the thought that I had lived through the immediate preceding days at some other time. But when and where?

The emotionalism at the football game in Jackson, with hundreds of waving flags and the introduction of a new state song, the words projected on a mammoth screen;

The Oxford incidents—the stonings, the chantings, the cursings and cryings-out of the Lord's name in vain;

The rantings against "outside authority;"

The horrible memory of James Meredith being transferred from class to class, hounded, treated like a dangerous animal escaping destruction to the peril of the public welfare . . .

None of this was new: I was certain I had experienced it before. But where?

Then I remembered . . . News reels, that was it. I had seen it all years before on news reels. Only that time, of course, the country was Germany, the peerless leader was Adolph Hitler—and James Meredith was a Jew.

Black Mayor Inevitable

We are in the lull between storms in Detroit, with the big winds of the primary behind us but with the thunder and lightning of the general election already disturbing the horizon. Before we sally forth to check the moorings one more time, this might be the appropriate moment for a little relaxed conversation. So pull up the footstool, settle into the easy chair and let's shoot the breeze. . . .

One of these days a black man is going to be elected Mayor. That brought your tootsies down off the footstool, didn't it? But it is going to happen, if not this year then surely within the next dozen. The registration of voters, black and white, is now almost even, which represents a tremendous gain for the black community—and the tide is still running.

Someone has said that the Nixon administration has finally stabilized urban neighborhoods by getting the interest rate on home mortgages up to 10 percent, thus making real estate transfers difficult to arrange, but this is probably a temporary situation.

Eventually, by those mysterious processes which control their operations, the money brokers will get the price of their product down to around seven percent, with plenty of it available, then the trek to the suburbs will resume in earnest and Detroit will become what is loosely called "a black city." Washington, D.C., is already in that category, and others are leaning, so we won't be alone.

But that is in the future whereas the pertinent question is now: Would the election of a black mayor kill Detroit?

Well, a similar experience did not kill Cleveland. True, there are those who say that Cleveland is dead, but if so its illness was terminal before Carl Stokes was elected Mayor. Cities do not rise or fall on the outcome of one election. Rather, they reflect the care or neglect they have had over a period of years, prospering or withering on the basis of what has been contributed to them, or what has been taken out, by successive generations. And in the long run that will be as true here, one way or another, as it has been in Cleveland.

Further, Los Angeles recently elected a black Mayor and at last report it did not figure on dying. There is the observation, however, that perhaps they were smarter than we have been, for they made the choice on the basis of ability at a time when blacks comprised only about 18 percent of the population.

This brings us to a thought I have not been able to shake in four years—that we should have elected Richard Austin in 1969, while there was still latitude for a decision not based on numbers. Please understand that I am not knocking the interim performance of Roman Gribbs. He has done the best he could under trying circumstances. But Richard Austin would have made a great "lead-in" black Mayor, and his election would have removed the suggestion that Detroit would not cross the color line until forced to it. If that mood persists in reverse, we may never elect another white Mayor, or one at the outside. Have you thought of that?

But 1969 is water over the dam. Now we face the election of 1973, and what are we going to do about it?

We have two unusual candidates—and the use of "unusual" constitutes an understatement. Coleman Young and John Nichols are from Hard Scrabble University. One of them became a professional politician and the other became a professional cop. Along the way, both of them probably had to say things and even do things alien to those who seek success in other lines of endeavor. You do not become a State Senator and Democratic National Committeeman by playing beanbag with the opposition; and the same was no doubt true of the route to the Police Commissionership. These are tough men out of rugged backgrounds; and from this standpoint either is competent to rule.

Which one has the best sense of where Detroit is and where it must go is a question to be decided by the campaign. The primary was the time for the testing of personalities, for perfecting the organizations while speaking in generalities. Now we must get down to the specifics of vital issues—of setting forth in detail the solutions to our problems.

If the city is tied in registrations, black and white, then we must settle this election on the merits of the candidates. And when you come to think of it, what is wrong with that?

Candidate Young

For a while we discussed the "important issues" of the campaign—who should be police commissioner and what should be done with the DSR—and then I said to him: "Senator, tell me about growing up in Detroit." And that was when Coleman Young became a spellbinder . . .

He has been with us about 50 years (there will a number of "abouts" in what follows), having arrived here at the age of four or five with his parents from Tuscaloosa, Ala. Even then Detroit was Mecca for those seeking social and economic improvement;

but then as now the words in the advertisements spread throughout the south sometimes contained more promise than possibility.

———————

Anyhow, they settled in a flat about two blocks south of where
Joe Muer's Restaurant is located on Gratiot, and there were days
to come when the residue of the red snapper served by that establishment succored the Young family.

Papa Young was a tailor by training, having completed a course
at an Alabama trade school, and for a year or so he altered
trousers at Sam's, which in those days featured pants for men and
little else. Then be became a guard for the Post Office and thereafter sharpened his interest in the finer things of life, including
stud poker and an occasional jug of whatever was available at a
workingman's price.

As the eldest of five children, Coleman had numerous family responsibilities, but these did not keep him from becoming an accomplished street fighter. These fisticuffs were carried out in an integrated
neighborhood, loosely speaking. Sometimes, he remembers, it would
be the blacks versus the Italians, with perhaps the Greeks joining one
side or the other as the mood seized them; and then again it would
be every youngun for himself and the devil take the hindmost. This
was hard on the nose, the eyes and the teeth but it gave a lad an appreciation of where he was and what he had to do to survive.

The neighborhood produced a few thugs, true, but out of it also
came some heroes of World War II. And from a similar section, under almost identical circumstances, came Joe Louis, heavyweight
champion of the world, who probably did more to electrify the
black community, and inspire hope and confidence, than any other
individual between Booker T. Washington and Dr. Martin Luther
King, Jr.

———————

Coleman Young was uppen atem from the age of six or seven.
He did everything he could within the bounds of reason to earn a
dime or a dollar, but so slim were the pickings that he has a vivid
recollection of the first $100 bill he ever saw. It was dropped into
the collection plate at St. Mary's church, where he was a junior
usher, by Frank Murphy, one of our legendary white politicians af-

ter whom our seat of justice is name. It caused a sensation—"Every sonofagun in the church saw it." Mr. Murphy, it should perhaps be noted, could give his opponents lessons in how to influence the electorate—and then beat them by a country mile on election day.

On a less auspicious occasion, Coleman Young also learned something of the difference between blacks and whites.

Having done well as a Boy Scout, he was promised a trip aboard the Bob-Lo. But when he arrived at the landing they would not permit him aboard the boat. Whites only. That made him look at the backs of his hands. Black? Not really. A very light tan. But there was a difference. And there may be to this day a scar from the difference.

No citizen of my experience has such a well-honed memory of Paradise Valley, which was once as famous in Detroit as Belle Isle, no less. For this and other historical reasons, we should get Coleman Young on tape, in depth. The Valley was where the dark folks and light folks mingled after the sun had gone down and it was full of restaurants, and hotels, and dancing girls, and games of chance, and ladies of the evening and countless other wonders guaranteed to make a country boy's eyes shine at midnight. It is gone now, largely bulldozed for urban renewal, but I have a map—his map—of it.

Well, this hasn't been much about Coleman Young, candidate for Mayor, has it? But early on the thought occurred that if you don't already know about the "issues" you aren't interested in them; so we have shared an intimate glimpse of a black child of this century who now seeks to lead us.

Addenda: He was elected. He served five terms. Even his enemies considered him an honest-to-God character.

A Man for All Seasons

Atlantis, Florida—Even when she has left home without leaving God a forwarding address, Irish insists on attending mass. Thus it was that a few mornings ago, we occupied a pew at St. Edward's Church, where the Rt. Rev. Thomas Daily, bishop of Palm Beach, was holding forth in favor of the poor.

As the Bible once estimated, the poor will always be with us—even in Palm Beach.

Bishop Daily, in his plea for the sharing of wealth, made a statement to the effect that "it takes a gentle person to be strong and a strong person to be gentle." It was then that all else faded from sight and sound and the memories of Soapy Williams came flooding back.

The governor is dead, I thought, and the world is diminished. Strange: He was an assistant secretary of state, an ambassador (Philippines) and the chief justice of Michigan's highest court, but to many of us he remained governor. That was the immediate reaction of Irish when word came through of his death: "He was the best governor we ever had."

She knew him before and during 1948, when he wheeled an ancient convertible into the outback of Michigan, campaigning on money raised by the mortgaging of his and Nancy's house. Somehow—no one ever quite figured out exactly how—he was elected, and then he was to withstand five more challenges at the polls, at times by margins so thin they resembled the butter on a boarding house sandwich. No Democrat in the state's history ever kept the Republicans in such an uproar, but now amid the thinned ranks of the survivors there must be those who recognize that there are times when defeat becomes sweeter than victory might have been.

———————

I first came upon the governor after arriving in Detroit in the fall of 1959, but it was not until President Kennedy sent him to Africa in the early spring of 1961 that I realized the full measure of a remarkable man. Soapy literally swept "the Dark Continent," as we were still calling it, off its feet, mingling with people in all stations of life as though he needed their votes at next Tuesday's election. In the 17 nations we visited, he left behind dazzled thousands, not sure, perhaps, of the exact identity or mission of the man they had met, but nonetheless aware that for an instant or two they had been in the presence of a rare individual.

To be sure, he unsettled some of the English, especially in Kenya, where a long and rather fruitful colonization was grinding down, and when he simplified his answer to a reporter's question by stating, "Africa should be for the Africans," the lid blew so high that

Kennedy had to snag it at a subsequent White House press conference. Soapy assumed that Africans could be white as well as black, as well they could, but in those days, as even now, the press had a way of jumping to the conclusions that kept steam in a torrid story.

Since then we have had no African affairs representative of equal horsepower; and on the personal side, I have written no story with such compelling appeal. Soapy and Nancy would whirl around until midnight, and then I would write and hunt for a cable office; and life seemed full of cocktail parties and small chops (the phrase for African meals at which less than an elephant was served) and days of constant movement, and below us as our old DC4 plugged along were the dark hills of Africa and the romance and mystery they protected from strange, prying eyes.

Surely the details of Soapy's public life have been written and rewritten about by this time, so I have kept this remembrance of a splendid citizen as free of repetition as possible. At our house, he was admired and deeply respected, and we are not likely to benefit from another leader of his capacities for a long, long time.

True, he could be partisan when pushed. Once at a "roast" for me, hectored by the likes of Neal Shine, J.P. McCarthy and Jerry Rideout, he said, "You have to vote like a Democrat so you can live like a Republican!" He became a defender of Lyndon Johnson, and I have always felt that he did more for Kennedy than Kennedy did for him.

Perhaps Africa was where he belonged in those days, though, for he was an American of great heart and patience and compassion—attributes as much in need then as now. Perhaps he spared some of the Dark Continent worse than it has known. From Florida, as the sun begins to shine again, I like to think that G. Mennen Williams was a man for all seasons, for all times.

A Man's Man

There comes now just another ordinary citizen to say so long and God bless to Henry Ford II.

I never knew him well enough to call him Henry. He was always Mr. Ford to his face even though I thought of him as Henry behind his back. Over the years we had several brief exchanges plus one long interview that led to two columns, but I never felt entitled to breach the barrier of old-fashioned etiquette. Mr. Ford, Henry, you old rip-snorter.

Familiarity breeds uncertainty, if not indeed contempt, so it was probably very difficult for the average Michiganian to realize that in his heyday Henry Ford II was the crown prince of international wheeldom, as much a celebrity in his field as could be found in any other, politics excepted. Part of this attraction came to him through a bloodline extending to the original Henry Ford, of course, but he picked up the family name and enhanced it when his turn came. He was the Ford in the future, and the name did not get rusty during his tenure.

There are a good many stories, of course, about his gong-kicking and hell-raising during the wee hours of more than one morning, but in one phrase he disenfranchised himself from martyrdom: "Never complain, never explain." He was not a candy-ankle where the press was concerned. If they wanted to hang it on him, he had broad shoulders.

Despite all of this, whatever little or much it meant, he was the No. 1 personal automaker during the prime of his years. General Motors was bigger, but it produced no figure of equal stature. Chrysler might have been more in the headlines at times, but Lee Iacocca never laid a glove on Henry Ford II as a member of what might be called "the industrial royalty."

The way the automobile business is helter-skeltering, like squid alarmed by seals, it is doubtful it will ever again produce anyone entitled to the crown princedom. What we have now are bottom-liners intent on making a profit if it takes every foreign price-cutter they can put their hands on. Well, Henry Ford II saved his company with Michiganians in the main when the U.S. Navy finally realized that it had plenty of lieutenants junior grade, but that there was no one in a position to chase the rascals out of the River Rouge and environs.

He was a tough young man in those days, Mr. Ford, and was smart enough, and unpretentious enough, to surround himself with a crew of ambitious young rise-and-shines who knew where their main chances were. From what you hear, working around world headquarters in the years immediately after the war was not exactly easy—or the least bit dull.

It is difficult to assess what effect Mr. Ford had on the lot of the working people who passed through his offices and plants over the years. Certainly there has been an outpouring of sentiment since his death, much of it from the rank and file of workers, but we cannot yet judge whether he established principles that will transform the monotony of mass production in the years to come.

You must remember that not too many years ago Ford Motor Co. was in a precarious position, with little to sell that met the challenges of an international energy crisis. Models had not yet been downsized or front-ended, and it was said that the chairman himself had been responsible for some of the stand-pat decisions.

Yet here we are, these few years later, with the company not only more than holding its own in the marketplace, but taking the lead, as well, in the writing of a union contract that will give more security to hourly workers. Somewhere along the line after his retirement, Henry Ford II must have had something to say, or do, with the decisions that turned the company around and brought it, quite possibly, the best labor relations in its entire history.

You know what Henry Ford II was? He was a man—a man's man. Michigan has no pretenders as his successor.

Citizens Are the Problems

I have been thinking about Richard Nixon, which will doubtless cause some readers to suggest that there must be a better way to spend a sunny April afternoon, but this reverie has not been without its constructive side. I have come to the conclusion, for instance, that there is absolutely no future to being President of the United States.

Talk about a job with a dead end! The best any President can hope for is mild praise when things go right, countered by Hail Columbia when they go wrong. It is one of the great mysteries of the times why anyone should want the office, yet here we have Mr. Nixon making plans for re-election while a whole wolf pack of Democrats are tearing around the country spending borrowed money in the hope of winning the nomination. There must be more to living in the White House than meets this jaundiced eye.

The trouble with being President, dear friends, is that you are at the beck and call of the largest assortment of crybabies, soreheads, fair weather friends and goodtime Charlies the world has ever known. I am speaking now of the American public, myself included, a whimpering lot of spoiled brats who have somehow come to mass agreement that they are God's chosen children and are therefore immune from adversity in any of its myriad forms.

America today, beset with difficulties as it may be, is still the finest place on this earth to live and prosper, with twice the opportunity per capita of any other nation saving, perhaps, Australia.

A young citizen, willing to prepare himself for the future and capitalize on opportunities as they occur, has horizons unlimited. No class or caste barriers stand in the way of progress. It makes no difference who your father was or from which side of the tracks your mother came. The only thing that matters, really, is can you cut it, and if you can, there it is—a better-than-fair portion of the bounties of civilization at your feet.

The vast majority of Americans, in short, are blessed beyond the imaginations of the teeming billions in Africa, Asia and Latin America, yet how much appreciation of this do you hear? Instead, it is pick, pick, pick at the President, regardless of whom he may be, when things do not go to suit us. The President has become the symbol of government, and government, God help us all, has become the pacifier of the people, the security blanket

202 Lessons Learned During a Wasted Youth

toward which they scurry whenever the wild winds threaten to blow. "Let Washington do it" used to be something of a joke, but now it has become a way of life, with the President the fall guy on bad days.

There is a persistent myth to the effect that "If we could elect the right President, everything would be all right." The recession would end; Hanoi would agree to reasonable peace terms; the Russians and the Red Chinese would reform themselves; the millennium would be upon us.

What nonsense. A nation is what its people are; the world is what they help make it. There are no substitutes, short cuts or magic formulas. Flip Wilson's observation, "What you see is what you get," is correct, and so is a paraphrase of it: "What you put into society is what you take out of it."

As an example of this, consider for a moment the great and troubled City of Detroit. For the 12 years of your commentator's residency, we have been weeping and wailing without respite because of the deterioration of entire neighborhoods. Scarcely a week has passed without a public statement deploring this decay, and if all the editorials, speeches and columns on this subject were stretched end to end, they would reach from here to Paw Paw.

But a question, please: Have we, the inheritors of this city from those who built it with their dreams and enterprise, made a serious effort on our own to rectify the ruin which grows around us? No. But how piteously we have implored Washington for succor. And how disappointed with three Presidents we have been when it was not forthcoming.

Cities—people: They are the same. The bold and brave ones prosper, the mewlers and pukers languish. And there is darned little the President can do for the latter, curse him though we may.

Big Shots

From the standpoint of economics it is the same old story. While the rest of the country drinks fruit juice and gulps aspirin to combat the cold of a recession, Michigan is in the oxygen tent with another full-blown case of pneumonia, meaning depression.

This dismal bedside report is reflected in the latest unemployment figures, which put us about four percent ahead of—or should we say behind?—the national average. Once again the fall after the rise of the automobile industry is largely responsible for our extreme trauma, and there are at least a few people around who have grown sick and tired of it.

The other day, as an example, we asked a prominent entrepreneur what he thought of the decision by General Motors to transfer the bulk of their Pontiac operations into a neighboring area. Stand by for a shock: "What they ought to do," he said, "is move the damned plant to Missouri, or some place, and take Chrysler and Ford with them!"

Well, now. Such a campaign would get him about as much support as Gov. Jerry Brown of California generated in the recent Iowa caucus, but perhaps it does reflect a wider attitude to the effect that the industry needs a good deal more stability than it has exhibited in recent years. And there may also be a few critics who can remember, or have been told, that Michigan was a thriving state, and Detroit one of the nation's finest cities, long before the original Henry Ford perfected the production-line technique.

That was in the dear dead past, of course, and we aren't going back to it. But surely there has been enough boom-and-bust hereabouts in recent years to warrant the feeling among the most patient of us that "something ought to be done." It is perhaps fortunate for some of the tycoons of the industry that they do not have to run at large for re-election, as politicians do, else they would have been turned out of high office long ago.

———————

In business or government a cardinal weakness of leadership is the failure to recognize serious competition and nip it in the bud, if at all possible. This may catch up with President Jimmy Carter before November has waned, and it is a standing indictment of the American automobile industry.

Think back a moment. For how many years did imports, and one thinks now of Volkswagen in particular, flourish in this market because our companies had nothing to offer as an alternative? And then came the Japanese, swarming and persisting, and now the situation is so bad that Douglas Fraser of the UAW is going "over there" shortly to plead for an infusion of their money and technology into our industrial complex. We have already wished him luck.

Thirty years ago the late Walter Reuther, who practically invented the UAW, was considered a troublemaker and worse—a blasted communist, in fact—because he insisted that imports should be met head-to-head, with products to match; and for that matter you cannot count on the fingers and toes of the members of your family the number of times this column was devoted to the same general subject.

Early on, the prevailing attitude seemed to be that "young people" were buying imports as a way of "thumbing their noses at the Establishment," but that turned out to be a crock of sorghum, didn't it?

Even when gasoline was 35 cents a gallon, or thereabouts, there was a growing market for economy and efficiency, and it has expanded now to the point where nearly one out of every four cars sold in America bears a foreign imprint. Moreover, our industry, with a reduced exception for General Motors, is still playing catch-up, and we are faced with the expedients of either higher tariffs or financial invasion by invitation.

There are counter-arguments to all of this; that labor has been irresponsible in its demands and careless, or worse, with the quality of its performance; that government regulations and controls have been excessive; that inflation has limited competitive pricing.

But you must remember that labor learned long ago to read stock market reports and annual bottom-line statements to stockholders and has found it satisfying to meet excess with excess; that imports have thrived while meeting all government standards and edicts; and that inflation here has not been without parallel abroad, especially in Japan.

Seventy years ago Michigan married the automobile industry "for better or worse," and it is too late for divorce.

Sad Saga

These are trying days for the automobile companies, which are the targets for criticism from just about every conceivable angle. One is inclined to say that the top brass are now earning their salaries and fringe benefits, regardless of what they total.

During this past week, for example, the tycoons of the industry were accused of stalling in their negotiations with the United Auto Workers; of being crassly insensitive to the perils of air pollution; and of pricing their products so high that there is no chance of heading off the inroads of foreign imports.

There were also some lesser charges hurled at the companies, but we have now reached such a state that unless a complaint rates comment on a national television news program, or a headline on the front page of the New York Times, it is too minor for serious consideration.

All this rancor is being heaped on an industry which is not yet accustomed to it. The railroads, one might point out, have been absorbing similar slings and arrows for many years, as have the steel companies, lumber barons and coal operators.

In the process, they have become thick-skinned and belligerent, perfectly capable of slugging it out toe-to-toe with any foe, politician or otherwise.

In contrast the auto makers, while leaning toward belligerency, are still thin-skinned. They wince when lanced by a Ralph Nader; they scream when elbowed by a Sen. Muskie; they grouse when taken to task in an editorial. A giant given to pain and anguish, you might say.

And this could be good—for the automobile companies as well as the country. It indicates that perhaps times have changed, that now more than ever before the largest and strongest among us is sensitive to public opinion. If so, the industry may escape many of the reprisals and punitive measures which were directed against its predecessors in bigness.

Aside, perhaps, from the railroads, which thrilled and excited the imaginations of generations of Americans, the automobile in years past had the best public acceptance ever accorded a major American product.

———

Henry Ford in his heyday was a towering hero and his Model T was a legend in its own time. Walter P. Chrysler, William S. Knudsen, the Dodge brothers, Ransom E. Olds, Charles E. Wilson, Barney Oldfield, Eddie Rickenbacker—household names all, these, in their primes, and surrounding them was the luminous radiation from an industry which signified pleasure as well as transportation. It made no difference that many of these men became millionaires and lived aloof from the rank and file. They were heroes because they made significant contributions to an industry which stood for romance, adventure, progress.

More than any other complicated device invented by man, the automobile changed America. It took us out of the mud—if you had a car, you had to have roads. It revolutionized mass production and upgraded the wage scales in all of industry. It created the need for vast satellite industries—petroleum, for instance. Ah, the automobile was good and the makers of it basked in public affection.

———

But that was yesterday, or just the day before. Then, quite suddenly, there came a change. All at once there were too many automobiles and pleasure driving became a hazard. Harry Truman pointed out that more people were being killed on the highways than were dying in the Korean War. You heard complaints that because of the automobile other means of mass transit were being downgraded and the cities were suffocating in unnecessary traffic.

Then, finally, came the ecologists and a seldom-used word, "emission," became popular. New York City and Tokyo banned automobiles on given days from certain streets—and the people cheered. Quite a change!

This is where we are today, with the automobile companies facing rising hostility, and they don't know how to handle it. They are puzzled, hurt, confused and inclined to strike back at their critics.

What they need most of all, of course, is a new emission-free engine, plus a little more patience with those who keep insisting that they should be able to produce one in short order. Such insistence shows that the belief in auto company miracles is not dead. This may be a weak substitute for yesterday's hero worship, but times, as noted, have changed.

A Farewell to Youth

There were some poignant unrehearsed moments near the end of his speech, for then he came to the time of confession. "Look," he seemed to be saying, "I knew it was going to be rough up here, but I didn't expect it to be this difficult . . . "

The hydraulic, downward-pushing, never-ceasing weight of this office has settled around the shoulders of John F. Kennedy, and now in the White House we have a man young in years who has said goodbye to youth.

Never again will he know carefree days. From now on, his sharing of the burdens will consist of a ton for himself and a peck for his associates.

Congress may legislate, the courts may function, the politicians may manipulate, the people may rally or sit morosely on the sidelines, but into the path of John F. Kennedy will fall most of the clods of responsibility tossed up as the world plows steadily toward the brink of madness. It is lonely as well as frightening where he stands, so no wonder he said: "I need your good will and your support—and above all, your prayers."

Many of us would have preferred another in his place. But now he is our man, as we are his people, and we must face this thing together. It won't be easy.

Days Ago . . .

. . . at the House on Grandmont we talked of what we would do if the nuclear attack comes. It was not an easy conversation; no one can confront the ultimate in horror without feeling that he is participating in make believe. But there ought to be some water, we agreed, and some food, and perhaps that corner in the basement.

I wonder how many similar conversations there have been this sweet, fine summer as America has laughed aloud at the joys of living while worrying inwardly about the odds of survival? Civil defense may not have caught on as a national program, but I suspect that it has been the private concern of countless millions.

She has thought: he may not be able to get home from the office in time, but he will be all right . . . perhaps. And he has thought: even if I don't make it, she and the kids will be safe . . . perhaps.

I would guess that in this instance, as in so many others, the people, acting so unconcerned and carefree, have nonetheless been far ahead of their leaders. This is trite, but true: there is good fiber in the mass of Americans. They can face up to danger. They are not swayed away from what they consider right and just by bluster or bombast.

Some of this came through Tuesday night in the President's address—a speech written and delivered, no doubt, as much for Russian consumption as for the rallying of his own people.

He was right in saying: "We do not want to fight—but we have fought before. And others in earlier times have made the same dangerous mistake of assuming that the West was too selfish and too soft and too divided to resist invasions of freedoms in other lands."

That was a good paragraph. The Russians should study it and be guided by what it says.

For Now America

. . . has come to initial grips with reality. The President's speech was not a declaration of war, it was not a deliberate flaunting of our enemy, it was not even a final blueprinting of what we shall do under all circumstances. There is room for negotiation.

Still, it was a definite commitment, agreed to by the Congress, which shall appropriate the money and pass the legislation, and concurred in by the people, who shall pay the costs, whatever they are. We are going to get ready for any eventuality . . .

In the mid days of this sweet, fine summer, a President and his people have reached a new maturity. Many things have changed overnight, including "politics as usual." For the duration of this crisis, only America matters.

The 60s Are Over

At station 35 in that vast, cavernous old building, the car began to take shape.

There was a clanking of chains, a whirring of pulleys, a reaching up of sure hands, a stretching of rippling muscles, a guiding with practiced eyes—and, all at once, as though it had been conjured out of thin air, the engine was in place.

Now the chassis no longer resembled the picked bones of a flat and monstrous reptile. It had form, the beginning of purpose, and I thought I detected the first surge of animation as men climbed over it, strong fingers probing, backs bending, arms flashing in the bright light.

There were sounds, many of them, as this skeleton moved slowly yet determinedly along the assembly line.

Above all the clangorous noises there was this one: "wheerrrr-ong!" it went, persistently, nipping in and out of the other sounds, signaling that harnessed air under pressure had been unleashed to snug nut to bolt.

———————

At station 35 the steering post appeared, mysteriously, and for some reason I was reminded of a long, jagged stick that was flung dagger-like into a South Carolina beach one afternoon by a capricious wind. But the sound was not of the wind or the surf: "wheerrr-ong," it said, and the pile of bones kept moving, relentlessly.

Suddenly there was a flash of red edged with chrome, and, from overhead, again as if by magic, the body appeared, the doors closed, the headlamps fixed, the windshield wearing the vapid stare of a window in an abandoned farmhouse.

It hung there for a few seconds, this mass of iron and fabric, quivering and wobbling, then it plummeted into position and again there were the probing fingers and flashing arms.

The wheels, red to match red, went into place and once more there was that dominating intrusion: "wheerrr-ong, wheerrrr-ong, wheerrrr-ong!"

I noticed a sign and laughed: "If you drop it, pick it up!" Funny guys, these auto makers . . .

———————

The hood plopped down and was bolted into position, swiftly. Floor mattings appeared and were flung into front and rear. Men did I know not what to interior fastenings and fittings, and now it looked like a car, sleek and poised, and where would you like to go this sunny afternoon, Mrs. O'Leary?

There was a word in script—I noticed it for the first time—on the left front fender. "Galaxie," it read. Stars in your eyes, too, Young Henry . . .

At station 14 the car was off the line, traveling on a horizontal escalator. Men in a long, trench-like pit were working furiously with screw drivers and small, shriller "wheerrrr-ongers." The tempo seemed faster, reaching now toward completion, the pace accelerated to make room for other inert newcomers crowded hood-to-rear along the line.

"Move it," someone shouted, and the motor of the red "Galaxie" caught and held, beating pulse-like, low and regular, against the backdrop of sounds.

It rolled away into an area reserved for "wheel alignment," and a blue "Fairlane 500" took its place.

Later, a few minutes after the last car had come down the line, a whistle blew and a strange, uneasy silence settled throughout the building.

———————

Workmen in white coveralls, lunch buckets under their arms, headed for the exits.

"That does it," one of them said. "That's the last of the old models . . . "

Thus in the early part of the ninth month of 1960, a year ended at the Dearborn Assembly Plant of River Rouge.

The red "Galaxie," sitting in the warehouse area, looked and smelled new, but it was old, really. With one swift, final "wheerrrr-ong!," time had left it in the lurch.

That is the way it is in the automobile business.

Make Your Influence Felt

Of late there has been a small flurry of mail from constituents with a common concern: They want to know how they can break out of the "silent majority" and play a more positive role in the affairs of their country.

The answer, of course, is "participation"—taking part in civic and governmental affairs at any and all levels, wherever there is a void or the need for another pair of hands or another active mind.

There is rarely a time, for example, when the political parties do not need help at the precinct or district levels. We sometimes forget how important this work is: We fail to recognize that decisions made in the 17th District, let us say, may eventually pervade the entire organization, up to and including the national movement. A precinct committeeman may not rate a 21-gun salute in the political pecking order, but there may be times when his voice is pivotal in party affairs.

Parents should be deeply concerned about what is going on in the schools and they should participate through the various means open to them. It is sometimes said that parent-teacher organizations are "meaningless," but wherever this is true it is probably because public interest has waned and control has been defaulted into too few hands. We will get back to this in just a minute.

Businessmen should support their professional organizations and the group movements, such as the Chamber of Commerce, open to them. And the various civic clubs offer a means of participation once they are moved off dead center. Read the by-laws of Rotary, for instance, and you will find that it was conceived as much more than a "meet, eat and sing" outfit dedicated to inane programs.

Many charitable organizations need help. The churches, at last count, were in desperate search of lay assistance. On all sides there are opportunities for the citizen who wants to be heard, who desires to make a contribution, who is sick and tired of being counted as a supine member of the "silent majority."

But remember this. If you decide to come out of hibernation, the organization you choose is not going to be instantly overwhelmed by your presence. They aren't going to change the constitution at the first meeting to suit your pleasure. They won't elect you president within a month or name you to the board of directors the first time a vacancy occurs. After all, where have you been all these years? You must work a while in the vineyard before you become the chief ramrodder.

Sometimes a fellow will write a letter to his Representative or Senator and then scream and holler when that worthy fails to follow through as advised. Democracy is dead, the writer will moan— I have no voice left in public affairs. Come, now: Does one letter constitute a contribution to democracy? And where have you been all these years?

The point is that no one—not even a newspaper columnist!— can hope to sway the course of events by a single act or a solitary contribution. Democracy is a vastly complicated process. It rewards those who love it enough to nurture it and protect it over the long haul.

Someone has said that you get out of life approximately what you put into it. This is true in public as well as in private affairs. End of lecture.

Mud in His Eye

To arising at crack of dawn (well, before 9 o'clock, anyhow) on Sunday morning and to reading Gallup Poll which indicated that

12 percent of all Americans would prefer to live elsewhere, but especially in Australia, Canada, Britain or Switzerland.

To thinking that too many people are selling the country short these days, permitting a few disadvantages to discolor the many advantages, and to vowing to outline piece to that effect just as soon as Ramrod Eight was fetched home from car wash.

To driving, then, to car wash, tooling through a fine residential area brightened by the gallant rays of Spring's first sun, and to declaring to no one in particular that only in America do so many people have it so good, and God bless the people one and all, as Tiny Tim was supposed to have said before he learned to play the ukulele.

———

To arriving at car wash and being first in line, which was like finding a small ruby in a pint box of strawberries, and to watching as thick layer of winter's grime was removed by assortment of brushes, sprays, padded discs and other mechanical wonders. To delivering underbreath oration in favor of Yankee ingenuity and to swelling with modest pride as Ramrod Eight emerged from bath glistening at every pore. To deciding it would last at least another season and to praising manufacturer for quality of paint job.

To getting into Ramrod Eight and driving to end of car wash runway, which intersects with busy street. To noticing large mud puddle on left but paying it no particular mind inasmuch as it seemed removed from line of traffic.

To sitting there, thinking other sweet thoughts, while hot-rodder approached from left, motor roaring. To observing that it certainly is strange how some people like to make tremendous racket on peaceful Sunday morning.

And to still sitting there, petrified, while hot-rodder deliberately cut to right, running wheels through large mud puddle and spraying 40 gallons of dirty water all over newly-washed Ramrod Eight.

To swearing mightily, to damning younger generation from hell to breakfast, to pounding steering wheel and to vowing by all that is holy to sell house and chattels and leave for Australia on next boat.

Lee and Ronnie

Man's Need

Just to need to be needed by someone
Is the whole of man's mission on Earth.
It's the total, the sum of his purpose,
It's the ultimate goal of his worth.

In a world that is wanting in freedom,
In a nation with pockets of poor,
In a city with problems a-plenty,
There is need for man's goal—to be sure.

There is need on the busiest homefront.
There is need where it's quiet and alone.
He who finds him a spot where he's needed
Fills the paramount need of his own.

—Margaret Rorke

A couple of rather earthy old dudes who have been needed—Lee Iacocca, industrialist, and Ronald Reagan, politician—pushed their ways into the limelight a few nights ago by dominating television programming.

Mr. Iacocca used an hour's free time to tell us how you go about reviving an automobile company that is run down at the heels and ripped and raveled at the seams; Mr. Reagan purchased five minutes with money from his campaign kitty to tell us what a scintillating president he has been, and why he should be re-elected.

Now both of these gentlemen have detractors. There are those in the automobile industry, for example, who will tell you that Lee Iacocca squeezed the gizzards out of a lot of good people, including workers, executives, suppliers and dealers in his fixated determination to save Chrysler from the auctioneer's gavel.

As for Ronald Reagan, there are a whole slew of folks, perhaps as many as 25 percent of the population, who would rather see Jimmy Carter or Richard Nixon back in the White House. Yet here he is, running for another term at an age when most men are concerned about an entirely different sort of hereafter.

All things considered, then, why are they such limelighters? They are, or at least they were, needed.

———————

Lee Iacocca is sort of the Winston Churchill of the automobile business. There was a time in the 1930s, remember, when very few Englishmen took Winston seriously. He had seemingly used-up all of his bombastic energy on projects which had not quite jelled, and if he hadn't been excellent as a writer, he and his family would have been on their uppers. Then Hitler came along, the Empire heaved and rolled, the moment had arrived for a leader of mystical qualities.

The parallel between Winston Churchill and Lee Iacocca is not exact, of course, but in some respects it is not far-fetched. No one has ever said so precisely, but when you come right down to it Lee Iacocca was fired by Henry Ford II for being uncouth. This was an Italian boy out of nowhere reaching for the stars in a corporation dominated by an old-line, hard-nosed pioneer family, and the possibility of it, the dazzling irony of it, simply would not play in Dearborn or Peoria, or so it was thought.

So Lee Iacocca went into eclipse at almost the time when Chrysler was headed for the economic compactor. There were those that said this feisty, profane man and this tottering giant bled white by poor management needed and deserved one another, and if all the wakes for the two of them had been held simultaneously, and the tears preserved, there would never again be a shortage of water in Lake St. Clair.

Well, he pulled it off, didn't he?—this cigar-nursing, furrow-foreheaded, cussing and gesticulating invader from Lehigh U. He saved Chrysler, at least for the nonce, and in the process probably saved himself. When you bring the "needed" together, miracles can occur.

———————

By the logic of the polls, which is to presume that polls have logic, Ronald Reagan will be re-elected. There may be another reason, not generally noted: The people have been disturbed, upset, by the turn-over in the White House, which has not had a two-term resident since Dwight Eisenhower. The presidency is a job which can be learned only by being on the job, so there is something to be said for tenure.

Beyond that, Ronald Reagan was needed, and perhaps remains needed, to satisfy the whooping, and hollering and belly-aching of the conservatives, who had been saying for years they could run the country slicker than the Toonerville Trolley if just given the chance. Have they; can they? They are going to say they need another four years in which to prove their assertions.

Ralph Waldo Emerson wrote that "All are needed by each one; nothing is fair or good alone." Powerful stuff, need.

Great Moment of Truth

Afterward—after that sinister, needle-like instrument had gone "whoosshhh!" and Comdr. Alan B. Shepard, Jr., had been recovered from the sea—I walked through the downtown area, too full of emotion, too close to tears, too elated to confront this typewriter.

There were others verging on the same state. At the bank, my favorite money-changer said: "I'm so glad you have come in. Tell me about it!" So we talked and I tried to put 30 minutes of the best of everything into words for her, but not too well, I fear.

On a street corner, the Free Press was already there—"SPACE SHOT OK!"—and a passerby, caught by the headline, murmured: "Thank God." Yes, thank the Lord. And all at once I felt taller, stronger, braver. . . .

Back at the Office . . .

. . . the city desk was answering a flurry of telephone calls and one of them was from Jean Pearson, our Jean, who had stood in the bright sunlight at Cape Canaveral while they cranked up that infernal machine.

She told her story crisply, coolly, one-two-threely—what a gal!—and there was no chance for me to say: "Hurry home, doll, and I'll buy the lunch!" But when she gets back, nose peeled, cheeks aflame, the invitation will stand. . . .

And now with this on paper, with a fleeting portion of a great city's reaction to a courageous Navy lad recorded for whatever "posterity" awaits—now, perhaps, it is safe to talk of other related things. . . .

Before Alan Shepherd . . .

. . . was hurtled into history, I had been troubled about the truth—the truth as the newspapers have been seeing it and reporting it.

There had been letters, one of them from a Flat Rock housewife (Mrs. F. P.) who wrote: "Take our astronaut launching, for example. How many times did Russia fail before she launched Yuri Gagarin? Thanks to her restricted press, as far as the world knows she was successful on the first day. But about our impending launching: thanks to our over-advertising, the whole world is waiting to laugh at our failure, or shrug us off as second best. . . ."

Well, from the "counting" standpoint—one, two, three—the lady is right: we still stand second best. But from the viewpoint of truth, it seems to me that America has scarcely known a finer half-hour.

For at Cape Canaveral on Friday, May 5, we put everything we have been, everything we are and everything we hope to be on the line.

With the correspondents of the world as our invited guests, we said, in effect: "Look—we kid you not. In a few minutes, Alan Shepard, astronaut, Navy officer, family man, is going to entrust his life to science. We think he will be boosted into space: we think he will be rescued unharmed from the ocean. We think, in short, that this thing will work. If it does—rejoice with us. But if it doesn't—you may still write the truth. . . ."

So It Worked . . .

. . . So Alan Shepard, who probably gave no indication during his younger years that he was destined for it, has become a part of the future lore, the folk songs, the ballads, the poetry, the warp and woof, so to speak, of his country.

And whatever it was he did that May 5—again, science must be the judge—the world saw him, alone and abandoned in those final minutes, the complete servant of his nation. Poised high above the sandy shore of the Atlantic, later thrust through a lonely sky, Alan Shepard was the truth, the American truth, maligned and disputed of late but still proud, fearless, unashamed.

In a very great sense he was the reply to those who say, "We print too much, we know too much." To a world desperate for the truth, he was the answer to propaganda, the half-lie, the blandishment, the slick promise.

EIGHT
Lost in the Horse Latitudes

Washington—Holy Smoke!

Washington—On a cold and windy day, let's take a stroll through that lemon orchard called bureaucracy, which flourishes in all seasons . . .

We have crossed famed Pennsylvania Avenue, heading south on Northwest 14th Street, and at the corner of Northwest E—we have on the right the Department of Commerce, the Hon. Secretary Hodges presiding.

———

In the normal course of things you do not hear much about Commerce. Yet its facilities here—and they are augmented elsewhere—are imposing. The building stretches for a solid block along Northwest 14th, and dips laterally for several hundred yards. I have attempted by telephone to learn how many employees it houses, but to no avail.

Across from Commerce, facing on Northwest E, is a large marble-faced structure bearing a sign—"District Building." I presume this has something to do with local government, which is a separate little empire unto itself. Let's keep walking . . .

We arrive at world-renowned Constitution Avenue, with Commerce still on the right, remember, and the Labor Department, the Hon. Secretary Goldberg installed, on the left. I happen to know that it shelters about 3,500 job holders, with more in the field.

Sort of kitty-cornered from where we are standing, in a wind-swept tract all its own, stands the Washington Monument, a marvel of architectural achievement in its day.

A thought, while gazing skyward, where a bleak, frigid-looking cloud hovers over the peak of the slender shaft . . . I wonder what the Father of our Country would say about the fact that the total expenditures of his administration, plus the costs of all Federal government through 1849, including the Mexican War, were less than one-sixth of what our deficit—just our deficit—will be this fiscal year . . .

Heading east, roughly, on Constitution, we find that Labor runs into a "Departmental Auditorium," also massive, and next we come to the Interstate Commerce Commission, small by comparison with its brother bureaus, but not so small as to shame an employee. We arrive at the junction of Northwest 12th, which dead-ends into Constitution.

Internal Revenue is next and it is a whopper, bigger than Commerce, filled no doubt with electronic monsters that will get you if you don't watch out. Facing on the other side is the Museum of Natural History, with a new wing under construction.

At Northwest 10, the Department of Justice, the Hon. Mr. Robert Kennedy in charge, and this runs for a solid block along Constitution. Next to it is the National Archives Building, while directly opposed stands the National Gallery of Art, a gift of that archreactionary, the late Andrew Mellon.

We continue, coming finally to Northwest 7th, where sits the Federal Trade Commission, but now I am going back to the hotel because my feet are killing me.

This has been the 50-cent tour. We have not come upon the Department of State, where dwells the Hon. Soapy Williams and about 6,000 others, and we have omitted the Pentagon and innumerable other havens where dwelleth the bureaucrats in staggering numbers. But perhaps what we have seen will tell you why Washington, with just one industry, government, is considered the richest city in the world.

A Bowlful of Blah's

This is being whacked out of the typewriter the day after "Super Sunday," and one has the feeling that the mood of the country is somewhat flat. It is as though all of us had been invited to a party which failed to live up to its advance billing; the food was cold, the booze was diluted and at least one of the entertainers, an import by the name of Yepremian, had two left feet.

Once again the Super Bowl Game has turned out to be a sterling example of what happens when propaganda is encouraged to run wild. We had two weeks of unabashed tub-thumping and incense-burning during which quite ordinary mortals were advanced to the realm of god-dom; the business interests, always eager to be associated with virility, were conned into coughing-up $10 million for television commercials; surely this was going to be a spectacle that would leave the yokels bug-eyed until late summer, when the pre-liminaries leading to another extravaganza would start again.

Well, it turned out to be a mighty dull way to spend a Sunday, even a Michigan January Sunday. But we must not despair. They will try it again next year; the same tom-tom beaters will be gathered, even though some of them may be feeling a bit crummy about their connection with this fiasco; "Super Sunday" is here to stay. It is too profitable, too utterly and absolutely laden with fantastic possibilities, to be abandoned. One of these years a decent football game may be held in connection with it, and then the whole country will stay daffy for weeks thereafter.

One has now advanced into "Morose Monday" in the grip of senseless speculation. What would happen, one wonders, if we could rally such overpowering forces to combat some of our social problems? Let us take hunger, for example. Surely stamping out hunger would be better business in the long run than providing the sponsorship of a football game, but unfortunately for hunger, it lacks pizazz. If you get intimate with hunger you end up dealing with all sorts of unhappy situations, and who wants to watch that on television, especially on Sunday?

Disease and second-class education lack pizzazz, too. If you tried to raise $10 million to sponsor a program over 200 stations on the subject, "This Is Why Johnny Can't Read," how far would you get? And one of the reasons why you wouldn't get very far is because scarcely anyone would watch it. Including Johnny.

That's the way it goes. The peerless leaders of ancient Rome knew what they were doing when they provided circuses for the people, and who are we to spit in the eye of tradition?

Long live Super Sunday, which has the full backing of our President, our business leaders and all others who know how to make the mare go, as the fellow said.

A Scandalous Assault

Michigan, My Michigan

Home of my heart, I sing of thee,
  Michigan, My Michigan;
A colder land there ne'er could be,
  Michigan, My Michigan
Nine dreary months of snow and sleet,
  We limp around with frozen feet,
Your derned old climate can't be beat,
  Michigan, My Michigan

Your loyal sons will ne'er forget,
  Michigan, My Michigan;
This year the coldest winter yet,
  Michigan, My Michigan
Your cold winds howl around our knees,
  We poke the fire and sit and freeze,
Oh, what's the use of my B.V.D.'s
  In Michigan, My Michigan!

Note and Comment . . .

The author of the aforesaid scandalous assault on our lovely wizard water wonderland is unknown, which a good thing for him. Otherwise, at least a half-dozen Chambers of Commerce which promote skiing, bobsledding, ice skating, and snowmobiling would be after his hide, tooth and nail.

On second thought, even if the culprit's name were known he would probably be spared punishment on this mortal coil, for this is a rather ancient version of "Michigan, My Michigan," and the chances are that the composer has long since gone to his ultimate reward. Leastwise, this is the estimate of Herbert P. Wagner Sr., who found the lyrics in the back of an old song book and sent them along in order that we might share in the hissing, booing—and chuckling. (It is funny in places, isn't it)?

Mr. Wagner, verging on his 81st birthday anniversary, is the songleader at the Ann Arbor Rotary Club, and he tells us that the members sang "Michigan, My Michigan" in advance of a recent program which featured a Red Cross report on the Great Blizzard of 1978. He does not mention the tune to which the lyrics were set; but he points out that the advanced age of the work is attested by reference in the second stanza to B.V.D.'s, the male unmentionables that went out of style a goodly piece ago. (Note: Your scribe can remember wearing B.V.D.'s as a nipper, but cannot recall when he stopped. It is likely that the abandonment of this traditional garment occurred shortly after the attainment of puberty, so now we are really dipping into the Dark Ages.)

Finally, Mr. Wagner's letter and enclosure (he is Michigan, Class of '21, incidentally) reached us on the day when our neighbors down the road, Hal and Rose Ware, pulled stakes after 24 years of pioneering and moved to Pensacola, Fla., lock, stock, and barrel. The night before they left, Hal had a few remarks to make about cold winds howling around his knees, just like it says in the song. We are reminded again that there are some things in life which do not change for the better.

Oh, yes: At the Rotary meeting in question, the members also sang "Blow the Snow Round," but let's not get into that in the middle of June, for crying out loud.

Salute!

Salute the stars that draw the mind,
The blue of peace and right,
The red of courage, raw, refined,
The purity of white;

The blend of heaven and of earth:
The symbol freedom flies
Above a nation blessed with worth—
Beneath its Father's eyes!

—Margaret Rorke

With "Salute!" Mrs. Rorke reminds us that Wednesday will be Flag Day. Give Old Glory a chance to dance and wave and shimmer in the breeze while you admire its beauty. The spectacle will be good for you.

There are some of us, hidebound and old-fashioned, perhaps, who will never be able to look upon the flag as "just another symbol." To us it represents the America we have loved from our beginnings, in good times and bad, right or wrong.

Jimmy Carter, Jimmy Carter

In 1948, while en route by shank's mare to the voting place in a small Ohio community, your commentator was thinking Tom Dewey. There is a perfect recollection of this: On that autumn day, afoot through a business district three blocks long and two blocks deep, nodding right and left to friends, acquaintances and delinquent subscribers, a country editor headed for the polls to deliver his franchise to the gentleman from New York.

But hark! Upon entering the sanctum reserved for free citizens, and upon being confronted by the paper ballot, an instinct beyond explanation moved the pencil to the box reserved for Harry Truman and an "X" was formed therein. It has since been said that this was a common miracle throughout America, leading to a considerable upset of political form.

Immediate history, which is little better than folklore, now applauds that shift away from Tom Dewey. Harry Truman, we hear on all sides, was "one of our great presidents." Was he, really? More serious students of the coursing of events are beginning to cast seeds of doubt. Mr. Truman, it is being murmured, may have

been too bellicose for his britches. A bit more patience on his part
might have saved us some of the unnecessary consequences of the
Cold War, including the disasters of Korea and Vietnam.

Such is the speculation of the historians. It leads us to this point
in time, as that fellow now isolated in California used to say—to
next Tuesday, when once again millions of uncertain Americans
will be wending their ways to the voting booths. Again, what is a
poor citizen to do? How does he know when he is right—or
wrong?

The country editor we met a few paragraphs ago, now clipped
and hammered by time, his backswing shortened and his patience
frazzled, will ride to the polls Tuesday. Another state, another ballot, another name is in mind—very tentatively in mind, it should
be admitted: Jimmy Carter, Jimmy Carter.

Will the hand that rocks the voting booth be staved this time?
Possibly. In some respects, this election has 1948 written all over
it. But for the nonce, at least, there is an inclination toward the gentleman from Georgia.

Why, you may ask? Well, why not? It might be argued that one
question is as solid as the other. But since you have doubtless had
enough of ring-around-the-rosey in this campaign, a few specifics
will be attempted.

Since everything gets back to sports these days, including Joe
Garagiola's role on behalf of Gerald Ford, America might be
likened to a baseball team that has finished third (or fifth or sixth)
several seasons in a row. Patently, something should be done, for
the fans are grumbling, and confidence in the future is at low ebb.

You can't trade enough of the players to make a perceptible difference, so you seize the only other recourse and tie the can to the
manager. Maybe—just maybe!—Jimmy Carter will turn out to the
Sparky Anderson we so sorely need.

This country is in the doldrums, and one grows a bit weary of
those who say, "Yes, but we are better off than England, France or
those other places!" The answer is that we ought to be better off,

for heaven's sake, considering our location, our population, and our natural resources, but even this is not the whole of it.

In any other industrial nation, had unemployment gone beyond eight percent and stayed, as it did here, the government would long since have been out in the street. Rather blithely, we are asked to put up with seven percent or more joblessness until "the economy rights itself." This isn't quite as sneaky as hiding prosperity around a corner, as was attempted in the early 1930s, but it will do until something worse comes along.

———————

Still persisting in the mentality of some of our peerless leaders is the "trickle-down theory" of economics, which holds that after the Big Boys have been satiated there will be spillover for the poor. One reads the papers and notes that the Chrysler Corp., as an example, has already made more money in 1976 than in any other whole year in its existence. It is natural to wonder how many furloughed workers they called back yesterday morning.

What the poor need has not changed much in this lifetime, unfortunately. They need jobs, the pride which comes from contributing to society and the assurance they are needed, wanted and appreciated.

We are out of space. The trek to the polls is contemplated with a strange name in mind—Jimmy Carter, Jimmy Carter.

What's Fair for Farmers

Out our way as these lines are written the rain is falling on the just and the unjust. If any good is to come from it, the farmer who goes to town to drink beer and play pinochle with his cronies will derive as much benefit as the one who stays home and helps take care of the kids. Partly, this may have been what John F. Kennedy had in mind when he said that life is unfair.

The rain began early last evening and has continued into midday, gently but firmly. Quite likely it will intoxicate our trees, plants and shrubs into a wild orgy of early bloom, then along will come a cold snap and wipe out everything in sight, including the peach, cherry and apple crops. Writing a column may be a silly way to make a living of sorts, but it sure beats farming.

Of all the Americans subjected to the so-called laws of supply and demand, the position of the farmer is the most untenable. If a manufacturer, by comparison, misjudges the market and produces too many widgets, he can store them in a warehouse and pray for an upward trend. But what do you do with an over-supply of lettuce, onions, pickles or whatever? Why, you take what you can get and hope that mercy will somehow find its way into the innards of your banker.

On yesterday's Board of Trade in Chicago, May futures in both wheat and corn were less than $2.70 per bushel in large lots. If memory is correct, prices were nearly that high 20 years ago. Who else is trying to run a 1977 business on 1957 prices? It is a miracle that agriculture has survived.

Sure, you say, production per acre has increased since 1957, but so has production in almost every other industry. Yet the farmer has been left holding the bag where technology is concerned. It has saved his hide, perhaps, whereas other lines of endeavor have reaped vast windfalls from it. The farmer paced the breakthrough into efficiency, but has received far less for it than he has deserved. The packer or canner, the distributor, the trucking industry, the unions, the merchandiser—if you want to complain about the price of food be sure to aim your sling and arrows in the right direction. The farmer hasn't ripped you off, not a dime's worth.

The farmer may be the only American who has lost ground on a trade-off basis—either hours of work or results of production as compared with what he has to buy. If at one time he could purchase a Tin Lizzie for 400 bushels of wheat, how many bushels must he grow today to meet the price tag on a Ramrod Eight? Or to trade for a tractor? Or remodel his home? Or send his children to college? Or pay his taxes?

Ah, yes his taxes! One of the worst things that can happen to a farmer is to have his land located near a community where commercial and residential development are afoot. All at once those acres attract the avid attention of the assessor, who whets his pencil and increases the value on the tax duplicate.

Thousands of farmers have faced this dilemma and have been forced to sell their property. They made a one-time profit. True. But in many instances their children were also driven off the land, the "cause" of agriculture was weakened as the result of this pressure, and there may well come a day when all of us will rue the loss of this source of food and fiber.

For these reasons and others, the remaining farmland of our nation is falling into fewer hands, and the time may come when most agriculture will be corporate in structure. Then you will see changes in prices and the division of profits.

Worse, this transformation will also alter the social balance, removing from it a type of citizen who has made the tremendous contributions to our political and economic stability. America without farmers as we still know them will be a different, and perhaps rather risky, place.

The farm vote, as we have called it, has served as a windward anchor during some of the storms of change which have blown across our country, tempering either idealism or radicalism to bearable limits. Those close to the land, as Lenin once noted, make poor revolutionaries, being more inclined toward possession than upheaval.

From the land has also come millions of transplants who have blended into metropolitan life, bringing with them the strengths and sensibilities which are nurtured by association with the soil. Indeed, the thought occurs on a rainy day that our debt to the farm folk will never be repaid.

Heroes—The Market's Glutted

Quite often we hear the cry, "Where have all the heroes gone?" and the lack of response leads to the possibility that they are dead. Well, some of them are: Thomas Jefferson, Abraham Lincoln,

Charles Darwin, Franklin D. Roosevelt, to offer an abbreviated personal list.

Now we go to Webster's for a definition of "hero," which in this instance will also embrace "heroine," and we come to this: "The central figure in any important event or period, honored for outstanding qualities." Apply this to society as it now exists, and it tells us what has been happening to heroes: They were here yesterday, but they will be gone today and forgotten tomorrow.

It is next to impossible for a hero to acquire longevity in the era of mass communications. Let us say that if a fellow came along with a sure-fire cure for hard times, and put it into effect, and cut the unemployment figure to four percent—but in the process had to spend much of his time explaining his plan to the media—within six months the people would be sick and tired of him.

———————————————

They would switch to another channel when he showed up on television, complaining because he had usurped the time ordinarily reserved for a game show or a pie-throwing comedy; they would write letters to the editor berating the amount of space devoted to the hero's background and family life, especially if there was no juicy scandal involved, and the news magazines would stop running his picture on their covers because of swooning newsstand sales.

Within a short span, then, another hero would have flared comet-like, then faded away. It happens all the time. The media, which reflect popular taste, make and abandon heroes without strain or pain. It has become a very fast track for heroes, a pertinent reason why only one president since Dwight Eisenhower has been re-elected.

Whereas heroes once came mostly from politics or war, or a combination thereof, now they are apt to spring up almost anywhere. This has become a society of widely divided interests, with some of the segments reaching into the millions of population, and the media try to touch all bases. This leads to competition among heroes for attention and has helped create an entire industry called public relations. It has also hastened the demise of some luminaries who might have lasted a bit longer had the field not been so crowded.

Now we have heroes in classical music (it is said the two leading tenors wish each other laryngitis); in rock 'n' roll, country western, guitar picking, fiddling, piano thumping and so forth. When the public tires of one, there is always an alternative. The world of sports has become even more diffused, with heroes in football, baseball, basketball, hockey, boxing, track, tennis, golf, skating, skiing, racing, marathoning and just about every other form of locomotion not considered scandalous. This is why newspapers devote more space to sports news than international news, and it accounts for the presence on the airways of sportscasters who are more highly paid than college presidents or even college football coaches.

—————

The environmentalists have heroes, and so do the unions, the various professional societies, the money managers, the industrialists and almost every other group except the militarists, who are in the doldrums at the moment. But give them another war and they will be back in the running for top honors. Who knows? They might give us another Alexander Haig or William C. Westmoreland.

As you can see, on any given day the country is apt to be teeming with heroes, each representing a specific bloc of our citizenry and entitled to full honors as long as they can keep footing and place. Moreover, every so often one of them puts several blocs together and gets elected to high office, and then he has the feeling that the skids are really greased. That was what happened to Ronald Reagan, who was having a lot of fun on the chicken-and-pea circuit until some folks started taking him seriously. Now he is hanging on for dear life, trying to remain a hero. It is a tough life.

The Willies

Something tells me this going to be as eerie as walking past a graveyard at midnight while a hound dog bays at the moon . . .

About three months ago an astronomer by the name of Fred Kerner wrote a series called "The Stars—Key to Our Future?!" The Free Press bought the articles, printed them last week.

The concluding piece, dealing with President Kennedy and his family, appeared last Thursday. In going through the copy prior to sending it to the printers, one of our editors came upon one line that gave him pause.

He studied it for a minute, finally decided that it was "too rough," and penciled it out.

This is what he deleted: "She (an astrologist named Stella) says "There is an indication that there may be sorrow through a child . . . " "

Now remember the date of that editing—it was last Wednesday in preparation for Thursday's paper. On Thursday, it was announced that Caroline Kennedy had been pulled out of a swimming pool just in the nick of time!

And away we go . . .

I Know Little . . .

. . . about astrology, I rarely read the horoscopes. I do not consider myself superstitious—but there are times when I get the queezies, nevertheless.

When my father, name of Thomas Frank, was a mere lad, about 12, he was out chopping kindling one day when suddenly a 'voice' said to him—Thomas Frank, you are going to live to be 50 years old.

Well, that stuck with him the rest of his life. When he was 30, say, and somebody would remark, "Thomas Frank, you sure look fine, you ought to live to be 95," Dad would reply, solemnly, "Oh no, I'm going to die when I'm 50."

The family hee-hawed at him, and got put-out with him, and tried to talk him out of his "premonition," but he never expected to go beyond the half-century mark.

And he didn't, either. He died when he was 50 years and two weeks old.

When My Mother . . .

. . . bless her soul, was a young girl, she was fast asleep one night when suddenly she awakened with a start.

A finger of flame was flickering across the wall in front of her, and as she watched it fluttered into the ceiling.

She was about to jump out of bed and sound the alarm—"fire"—when the flame left. It just disappeared, sort of oozing into the ceiling. Her parents slept directly above . . .

The next morning she told her mother of the flame and said, "Something is going to happen today," but Grandmother Dillon replied. "Hush, child, don't be silly . . . "

Grandfather Dillon, a tanner, went to work the same as usual. A few hours later the blade of a buzz saw disintegrated and a big piece of it pierced his body, killing him where he stood.

What's This . . .

. . . all about? Search me. But whenever someone says, "I had a dream last night," or "I see by my horoscope, etc.," Old Arney doesn't snicker or guffaw. He just tiptoes away, easy like. You can never tell when some poor fellow is snake bit.

Look . . . I'll walk under a ladder with you; or light three off a match (although I am a bit leery of this, having once busted an arm five minutes after doing it); or cross the path of a black cat; or flaunt most any other superstition.

But stay away from me with those "premonitions," please. They give me the galloping willies. Besides, you never know when one of them might rub off!

Lessons of a Lifetime

Some lessons learned during a lifetime, including a wasted youth . . .

1. It is never too late to develop new interests, even to the point of changing the direction of your career. Many people are "slow starters" and do not find their proper place in the scheme of things until their mid-30s, or even later. It takes courage at that juncture

to break away from established routine, but the alternative can be devastating. Have you ever known a happy individual who was following a line of work he (or she) detested?

2. The liberal arts degree awarded prior to World War II was the finest all-around education our colleges and universities ever offered.

3. Given a child who loves to read and is fascinated by the wonders of nature, you are blessed indeed.

4. More hot air has been pumped into high school athletics as "a builder of character" than into all other phases of public education combined. Games are good for our people, young and old alike, but the emphasis we have placed on them to the neglect of arts and recognition of scholarship has amounted to sheer madness.

5. Most successful politicians would have done well in other walks of life. It takes a combination of energy, persuasiveness, determination and combativeness to prosper in public life, and those are attributes needed in business and the professions. The real danger of Watergate was that the people would come to look upon all politicians as cheats and sneaks, but this seems to be abating, thank goodness.

6. The best president of this lifetime was Franklin Delano Roosevelt, beyond comparison. He came to office when revolution and anarchy were sweeping the world, yet he helped preserve the best facets of the system. Simultaneously, England was losing its empire; France was corrupted by internal weaknesses; Germany fell under the spell of a madman; Italy succumbed to fascism; Japan turned to militarism; Russia reeled under tyranny. The period 1932–1945 was the worst by far in this century for freemen and their institutions, and only brilliant leadership spared us the liberties and privileges we enjoy today.

7. The worst president? Warren G. Harding, probably, because his administration lacked all of the saving graces during a post-war period when the world desperately needed American leadership. Richard Nixon turned out to be a zombie, but during his bright years he was alert to main chances in foreign affairs, particularly in Red China, and he had the courage to pursue them.

8. The best movie was "Gone with the Wind," primarily because it utilized every ounce of the then-available technology in

sound and photography; the best novel was "The Grapes of Wrath," which did more to awaken the nation to the consequences of the Dust Bowl than any other source; the most interesting professional sports team came out of St. Louis in 1934—the original Gashouse Gang featuring Dizzy Dean; and no one ever hit the golf ball better than the fabled Bobby Jones, who was still using hickory-shafted clubs, for crying out loud.

9. In communications, television has been the most jarring force unleashed on humanity, and you could argue that it descended upon us about 30 years before we were ready for it. As an intellectual force, television is about where yellow journalism was at the turn of the century, so you keep hoping it will improve in the years to come. There is a modicum of consolation in the thought that in some ways it can't get any worse.

10. Of the old nations now in the doldrums, England may well make the most spirited recovery before the year 2000. The English are a rugged and intelligent lot, and one of these days they could find the right blend of socialism and free enterprise and start "putting it together" again.

11. The most essential ingredient in happiness is a good marriage, regardless of which one it is—first, second, third, you pick it. This thought will disturb some of our young friends, who are showing little appreciation for marriage as an "institution," but let them get a little older, and a little less enamored of the joys of wanderlust, and they will start heading for the parson. It is the nature of most of us to need and seek stability, and since the beginning of time no substitute has been found in this respect for marriage. We are advised in Genesis that "It is not good that a man should be alone," and there has been no better phrasing of it.

12. Over the years we have been owned by four dogs, and in their own distinctive ways they have given us more enjoyment than all the rest of our "possessions." Today, when Old Yeller comes around of his own free will and accord to share his affection, even inflation seems bearable.

13. Make a semi-annual commitment out of taking a priest, preacher or rabbi to lunch. Not only are they good company, but the way of the world has been such, and remains such, that they probably need kindness more than you do.

14. Time usually shows that the Supreme Court was right in its decisions.

15. Never sell America short. Never. And aggravating as they sometimes seem, this may be the best lot of Americans ever.

Wintry Observations

I am trying to be a true-blue citizen—Michigan, My Michigan!—by reacting with calm fortitude toward the season's first snow, which began the morning of this writing and is continuing at mid-afternoon.

All in all, it has been a rather trying day, with rain early in the morning; followed by snow; followed by sleet; followed by snow. One needs a touch of levity to keep up his cheer during such a calamity, so a while ago I forced myself to recall Bob Hope's famous weather forecast—"High winds, followed by high skirts, followed by me." It didn't help too much, however, for what's a high skirt these days? Dime a dozen, that's what they are. Shucks, a fellow can walk down Washington Boulevard on an absolutely windless day and see enough high skirts to last him for a month, unless he's a pig. That's what this permissive society has brought us to: Nothing to look forward to on a cold and windy day.

———◆◆◆——— ———◆◆◆———

But one must prevail, one must remain a Civic Booster, one must never admit that things might be better in Florida, one must seek out and find the Positive Attitude. To this end, let us dissect winter, dear friends, piece by piece, and take comfort from the findings.

SNOW—Anyway you look at, snow has been vastly overrated. Poets have eulogized it, critics have condemned it, yet when you come right down to the nitty-gritty, snow is just water that has turned cold. This is why it rarely snows in Florida—they can't get up a good head of cold. It is also why it snows so much in the Upper Peninsula—they have cold coming out of their ears. So don't be awed, or cowed or romanticized by snow; don't curse it, or stamp it, or try to kick it in the teeth or wish it on your worst enemies. Just remember that if the temperature stood at 70 degrees at this moment, it would be raining violets. This was what the fellow meant when he said, "You don't stand the chance of a snowball in Hell." When the heat is on, snow takes a powder, so to speak. It is not a trustworthy substance, and for that reason you should not be intimidated by it or attracted to it.

SALT—This is what we use around here to remove snow from the streets, and I would be inclined to offer a lengthy paean of praise to it were it not for the fact that in the process of removing snow, salt also removes your tailpipe, your fenders and the paint up as high as the windows. When you see a fellow driving around with his doors closed but his feet showing, you know right off that he and his jalopy have spent several hard winters. If you think we are going to have a lot of snow this winter, take a flyer in salt futures. Blizzards may strand motorists, stop the mails, delay your newspapers and dull your snow shovel, but they make the salt companies rich.

SKIING—This is something that is done in the winter, because of the snow. If you could do it in the summer, more of us would be in favor of it. One gathers there all sorts of skiers, ranging from terrible to terrific, but unfortunately they have never worked out a rating, or handicap system, so you can tell how awful or agile a participant really is. This makes it possible for characters such as disc jockeys to fib by the hour when you ask for a report on their degree of dexterity.

Skiing is also the only sport where it is considered chic to end up with a busted arm or leg. If a friend rode a bicycle into a tree and fractured his knee, you would consider him something of a nut. But just let him go skittering into a chasm, bedslats akimbo, on a day when an Eskimo should not be abroad, and you take him a $12 bottle of Scotch and autograph the 40 pounds of plaster in which he is encased. Skiing seems to be growing in popularity, which may speak more for the blithering state of mankind than any words we might conjure up in this limited space.

FIREPLACE—This is one of man's smarter inventions, especially if you can find some well-seasoned logs to burn in it. Use of the fireplace when it is snowing is highly recommended. It won't keep you very warm, especially on the back side, but the flames symbolize man's hope that decent weather is just around the corner. Truthfully, though, I have never understood how Abraham Lincoln learned to read by the light from a fireplace. He must have been made of very stern stuff, including 40-40 vision.

SPRING—This is what comes after winter. It is a long way off, but we will make it if we adopt a Positive Attitude. Starting tomorrow morning, Think Spring.

Women, Women, Women

Traffic is light this morning as your commentator peers from the window of his second floor aerie, but wait until this early evening when the offices and shops release their hired hands. Then the traffic will be bumper to bumper, and a marvel will be apparent to all who have eyes old enough to remember other days.

Many of the Ramrod 8s, perhaps a majority, will be piloted by women, most of them young, most of them alone, and most of them the owners, at least on the installment basis, of well-shined velocipedes in the $10,000-and-up range.

They go smartly, holding their lanes on the clogged thoroughfare and neither asking nor giving quarter. They are not afraid of traffic. If the truth were known they probably aren't scared of anything. Where are they going? Most are probably going home. And where and what is home?

It may be one of the apartments or condos that cluster in Clangville. Or it may be to a house, snugged into a side street and blessed with shade. And waiting may be a husband. Or perhaps a husband and children. Or maybe just children. Or in some instances, just a guy. Or no one. It is really none of our business, although human nature has not yet changed enough to outlaw gossip.

The thing is that we have already witnessed the marvel: Women by the millions, here and elsewhere, have returned from a day's work, and the country hasn't gone to hell as some thought it would when the practice first began.

On a per capita basis, there has scarcely been a year in this century when young women did not outscore young men in high schools or college. That is still true.

Yet when Margaret Rorke, the poet laureate of this pillar, decided to go to law school, the University of Michigan had to establish separate facilities for her and six—just six—others. And when Catherine Blanche Wynne, the mother of Irish, received a bachelor of arts degree from the same institution in 1918, it was a stunning achievement, almost as though she had swum the English Channel underwater, both ways, in mid-winter.

Fresh out of high school, my late wife, Fern, attended "summer college," received a teaching permit, and that autumn took over a country grade school where several of the students were older, and some thought tougher, than she.

Later, she part-timed her way to a full degree, and when we had weekly newspapers she would fetch in so much advertising that her husband would swear, add two more pages, and frantically hunt around for enough boiler plate to fill the nooks and crannies of 16 more columns.

That's a sampling of women for you, though we must not forget Irish, who will battle her way home this evening through the traffic already mentioned and add a new dimension to this establishment; nor my mother, who struggled to survive during the dark ages of society, and was not permitted by national law to vote in a presidential election until the choice was Warren Harding or James Cox, which was a ton worse than Walter Mondale or Ronald Reagan, unbelievable as that may seem.

American industry is often accused, and rightly so, of hugging the bottom line and cherishing the conglomerate which tends to shrink the work force, but it has done a fairly decent job in recent years of admitting women into its sacred realm.

Part of this may have been price—women were paid less in the beginning and still are if not unionized—but in general there has been an awakening to talent that was once largely confined to teaching, nursing, beating the typewriter and getting pregnant.

There remain scattered reservations in this quarter. The Navy has some seagoing women, and one wonders how this might turn out if it comes down to the rocket's red glare. But, then, they might do as well as this old salt, who was always scared stiff when Japanese planes showed up on radar.

Fairs Are Higher

Some time before World War II (I'm too lazy to look up the exact year since it is of little consequence, really) there was a World's Fair in New York City and this became a Big Thing within the family circle because my brother and his wife decided to attend.

People of "the working class" to borrow a rather hideous British phrase, didn't dash off to New York, willy-nilly, in those days. A trip there was a once-in-a-life-time expedition full of nameless, formless, delicious dangers, and planning for it was almost as much fun as going. And afterward, of course you talked about it for months . . .

Anyhow, Brother Jack and his wife had less than $100 in cash, but they possessed that greatest of all fringe benefits in the eyes of a railroader—an annual pass, good over competing lines.

Later, home safe and sound from two nights and three days in the Big City, he filled us in on the details at a meeting of the clan.

"We saw it all," he reported, "every stick and stone of it. We went to the fair, toured the city, had our meals at fine restaurants, stayed in a good hotel and rode in some taxi cabs. What a trip. I don't have a single regret even though we did spend Sixty-Two Dollars!"

"Holy Mother of Mercy," someone whispered. "Sixty-Two Dollars!" But it was an expression of awe, not of rebuke. In those days, it was generally agreed everyone had a right to live once.

Anyhow, a While . . .

. . . back I took to reading Look magazine and there was a report by Fletcher Knebel on a trip he had made to New York City at the suggestion of his editors. He was supposed to go there with his wife and do the things that would interest a tourist, living well but not lavishly, being thrifty but still not parsimonious. The following is his expense account, for two, for one day . . .

Hotel, $15; hotel-room tax, 75 cents; newspaper, 10 cents; breakfast for two, hotel, $4.70; breakfast tip, 50 cents; luncheon for two at "21" (one drink each, beef stew and turkey hash, one vegetable each, coffee) $16.80, tip $1.75; luncheon hat-check tip, 25 cents; window shopping, Fifth Avenue, on the house.

Visit to Wall Street (four subway coins), 60 cents; cocktails at Toots Shor's (two martinis each), $4.65; tip to barman, 50 cents; hat-check tip at bar, 25 cents; cab to restaurant, 50 cents; tip to cabdriver, 25 cents; dinner at Le Marmiton (one drink each, soup, frog legs and scallops, dessert, coffee), $15.84; tip to waiter, $1.75; hat-check tip, 35 Cents; cab to theatre, 65 cents; tip to cabdriver, 35 cents.

Two orchestra seats ("How to Succeed in Business Without Really Trying") plus broker's fee, $20.90; lemonade, intermission, 60 cents; cab to nightclub, 17 cents; tip to cabdriver, 25 cents; visit to Upstairs at the Downstairs (night-club), $5 minimum, plus tax, $11.50; tip to waiter, $1.50; cab to hotel, 55 cents; tip to cabdriver, 25 cents.

Total bill for one day, $102.34.

As that relative whispered so long ago—"Holy Mother of Mercy!"

Somalia Got Its Army

All in a Lifetime . . .

This is one of those "I remember when" things, of no particular importance except that it does demonstrate that sometimes the utterly fantastic comes true . . .

One evening a group of us, perhaps a dozen in all including scribes and second-string embassy people were sitting under at tree in Mogadiscio, the principal city of Somalia, awaiting the call to dinner.

Among the guests was a gentleman from the local legislature, a member of the opposition party, and with a minimum of encouragement he took to talking about what his country needed in the way of foreign aid.

"What we want more than anything else," he said (I am giving you the short form of the conversation), "is a standing army of at least 8,000 men."

"We have had a border dispute with Ethiopia and some of us are never going to rest until it is settled—on our terms."

Then he added the clincher: "I'll tell you something else, If the United States won't give us the army, then I am in favor of accepting the money for it from the Soviet Union."

That Dialog . . .

. . . stays in my memory because of other incidents which occurred the same day. I had traveled around Mogadiscio, visiting the wharves and other areas where you would expect to find commercial activity, and for the first time in Africa I had come upon adult males sleeping on the sidewalks, on the steps of buildings, wherever there was sufficient shade to ward off the blazing sunlight.

"These people are resting," one of our chaps explained, "because of deficiencies in their diets. They simply run out of energy before the day is half-done . . . "

Somalia, I had also learned, is largely arid, with barely enough land under cultivation to feed its two million inhabitants. There was no "major industry" and the illiteracy rate was appalling. Man, here was a country, newly come to "independence," desperately in need of help!

But now, in the comparative cool of the evening, with the wind gently disturbing the palms, here was a politician, a learned man, a leader of the people, saying that what Somalia really needed was an army. He had to be kidding . . .

He must have caught some of my disbelief, for before we went in to dinner he repeated himself: "We want enough money for

8,000 troops—and if we can't get it from you we will take it from the Communists."

Well, the other day Somalia got its army—from the Russians, who outbid us. The wire services had the story: The United States, West Germany and Italy offered 18 million dollars in military assistance, but the Soviet Union promised 30 million. The politicians accepted Moscow's greater generosity.

So the Soviet military advisers will come in due course to that crude land. Somalia, where men sleep on the sidewalks because their bellies are empty. Those who do not know the alphabet, or their numbers, will be taught, nonetheless, to maim and kill.

On the Horn . . .

. . . of Eastern Africa, with harbors on the Indian Ocean, Somalia will provide the Soviets with a new springboard into the inner reaches of the Dark Continent. The Somalians, who hate the Ethiopians, will burn with new patriotic fervor at this opportunity for "justice," little realizing that they are mere pawns in a much larger and far more dangerous and desperate struggle.

The world is a crazy, mixed-up place, isn't it? Men of so-called intelligence cry peace, peace, then vie with one another to supply guns for a country on the ever-edge of famine. Let us weep for Somalia, whose "progress" now includes an army.

Ouagadougou Gourmet

There is a memory of the day in 1961 when we arrived in Ouagadougou, the capital city of the Upper Volta, with the old Air Force DC-4 kicking up a dozen small whirlwinds of sand and gravel as the pilot braked to a halt.

This was to be the final official stop on a 16-nation tour of Africa, and the ritual—the protocol—would remain the same even though the plans for the day were a bit indefinite.

Soapy and Nancy Williams would be first off the plane, followed by their entourage of heavy thinkers from the State Department, and "the press" would bring up the rear. We lined up in the narrow aisle, stooping to peer out the windows, and then the sergeant opened the door.

Holy Toledo!

. . . The first blast of the mid-morning's heat rolled in from the desert, and the small talk died with the realization that this would be a real stinker. "It must be a 110 out there," somebody complained.

Two of us were left in the plane, finally, the other being Warren Unna of the Washington Post, and all at once it became a case of great minds running in the same channel. He took off his coat and draped it over the back of a seat and I followed suit. Then we peeled off our ties, opened our shirt collars and set forth to observe the wonders of Ouagadougou.

Thirty minutes later, at the home of the American consul, the word came that we were to have lunch at the palace. "The press" was invited, too. Someone noted that "the press" was not respectable. "The press," it was said, was not dressed to meet the mayor of Skid Row, let alone the leader of the sovereign state of Upper Volta. Could the consul do something to correct the disreputable appearance of the Fourth Estate?

He said he would try. Out of his wardrobe he selected a seersucker coat and a red necktie for Mr. Unna, and a white linen jacket and a blue necktie for this correspondent. Beggars cannot be choosers; we made no complaint of the fit of our garments, which had been designed for a chap only a few inches shorter than Wilt the Stilt. Mr. Unna, it should be noted, is approximately five-ten, while I am a bit less. It was on to the palace, with coat sleeves covering all of the fingers and the tails flapping around the backs of the knees.

What a feast had been spread for us. Long tables were dotted with dishes of Upper Volta specialties. And just before the call to action, four chaps came in with the pieces de resistance. In pairs, they were carrying roasted goats spitted by long iron rods. Chairs were reversed, back to back, and the ends of the rods were rested on them. Thus suspended, the goats were ready for carving.

The Serving . . .

. . . started. An attendant armed with a long knife sawed diligently at the flank of one of the goats, slicing off succulent pieces. The goat took to swinging on its rod, becoming the world's strangest pendulum. After a few minutes, one end of the rod worked off the back of its chair and the carcass fell to the floor, smack!

Conversation was muted. What would the attendant do? He simply lifted the ends of the rod back onto the chairs and returned to this carving. The line moved forward. When in Upper Volta, do as the Upper Voltans do. I had a helping of goat. It was very good . . .

Some days ago there was news out of Ouagadougou to the effect that "the rebels" had overthrown the government. I wondered which side the goat carver had chosen. I'll bet he stood with the rebels. And then the thought occurred that maybe I could write something about the Upper Volta.

These are the memories I have. They are unfair, as most memories of Africa are. It is an amazing place, Africa, beyond the ken of the average Westerner. We should remember that, always, whenever we read stories about its people and their customs.

Thrill of a Distant Drum

All in a Lifetime . . .

You are forewarned that this will doubtless turn into a "travel column," at least to the extent of carrying you to Concord, Mass., where on a sunny morning in April many years ago the first feeble flames of freedom were kindled. I hope you are not bored stiff by this junket, since it did me a great deal of good.

In America today it is fast becoming "square" (an ugly word!) to admit to patriotism. The flag, the anthem, the honor roll on the courthouse lawn, the recollection of Lincoln at Gettysburg, a forlorn man with a "weak" speech, or of Patrick Henry declaring for

Liberty above all else—good heavens, man, don't be such a sentimental slob! This is the Twentieth Century, the age of the cool cat,
when there is little honest feeling for people, even, let alone for the
events and trappings of the dim and distant past. It is so easy to become blase—inured to the meanings of history.

In Something . . .

. . . of this mood, old, and tired and a victim of the I-have-
experienced-it-all philosophy, I walked a few days ago across the
wooden bridge spanning the Concord River, thus passing from
what had been the "British side" to the "American side," and came
to the base of Daniel Chester French's statue of the Minute Man.

Looking up, an amazing thing happened. . . . All at once I was
an American again, a sentimental slob, if you please, remembering
his heritage, thrilling to the distant beat of the drum, caught up in
intrigue against the Crown, and cheering as Major John Buttrick
shouted: "Fire, fellow soldiers, for God's sake, fire!"

We fired. No, no—they fired. It was a ragged volley, only three
of the Red Coats were mortally wounded, the Concord Fight, to
last only three minutes at the most, flickered, blazed, then died, a
snap of the fingers as time is measured, but Emerson caught the
essence of it years later when he wrote: "Here once the embattled
farmers stood. And fired the shot heard round the world . . . "

It was the beginning, that flurry, that tremulous exchange of
musketry, of the bitter and pain-strewn road to Independence,
leading to Breed's Hill, better known as Bunker's, to Valley Forge,
the blood of men's unshod feet in the bitter-cruel snow, doubt and
confusion in the ranks, mewlings and pukings among the citizenry,
by God's grace it was a miracle, all of it.

It Was the . . .

. . . beginning, too, of everything we are now, and of everything
we shall ever be—Concord is a shrine, no less, albeit a nearly forgotten one. Why in the world John F. Kennedy, who was born near
there doesn't do something to maintain it, instead of running

around the country trying to find more worthless acres for the federal preserve is beyond me.

Very little of the Concord Battle Ground is encompassed in a national park, while the Lexington-Concord Road, down which the British fled in increasing disarray, is a shambles, a jumble of restaurants, residences, shacks, souvenir stands and the like. Most of the stone fences, from which the farmers bushwhacked the British, are gone—in general, the area is a mess. Concord has retained some of its Revolutionary "flavor," but Lexington is just another modern American city, common as Toledo.

Otherwise, we were in the East, Vermont principally, during the peak of the "color season," lucky tourists, for Mother Nature's annual style show came two weeks early this year and we blundered into it. They were blessed with the maple, glorious tree, in profusion, and the mountains were ablaze with gorgeous reds, purples, oranges, yellows, browns.

Aftertaste of Ashes

"Where are the bells?," she asked after the President had concluded his prophecy of peace with honor, but there were no bells. Traditionalists to the core, we opened the front door in anticipation of at least one small sound of gratitude. But there was a muttering wind, a slight skiff of snow, darkness.

And thus, a war which had started with a resolution from Congress—not a declaration, mind you, but a resolution—ended in silence. One way or another, all of us were cheated.

If nothing else, wars are supposed to leave the minstrels of the people, the story-tellers, with the drama from which sagas are fashioned. This war, we now understand, was as costly in battlefield deaths and wounds as World War I, but what is to be told of it when the hour comes for the gathering of the clan?

Where did we fight to warrant, to perhaps even grace, such a flowing of blood? The oldsters can tell you of Cantigny, Chateau

Thierry, Belleau Woods, St. Mihiel, the Meuse-Argonne, but what of charge and counter-charge in Vietnam? It is a terrible thought: We seem to have dribbled away all of those brave young men without having left a single path of glory. The Navy fought and died, too, but there was no Battle of Midway or Coral Sea. Instead, we have with us a blur, an endless recounting of ambushings savagely exchanged, and our minstrels are bemused.

There is also supposed to be a recounting of the gallantry of the people in any well-turned saga, and where is that? Mostly it is "over there," among the Vietnamese, friends and foes alike. True, thousands of our households were blighted by news of death or maiming, but for some reason those among us who gave, gave alone. There was a solitude in sacrifice unknown in any other war in history.

For those of who us did not give, it was business as usual, tubs of butter as well as armadas of lethal instruments.

The gross national product kept soaring and this war was "traditional" in at least one respect—it produced a new crop of millionaires. It also came dangerously close to bringing about the industrial-military complex against which Dwight Eisenhower had spoken, but that was not the common worry. Rather, most of us were concerned with the inflation which cut into our easy living.

Even our moral objections were at times blemished by the false assumption of virtue. Once the dangers of the draft had been limited, the outrage on the campuses was muted.

The young, who had initiated the early rounds of protest against the war, did not vote against it in overwhelming numbers last November. For our people, then, this was a strange interlude, a long and yet not too feverish nightmare, a time during which there was much advice from on high, but a minimum of great leadership. At the end, there was a hard core for the war, and a hard core against it, and a vast sea of impassiveness in between. It contaminated all of us, but deeply touched so few of us—in support of it there were few songs, few slogans, few articles of faith, little of which sagas are made.

The civilian pathos, the terror, the senseless slaughter and the gallantry were left to the people of Vietnam. South and North. Some of us will remember for the rest of our lives the television pictures revealing the devastation and the savagery unleashed upon the poor and powerless. They had such good faces, those people, those who were for us and those who were against us, and underlining each sequence of agony and waste was the thought that they should have been ours, all of them, to shield from the consequences of such madness. It was difficult to escape the thought that somehow we had lost our way "over there," that instead of pitting one good face against another good face, we should instead have been in the middle, the champions of peace.

As these lines are written Dr. Henry Kissinger is outlining the terms of this new contract, and much will be made in the days ahead of the nuances of its language. Is it a superior document to what we had in late October, when peace was at hand? I do not know; I do not much care.

It is peace, the best we could get out of a long and dreadful experience, and let us bless it even though the bells are silent.

NINE
Different Views

Ecology—The New Word

ECOLOGY—"A branch of science concerned with the inter-relationship of organisms and their environments; the totality or pattern of relations between organisms and their environment."—Webster's Dictionary.

To breaking bread a few days ago with Gus Scholle, chairman, and Ralph MacMullan, director, of the Michigan Natural Resources Commission, and to posing a question. Listen:

"Supposing I wanted to go out into our Water-Winter Wonderland, as we used to call it, and buy or build a cottage. Where could I locate that would be free of air and water pollution?"

Mr. Scholle, who is better known in this capacity as a Labor Tycoon, was silent, a situation so unusual for him that it may only be likened to Big Ben not striking on the hour. Indeed, he was so nonplussed that he half-turned in his chair and, with a wave of a hand, conceded the floor to MacMullan.

———————

The latter paused for a few seconds, obviously mulling the question, and then he gave it to me straight.

"There might be a place or two," he said, "where the open water would be relatively clear of pollution except for traces of DDT, but there would be no place where you could escape air pollution. It is everywhere, to one degree or another . . . "

249

Webster's definition of "ecology" heads this column because it is apt to become The Word of the future. Our environment—air, land and water—is in terrible shape and, to borrow that tired old phrase, "something must be done about it."

Like most pressing problems, it is not just local in extent or cure. Much of the Michigan air pollution that Ralph MacMullan finds "everywhere" originates elsewhere. In the western part of the state, for example, there are days when the wind drifts Chicago's smog over our landscape. We are, in short, in this thing together, all of us, and the solution must be reached on a national basis. In the meantime, however, how do we get our own environment in order?

Mr. Scholle and Mr. MacMullan agree that Michigan's laws in respect to pollution are among the best in the nation. The trouble is that this is akin to saying it is better to have diphtheria than smallpox. The truth is that there are no laws adequate to the correction of the conditions now swirling around us.

I could tell you (but won't because there are others in the same fix) of one lovely community in the north woods area that it is being blighted by the smoke from the stacks of a large and important factory. This condition could be eliminated by the installation of modern equipment costing, let us say, two million dollars.

Who is to say to management, "You must correct this within three years or close the plant"? The city fathers, who realize the payroll is vital and who fear the factory might move elsewhere? No. They can not do it. The state might be able to do it, up to a point, but only the federal government, by insisting on uniform standards, could guarantee against the possibility of management pulling stakes and settling somewhere else.

Michigan is doing a reasonably good job of cleaning its waters, with the result that by 1972 we will have "minimum standards." These won't be good enough, but at least we will have made a start.

However, the problems resulting from the use of DDT and other "bug-killers" run much deeper than is generally realized. Off our shores, there is contamination in lake life, some of it already head-lined. Off the Pacific, those denizens, of the deep, the tuna, are showing increasing traces of involvement with pesticides.

It is an alarming situation. But how do you get this fact across to the public? How do you convince the Common Man that unless he awakens to what is going on around him, this earth will be robbed of its beauty and perhaps even of its livability?

The trouble is that man is doing what comes natural to him. There has always been pollution. Even the Indians polluted the air and the water. But there were so few of them. Now, however, the nation and the world teem with humanity—there will be 14 billion of us by the end of this century. The dangers are frightening, no less.

Ecology. Remember that word. You will be hearing and seeing it often in the weeks and months to come.

Vietnam's Pain

All in a Lifetime . . .

I have been sitting here thinking about the Vietnam war, during which I was a hawk—turned doubter—turned bring-the-boys-home-er. Many Americans went through a similar cycle during that long and tragic misadventure, and the sudden appearance of Dan Quayle on the national political scene has no doubt stirred a pattern of memories.

With few exceptions, Americans became very sure of themselves—perhaps even puffed-up on themselves—as the result of World War II. After Hitler had been stymied in Europe and the Japanese had been frustrated in the Pacific, there didn't seem much that we, with the Allies lending a hand as needed, couldn't do. This needs a bit of explanation: We never fully appreciated the contributions of the British after the land war had started; and the heavings, and strainings and bleedings of the Russians were obscured by too many years of red-baiting and commie-hating. American home-consumption propaganda was very effective during the war, at times over-selling our victories and then again under-selling our defeats.

We came out of this, finally, very sure of ourselves, not only of our military prowess but of our political system. When it came to leading the world and running ourselves, we had the right stuff. To paraphrase Prof. Henry Higgins, why couldn't everyone including in due time the Vietnamese, be more like Americans?

To be sure there were a few, precious few, who warned us against Vietnam. Douglas MacArthur, old Dug-out Doug as the Navy referred to him, had spoken against fighting land wars in Asia and Dwight Eisenhower finally bailed us out of Korea after we had our noses knocked more than slightly out of joint in an excursion above the 38th parallel.

Still, John Kennedy sent advisers into South Vietnam and later his brother Bobby, paid a visit and announced that we were there to stay. It didn't seem like much of a war at the time: It was more of a training-camp scuffle in which we were loaning our system to the South Vietnamese, who had such staunch friends in our government and segments of the Catholic hierarchy.

It has since been said that if John Kennedy had lived he would have pulled the advisers out of Vietnam, but this is little more than talk-talk by his idolaters. By 1968, Bobby Kennedy was all stirred up against the war, but by then a presidential nomination was at stake and the cry, "Hell, no, we won't go," was ringing throughout the land.

How did all of that happen? Well, Lyndon Johnson said speed boats, or launches, or some sort of belligerent vessels out of North Vietnam had fired on our ships at a somewhat loosely charted spot in the Gulf of Tonkin, and it wasn't long before our planes were bombing, and our lads were knee-deep in rice paddies and the air was full of Agent Orange.

How about the Gulf of Tonkin incident? It seemed strange then and still does. I asked the late Sen. Phil Hart about it and he replied that only the president knew all of the facts. The vast majority of Congress seemed to be in the same fix and it was war—a little war that festered and spread like a carbunkle.

Hawk-'em, the World War II generation said. Our system, right or wrong, and after the Vietnamese are united they will be showered with the blessings of peace and solidarity. Not much was made of the fact that they had been fighting over there for centuries about this, that and the other thing.

Then the word came that we really weren't trying to win the war, that we were simply trying to guarantee democracy in the southern precincts, and that's when hawk'-em started fading to doubter. And when Hubert Humphrey, one of the few major politicians in this century with a soul, was hooted and hollered into defeat in favor of Richard Nixon and the Kissinger bunch, the war really got barbaric and it was time to bring 'em home. You know something? Jerry Ford should have been elected in 1976, but by then the country had turned to hand-wringing, soul-searching, breast-beating and Jimmy Carter.

Now, because of the sudden ascendancy of Dan Quayle, who didn't go to Vietnam although the door was wide open, the '60s and the '70s have come back to haunt us. It has turned this political campaign, which was supposed to deal with so many momentous issues, into what sounds like a tomcat fight at midnight. Here we are past Labor Day and if we had to vote next Tuesday, many of us would say, well, grandpa was a Democrat, or a Republican, and pull the lever. Vietnam set the system to reeling, and it hasn't recovered yet.

A Penny-Ante Caper

A few days ago, having a penny in his pocket and a cavity in his stomach, your commentator decided to invest the copper in the peanut vending machine located in the composing room of this megaphone of free speech.

In partial defense of this extravagance it might be noted that peanuts are good for you, being full of proteins and other substances which fortify the vital juices, and a craving persists for the goobers even though it is said that Adolf Hitler was nuts about them, ha, ha.

Anyhow, a firm stance, calling for just a slight hook into the wind, was taken in front of the machine; the penny was inserted; the lever which would release an avalanche of delicious nutrients was pushed; and the other hand was cupped beneath the chute to prevent spill-over. As the mechanics of the transaction were completed, there was the thought that a penny spent is not always a penny wasted.

Well! Seven peanuts—count 'em, seven!—came down the chute. There were five whole ones, about the size of immature garden peas, and four halves. It did no good to poke around in the contraption with a forefinger. Seven peanuts, that was the entire load. One left the composing room with the sinking feeling that all of the talk about the demise of inflation has been premature.

———————

This was substantiated a few days later when a housewife called to report a similar experience, although on a grander scale. And instead of peanuts, she became involved with pears.

As the keeper of the budget which must sustain six appetites, she came to the end of the week with enough surplus to provide a treat of canned fruit. Strolling through the market she chanced upon what seemed a rare bargain—a large can of pears for 66 cents. That would do it; the saints be praised.

Alas. For when she opened the can that evening she discovered that she had really purchased three pears, in six halves, plus about a quart of "syrup." Much of the latter is now in the refrigerator, awaiting inspiration. What do you do with a quart of pear syrup, for heaven's sake? She received condolences but little practical advice from this department. However, we did have a few good moments, chewing away by telephone at inflation.

———————

It has been said that if President Ford's energy proposals are adopted, the "average family" will pay an additional $22 per month for heat, lights and gasoline. None of this money will be retained by private enterprise. It will not, for example, benefit the utility companies, most of which are painfully short of capital for expansion. That money will have to come from additional rate increases. Either that or eventually we are going to face critical shortages of absolute necessities. Not enough has been written or said on this subject, primarily because for many years the utility companies have rated with diphtheria and the devil on the popularity scale. One of these days, perhaps sooner than you think, we may have to take a new look at these sources of energy, too.

Meanwhile, one suspects that inflation is far from whipped. What we may have at the moment is a lull in the storm. If this seems too much pessimism for a Monday morning, blame it on seven peanuts and three pears.

———

In rapid succession, we have had almost more "state of" messages than the nervous system can bear. First there was the "State of the State," by Gov. Milliken; then the "State of the Union," by President Ford; and lastly the "State of the City," by Mayor Young. One gathers they are in a mell of a hess, all of them.

Among other things, one does not pretend to know what is going to become of government. One suspects, however, that if hard times continue government will have to do what business, industry and many of our people are already doing—make-do. Find new uses for pear syrup, you might put it.

We moved into the 1930s with a total federal deficit of about $26 billion. We are now approaching $500 billion, as Mr. Ford warned in his address. City, county and state commitments have also soared into the wild blue yonder. Something has to give. The least you can forecast for 1975 is that it will be an interesting year. As the country editor used to say: "Pay your subscriptions!"

The Rise of Emancipation

On Wednesday the League of Women Voters will stage a parade on Woodward Ave. to celebrate 50 years of emancipation. They got the vote back in the autumn of 1919, the ladies did, and they have been owly about it ever since.

Your commentator has vivid and somewhat painful memories of the first national political campaign in which womenfolk participated as equals. That occurred in 1920, when Warren G. Harding opposed James Cox, and at the beginning of the school year Young Arn was drafted as a mobile billboard for the Democrats, much against his better judgment.

Right off the bat, ours was a House Divided, something Abraham Lincoln had warned us about many years, earlier.

Step Father, the owner of a general store (groceries, dry goods and staples), was a Republican. Like most Republicans before and since he was fed up with what had been going on in Washington; he had a belly full of internationalism as practiced by Woodrow Wilson; he pined for a return of isolation and business-as-usual; and the prospect of another season of "normalcy," a word and condition invented by Sen. Harding, suited him just fine.

In contrast, Mother was a Democrat for reasons lost in antiquity, although one presumes that spite had a good deal to do with it. The ladies were rather touchy in those days about having been denied the vote and some of them opposed the political views of the Old Man out of pure and sweet meanness.

After they had been granted "suffrage," as they called it, the women did not go around murmuring "oh, thank you," or words to that effect, to their lords and masters. Instead, they acted as though they had finally obtained what had rightfully been theirs for a long time, so to heck with gratitude. As for the men, 1920 was the year in which they came to the realization that "suffrage" was a terrible mistake, but by then it was too late.

Anyhow, in the golden autumn of that presidential campaign your commentator in all of his blissful ignorance was suddenly marshalled on the side of the Democrats. His Mother called him one morning into the parlor, and forthwith fixed a tin rooster into the lapel of his school jacket.

Now the rooster was in those days the emblem of the Democratic Party. Just why remains a mystery, for heaven knows the Democrats had never in the memory of man had much to crow about. At least not in Liberty Center, which was about three-to-one Republican, and counting.

Nonetheless, all at once your commentator, a precious lad given to the study of the violin and the gathering of posies in wood lots, became the symbol of the Hated Opposition.

Without quite knowing why, he fought a dozen pitched battles that autumn on behalf of Jim Cox and the Democrats. That damned tin rooster, if you will pardon the expression, like to got him knocked lopsided.

Sometimes he would come fleeing home, one jump ahead of five or six adversaries, to be saved by his Mother, who would say to his tormentors, "Get out of here, you Harding hellions!"

She was like the manager of the battered prize fighter, teeth scrambled and ears shredded, who would assure his gladiator between rounds: "They can't hurt us." Surely, that was the longest political campaign in history . . .

Well, you know the rest of it. Warren G. Harding, who looked more like a president than any other man yet born, won in a gallop.

The ladies voted for him in vast droves, and thus helped save the country. The judgment of Step Father and all other Republicans was vindicated, and they gradually forgave us Democrats, young and old, willing and drafted.

What became of that tin rooster escapes memory, but there is no recollection of tears at its disappearance. We returned to "normalcy," the lot of us, and only the die-hards contend to this day that Jim Cox should have been elected.

And now the League of Women Voters will parade on Wednesday, observing the Golden Anniversary of their equality at the ballot box. In 1919 they set out to change the nation, and who can say they haven't. Somebody did.

If your commentator could find a tin rooster for his lapel, he might join them for a block or two.

The Ruins of Home

Mutterings . . .

A friend inquired the other day if I had yet made a complete tour of those areas of Detroit destroyed in the recent rioting, and the answer was "no." Nor is there the slightest desire to retrace, step by step, the routes of the looters and burners. When you have seen one such ruin, you have pretty much seen them all . . .

In the mornings, five times a week, your commentator is east-bound on Grand River for approximately 10 miles, and in the evenings the trip is made in reverse.

This unsentimental journey provides all of the slum-viewing and ruin-gazing one moderately sensitive man can take. As a matter of fact, we have talked some of selling our house and moving down town in order that this junket through advanced blight might be avoided.

For at least eight years—long before the sackers and the burners were agitated—it has been suggested in this space that long stretches of Grand River were only a slight improvement on how Hell must look on a gloomy day.

The truth is that while a good deal of still-barely-taxable prop-erty was put to the torch in late July, very little of beauty was de-stroyed. The areas look tougher now only because new ruins always seem grosser than old ones.

If you will take the sections of Grand River under discussion and multiply them by one thousand, or maybe four thousand, you will have an approximation of what out-of-the-chic-area of metropoli-tan America looks like today. The last such figure I saw showed there were nine thousand acres of slums in New York City alone, and let us not forget that there are vast regions of Chicago—the whole South Side, loosely,—which will make you vomit in an un-favorable wind.

Los Angeles, Philadelphia, San Francisco—yes, beautiful, highly-overrated San Francisco!—Flint, Grand Rapids, Toledo, Miami, Akron, you name it—there are slums in this country where only a very few years ago there were sheep grazing or apples grow-ing—and it makes you sick when you think of what has happened in America, the Beautiful.

Who is to blame? Or what is to blame? Many people, many fac-tors. And you have heard most of it before: lack of pride; lack of incentive; lack of an inkling, just a glimmer, of light for tomorrow; lack of money, but least of all money, for there are people in this world who stay clean even though they do not have a sou, a cent, a mark; lack of belonging, lack of giving a damn what your neighbors think, because they are as short of gumption as you, and that is about as low as you can sink, baby . . .

I don't know . . . How can America go on like this; how can it prosper beyond the shallow glitter of materialism; how can it lead the inept and succor the helpless with which the world is overloaded; how can it provide morality in the event we ever need morality for more than a campaign slogan, which we probably will? How, how, how?

Do you worry about these things once in a while, Mr. Citizen? Do you then become depressed and vow to think of something more cheerful for a change? How nice that you—and I—can do this.

For there are those what can't. Their names are such as Jerome Cavanagh, and John Lindsay, and Richard Daley, and Lyndon Johnson, and George Romney, and Sam Yorty. They are our slum-viewers and ruin-gazers on a full-time basis, so think how lousy they must feel sometimes, too.

Life's Best Moments

Notes and Comment . . .

Upon approaching the intersection at Grand River this morning it was noted that the lone school crossing guard, a nipper about four feet high, was taking advantage of a lull in foot traffic to practice his baseball swing.

He would go into a crouch, knees flexed, arms high, the imaginary bat cocked behind his right ear, and then when the pitch came in he would lash at it with the ferocity of a tomcat attacking a French poodle. Whap! While I sat there awaiting an opening in the stream of vehicles he hit at least one homer and a pair of doubles. Get the showers hot for Denny McLain!

Later, following the second lane to the office while a million dollar rain fell upon the just and the unjust, the thought occurred that little boys never really grow up.

The other day, for example, while waiting for the light to change at Washington and Lafayette, I saw a fellow in his mid-forties, or thereabouts, who seemed to be taking languid swats at a bumblebee.

He would pull his right hand back high over his head, his body titled, and then he would swing his arm forward with some wrist snap near the end of the arc. Call the man in the white coat? No, no. It dawned on me that the fellow was practicing his fly casting. Look out, lusty bass!

I know a Michigan politician, who shall remain nameless, much given to rehearsing his speeches in front of a mirror. He goes through all the appropriate gestures while silently mouthing the words and phrases, jabbing his finger, cutting the air with his hands, arching his eyebrows and smiling in appreciation as the applause interrupts his peroration. Under those conditions he is the best the country has produced since William Jennings Bryan; but, alas, his delivery falls off when the audience is "live."

Your commentator, it must be confessed, quite often practices his golf swing in the corridors of this megaphone of free speech, especially while waiting for an elevator, and under those circumstances he can hit an eight iron 150 yards, drawing the ball into the proximity of the pin, where it falls dead as though constructed of cottage cheese.

He has decided, incidentally, that if he ever gets a hole in one, God willing, he will "play-act" when queried about it and swear that he used a five iron for the 190-yard stroke. Have you ever noticed how many four and five irons show up in the paper as the weapons used to propel the ball prodigious hole-in-one distances? Why ruin a good story by confessing that you hit the three wood, swinging from the heels?

It is recollected that in the days of this youth we spent a good deal of time shadow boxing, flicking the left hand straight out, splat!, then dancing out of harm's way before bobbing and weaving into position and throwing the cruncher—a right hand that sundered the air and left Jack Dempsey hanging on the ropes, beseeching mercy.

What did it matter that most of us, in actual combat, could not punch our way out of a wet paperbag, as the saying went? At shadow boxing we were fearsome indeed, veritable tigers, with tremendous footwork, and one presumes at this late date that it was good for the wind.

No matter what age, man can live neither by bread nor reality alone. Supposing I had stopped this morning and said to the lad who was knocking Denny McLain out of the box-"Son, you will never be anything but a banjo hitter!" What good would it have done? At best, he wouldn't have believed me. And at worst, it would have destroyed one of his illusions, leaving him that much less to go on as the totalities of life creep up on him, which they surely will without any help from strangers.

Thoughts of a "W"

There were words of encouragement a few days ago from a correspondent in Detroit. "I know from experience," he wrote, "that you will get along all right. After all, I have been a 'W' for 25 years . . . "

A "W"? Your narrator scratched what remains of the thatch on his pointy little head. And then the light came on. The man meant "W" as in "widower."

It is perhaps coincident with the actuarial tables compiled by the insurance companies that Webster's New World Dictionary of the American Language devotes 17 lines to a description of "widow," but only four to "widower." Men so rarely survive their mates (we do not know the precise percentage) that "widower" falls upon the ears as a somewhat uncommon word, akin to "iron-monger" or "falconer." This leads to the simple definition: "A man who has outlived the woman to whom he was married at the time of her death; esp., such a man not remarried."

This is neat and concise and perhaps as much as a widower deserves. Still, it seems a bit brusque to one who has but short tenure in the classification, so he arises in mild protest to state that widowers have more heart, soul and sinking feelings than society seems willing to recognize.

———

There is the matter of possessions. It is not ordinarily assumed of husbands that they match their wives in affection for the accumulation of household goods and the assorted bric-a-brac which make a house a home, as Eddie Guest once put it.

In truth, your narrator contended for a number of years that a newspaperman should own no more chattels than he could tie in a red bandana handkerchief, fasten to the end of a stick, and conveniently tote on one shoulder. He sometimes stood aside in wry amusement as trinket was added to doodad until his surroundings seemed to bulge with obstacles which threatened safe passage in the deep of night.

But now that he is a widower, and therefore in the potential position of having to dispose of his possessions, your narrator finds that he would shed blood to protect them.

All at once he loves his davenports, end tables, pictures, books, chairs, dishes, and multitudinous what-nots, and the thought of giving them away, or worse yet of subjecting them to the auctioneer's hammer, causes him to snarl like a lioness with an endangered cub.

And then there is the house, which once seemed of modest proportions but has now taken on the dimensions of Cobo Arena. It would be arrogant of a widower to assume entitlement to such an expanse of unused rooms, nooks and crannies, with an attendant high cost of upkeep.

———

We come to the dog, Schultz, a boon companion treated as a person, pampered and indulged. The other evening, for the first time ever, he was left alone in the house, and one returned three hours later anticipating havoc. There was none beyond evidence of nesting on a bed.

But immediately Schultz stationed himself in front of the widower and delivered a lecture of such intensity as to wring the soul.

For upwards of 20 minutes he barked, and whined, and muttered, and cried, and pawed, and said in effect: "Please do not leave me alone!" What would happen to him if possessions were sacrificed?

Another reader, a dear lady in Dearborn, has recognized the situation. "Schultz is a problem," she has written. "You can hardly stay where you are for his sake, though I would not put it above you! He might adapt himself in a new place with a new family who will give him a different kind of love. Do you know such a family? He will never forget . . . but he might adapt. He will plaster himself to you now. I'm 88-plus years old and I have seen a lot. You have a problem but it can be solved . . . "

Thus, the early reflections of a "W." He has made a case for his comrades in arms, knowing full well that he has been riding a weak horse. The next edition of Webster's New World Dictionary will still appropriately favor the widows, 17 lines to four.

Get With It

Of late and in a highly proper and platonic manner—and what else do you expect, pray tell, from a contemporary of the Town Howler?—I have been thinking about the dear ladies.

This pleasant consideration has been stirred, no doubt, by the recently sudden emergence of the Woman's Liberation Movement, an uprising which swept across the country a few months ago with all of the unexpected fury of an undetected hurricane. You know now—don't you?—why they name those storms after women.

Anyhow, I have probably been less shaken by Woman's Lib than men of more tender years inasmuch as this was not my first experience with it. Shucks, I have memories of 1919, when Congress was getting weak-kneed on the issue of the 19th Amendment, and there are vivid recollections of the campaign of 1920, in which women voted for the first time for—or against!—presidential candidates.

Somewhere along the line I have told you how my dear mother became obsessed in the autumn of 1920 with the notion that James

M. Cox, a Democrat, for heaven's sake, should be elected President of the United States.

We never found out what possessed her. As a matter of fact, no one in the immediate family had the nerve to ask. All at once she was for Jim Cox, whoop and holler, and on the lapel of my school jacket she pinned a tin rooster, which was then the insignia of the Democratic Party. I wore it with some pride until I learned the hard way that Liberty Center, O., was about 8-to-1 in favor of Warren G. Harding, with the school kids reflecting the somewhat violent judgments of their parents. Physically speaking, Mr. Cox lost no more in that campaign than I did.

You know the rest of the story. The women poured to the polls, increasing the vote by about 10 million over 1916, and they helped elect Mr. Harding, who was perhaps the most unsuited candidate for the presidency in our history.

These many years later it is time to ask a question. Would the men alone have elected Warren G. Harding in 1920? Of course they would have. And without any assistance from the ladies, the men would have elected Calvin Coolidge, Herbert Hoover, Franklin D. Roosevelt and all of the rest of our Presidents, great and near-great, up to the present moment.

Since 1920, women have become dominant, at least as silent partners holding great financial stakes, in business and industry; and their influence in other spheres of our social and economic life has been considerable, if not always spectacular.

The key word, of course, is "spectacular," and now let's get back to Woman's Lib.

If the movers and shakers of today's renaissance are trying to tell us that modern woman does not have, or cannot usurp, sufficient freedom, then my answer is: "Baloney!" But if, instead, they are saying that women have not fully utilized the freedom available to them, then my reply becomes "You are right, and something ought to be done about it."

There is, however, nothing that men can do. If the truth were known, there isn't much men want to do. Most of us are reasonably content with the status quo, and we are smug in the knowledge that the women of America have reaffirmed much of what we set out to do.

To be blunt about it, for 50 years the women have been our partners in every indignity which has been perpetrated in the name of "progress."

This has always puzzled me. I have never understood, for example, why women, who are such dainty and tidy creatures, would countenance the slums of America; or the pollution of our streams, lake or air; or the devastation of our countryside.

And why do women, who bring men into this life, speak so reluctantly, and with such an obvious lack of group purpose, on the issues of war and peace?

The spectacular use of freedom—that is what we need from the women of America. Until that occurs we are going to have the same old "sixes and sevens," as someone once described the course of life, for little will change until our last great source of public conscience—the women, God bless them—is activated to the fullest.

The Kook Klux Klan

Telephone calls to the Police Department and the Anti-Defamation League of B'nai B'rith bring a harvest of sweet tidings—there is no Ku Klux Klan activity in Detroit. Whatever else our shortcomings, we seem to be spared this form of craven lunacy.

The phrase—"we seem to be"—is deliberately employed in the event Klansmanship is now being practiced hereabouts under an assumed name, as is the case elsewhere. It is said that a number of societies, associations and sporting clubs with KKK overtones have sprung up in various parts of the country of recent months, but—again—there is no alarm in these precincts at this particular moment.

A look through the Free Press files leaves the impression that the Klan either expired or wiggled underground in 1940. In May of that year, a cross was burned beside a home in Ferndale, while in August there was a brief revival under the pretext of "mobilizing to battle the German Bund." As for later activities, there are those who suspect that remnants of the KKK inspired the terrible race riots of 1943, but of this there is no proof.

One of the documents in our morgue is a "confidential report" from a staffer to the city desk, dated Nov. 20, 1937, in which much of the background of the Michigan Klan was chronicled.

Most of the details remain rather sordid, but there is this somewhat amusing note: "In 1917, two Knights of Columbus organized the Ku Klux Klan in Michigan and walked off with $29,000 in fees and dues . . . " Quoting his source, the reporter also wrote that by 1930 "there were 162,000 members of the Klan in Michigan, 88,000 of whom were in Detroit." Some organization! Some bigotry! Some outrage on tolerance and public decency!

Of Personal . . .

. . . recollections concerning the Ku Klux Klan, there are two.

In 1958, a Georgia newspaper of which I was the editor had a cross burned in protest of something we had printed on the editorial page. The incident caused scarcely a stir, for in those days (was it really so long ago as all of that?) it was recognized by the community that the KKK embraced only the scum. I would pay $40 to see today's membership roster!

From a much earlier time, boyhood, comes the remembrance of the only Ku Klux Klan public demonstration to which I was ever attendant. Of an autumn night, big of moon, eeried by the approach of Hallowe'en, the assorted cyclops, kleagles and lesser minions, perhaps two dozen in all, donned their bed sheets and paraded the main drag of our town, clumping all the way to Houston's Field, where a cross was touched off. Some event! Some hokum!

For in the line of march it was easy to spot all of the town characters, the ne'er-do-wells and hot stove commandos, the boozers the dead beats and the loud mouths. There are no secrets in a small town, not even the way you carry your shoulders when you walk.

"Suck in your stummick, Willie!" someone yelled from the curb.

"You're lookin great out there, Jim. Too bad you haven't got a holt of a plow!"

"What you gonna sleep on tonight, Pete? You've cut holes in your only bed sheet!"

And more of the same. Our people were provincial; Rome seemed a million miles away and the Pope was a wispy figure presiding over strange rites. But there was awareness, nonetheless, that virtue at home was not enhanced by a white robe and a covered face, and that was the one and only show of force of the Ku Klux Klan in out town. They never burned another cross or issued another pronouncement which speaks well of the power of curbstone ridicule.

Elsewhere, of course, they have been a vicious and sullen lot, performing twisted atrocities in the dark of night, and Lyndon Johnson struck a blow for decency, honesty and forthrightness the other day when he called the KKK to task.

Tea Party's Over

William G. Coleman, executive director of the Advisory Commission on Intergovernmental Relations, is quoted in the New York Times as saying that "this is probably the most eventful year since World War II" insofar as state taxes are concerned.

Since January first, 21 states have either dreamed new taxes or have hiked the rates on old ones, while 38 states now have income taxes. New to the latter list are Maine and Illinois, with Mayor Daley of Chicago and Gov. Ogilvie having just disengaged from a wrestling match of such ferocity that it would have been barred from "Gunsmoke" as too bloody for public viewing. Now the Democrats of Illinois are trying to blame the Republicans for the income tax, and vice versa, and it is a fine uproar they have going.

North Carolina recently adopted its first tax on cigarettes, a landmark decision in a state where tobacco is king; Connecticut has passed the highest increases in its history; New York has upped its sales tax; and even staid old South Carolina is raising more money after a decade of passivity. Other states with 1969 increases are Alabama, Colorado, Delaware, Maryland, Missouri, Montana, Nevada, New Hampshire, North Dakota, Tennessee, Vermont and Wyoming.

In almost every instance, the people of the several states uttered the same piteous cry—"We can't stand any more taxes!"—as their legislatures considered new sources of revenue. But stand it they will, if for no other reason than that sanctuaries are becoming scarcer and scarcer. The cost of local government is booming everywhere with a few notable exceptions—Hawaii, where taxes have always been high; and Nevada, where legalized gambling pays a good share of the freight.

What is making the situation all the more painful is the fact that the federal government got in its licks first with a substantial income tax, and since then the rising costs of local government have been imposed on top of that initial burden.

Actually federal taxes are now devouring about 14 percent of the gross national product—down two percent since 1946. But over the same period local taxes have jumped from five to eight percent of the GNP—and this is the pinch being felt and opposed by the average citizen.

———— ⦿ ———— ———— ⦿ ————

What is the answer? There is no one remedy, but there may be several.

First of all, the people must understand that if they demand more service, the cost of government is going up. This seems so simple as to deny the need for explanation, but unfortunately the "Santa Claus syndrome" has a powerful grip on many of us.

A legislator or a congressman can vote with impunity for any new governmental service as long as he does not support a means of paying for it. The people, in short, will bless him for the service—but they will cut his throat at the polls if he tries to make them foot the bill. Literally dozens of our "greatest politicians" have made their reputations through fiscal irresponsibility. At one time, and even yet to some extent, "federal money" was a magic phrase meaning almost the same as "for free." Unborn generations will pay the price of that misunderstanding.

Local government has followed the federal pattern in that many of our bureaus and offices are vastly over-staffed. A few days ago I put the question to a city worker—"How many people in your department could you get along without and not impair service?"—and the answer was "Fifty percent."

This may be an "unusual situation," but the truth is that government at all levels has become so enmeshed in "civil service" and entrenched red tape that not even the department heads can do anything about it. In Washington, in Lansing, in Detroit—we need first-class house cleaning, but there isn't a solitary elected official, not even the President of the United States, who can bring it off. The President has, as I recall, about 3,000 jobs at his command. The rest of the "protected" functionaries can tell him to go jump in the Potomac, and frequently do.

How much control does Gov. Milliken have over the Lansing payroll, or Mayor Cavanagh over Detroit's? Very little. It is a myth that elected officials "run government."

And it is a myth that the cost is going to decline in the years to come. We are stuck with it, chums.

The Common Man

Let us return to a favorite subject, the Common Man, who is more apt than not to catch it in the neck as he plods through life.

The generals and the politicians make wars, and the Common Man fights them. (Only three draftee graduates from Yale, Harvard and Princeton have been killed in action in Vietnam. Who do you think has been doing the fighting and bleeding over there? The campus dissenters?)

Candidates for high office pledge a New Deal, a Square Deal, a Fair Deal, a New Frontier or a Great Society, and who gets rich? (The last statistics I saw showed that since the start of World War II we have "created" more than 1,500 new millionaires in this country—and not a one of them held a job on a production line.)

The labor leaders and the industrial tycoons call strikes, and the Common Man suffers through them. (How many members of the

UAW brass or the General Motors hierarchy will sustain pay cuts during the current unpleasantness? Ha!)

The Common Man, in short, has four principal prospects in his life—work, beer, television and sex—and all of them are uncertain for various reasons. The miracle, then, is not that the Common Man is so rambunctious, but that he is as complacent as he is. As someone was saying the other day, if those of us who frequently criticize the Common Man had to take his place in the factories, we would immediately start screaming for "10 minutes and out." To hell with 30 years . . .

All of these kind words directed at the Common Man do not necessarily mean that I think his side is right in this confrontation with General Motors. Rather, they indicate a sympathy for him because I happen to believe he has been mis-led, mis-governed and mis-used over a long period of years, to the point where he is the victim of circumstances far beyond his control.

Since midnight Monday there has been the usual spate of print and electronic stories detailing the reaction of workers as the strike deadline came and passed and we have been treated, in part, to accounts of the elation and esprit de corps with which this decision was accepted.

Well, baloney. What do you expect a worker to say to a reporter when his name is going to be in the paper or his face on television? "Leonard Woodcock has holes in his head"?

In contrast, I know of one plant where the workers turned off the machinery and punched their time cards before leaving, making sure everything was in order for "tomorrow," whenever it comes; and I know of another where 80 percent of the second shift reported at 11:55 and worked until midnight—five whole minutes! They, too, were hoping against hope . . .

So now they are pounding the bricks, you say. Again, what do you expect them to do? That is part of the drill, of what they must do to get strike "benefits," of the circumstances in which they are caught. They want to win, of course, and they will suffer privation if need be, but to suggest that they have no concern for their nation in all of this is to do them great wrong.

The plight of the Common Man in recent years might be likened to that of the beginning skier who somehow got started down the main slope after only one hour's instruction. Whoosh!

———————

The common man, let us remember, did not start the mad dash of inflation and there has been no way he could stop it. His only hope of averting disaster has been to let himself go, to bore through the wind and pray that he survives the crash landing. If he escapes this wild experience he will never intentionally go skiing again, but how does he get off the slope?

To this point the efforts to rescue him have been half-hearted, at best. The White House has been quiet during repeated price increase and wage boosts. The Congress in a number of instances has appropriated more money than a "balanced budget" called for.

If there has been a conclave of industrial, commercial and financial interests devoted to putting a stop to excessive profit taking, I have missed it. And that blasted war in Vietnam goes on and on and on, adding to inflation and frustration, with victory long since forfeited.

These, in brief, are the circumstances in which the Common Man finds himself. He does not enjoy his position. He is scared just like the rest of America. He would do his part to return to "normalcy." But who knows the way?

Who, indeed?

Too Much

This being a tough country full of resolute citizens, we have now survived the two major political nominating conventions. Another spurt of fortitude will carry us though the election campaign, and then we will be home free, as the saying goes, until our new president delivers his State of the Union address.

If this sounds a bit contemptuous of the political process, the plea is guilty as charged. One of the reasons we have too much government is because we have over-emphasized the importance of its functions and the significance of those who participate in it.

During recent years we have built the presidency into a sovereignty and mere congressmen are receiving more attention than good third basemen. You can make a considerable argument to the effect that the country was better off when Cal Coolidge didn't have enough to do to keep him busy eight hours a day, Mondays through Fridays, and Congress adjourned the first of May.

Some of this feeling—that government has become too big for its britches and too expensive for the benefits it provides—cropped up in the Democratic convention, while the Republicans were more emphatic about it during their sojourn in Kansas City. Expecting the politicians to cut back on their own activities is probably akin to anticipating that arsonists will grow weary of watching the fires they set, but if the present mood permits an opportunity to curb the proliferation of agencies, bureaus, empires and satraps, the people should not miss it.

With this in mind, the following suggestions are offered for the consideration of the constituency.

———————

Free enterprise—Either we have such a system and it will work if given a chance, or we don't. It is time we found out.

The cost of conformity with rules and regulations written, rewritten and then compounded by the bureaucracy is probably adding 10 percent to the price of everything we eat, wear, drive, burn, smoke, drink or gargle. There are no exact statistics in this area, but one suspects that if he could witness the amount of time and effort expended by General Motors in record-keeping for the benefit of government, his mind would be boggled, whatever that means.

We use General Motors only for the impact of size and recognition. Every business, from the hot dog stand to the telephone company, is swamped with paperwork which is non-productive in the final and absolute sense.

This shilly-shallying has become a tremendous factor in what we pay for the necessities of life, yet there is no way to negotiate it. The politicians say jump and business jumps, or else, and as long as this arrangement persists it is a myth that free enterprise is functioning as intended.

One final absurdity in what could be a thousand. Currently, our secretary of transportation, who drives a foreign-made automobile, incidentally, is weighing the prospect of the air bag. Should the automobile companies be compelled to install them, or shouldn't they? It really makes no difference that several of the companies have spent millions of dollars researching the pros and cons of the air bag, with somewhat controversial results. In the end, what the Hon. William T. Coleman in his infinite wisdom decides will be the law of the land, and if you don't like it you can lump it.

Just for a while, on a final trial basis, it would be fascinating to witness the performance of free enterprise without the assistance of the state, city, county and federal bureaucracies. A few years ago, it might be noted, agriculture was unleashed, more or less, and the farmers seem to have been doing rather well ever since.

The courts—Over the years there has been a considerable argument as to which direction dictatorship might come from, the right or the left, with little thought to the possibility that we could wind up with a tyranny of the judiciary. Yet today the courts seem to be the final arbiters of everything, from where the school buses shall run to what children shall recite in the way of thanks once they have been transported from their neighborhoods.

It might help the cause of freedom, and reduce the frustration of the populace, if the role of the courts were redefined, with emphasis on such common but vital functions as clapping those in jail who deserve it. Sometimes our esteemed jurists seem more interested in sociology than in justice, to the irritation of the police and the danger of those who must move about in pursuit of their daily bread.

In his keynote address to the Republicans, Sen. Howard Baker of Tennessee, who turned out to be more of a stemwinder than some of us anticipated, put it this way:

"The issue this year isn't virtue. It isn't love, or patriotism, or compassion. These are the common concerns of all of us, regardless of party. The issue this year, quite simply, is this: How much government is too much government? How many laws are too many laws? How much taxation is too much taxation? How much coercion is too much coercion?"

The Republicans, who seem to have very little else going for them, might well seize upon "How Much?" as their campaign slogan. The results could be astounding, for one senses that Americans of all political persuasions are asking the same question.

Catton's Memoirs

Sometime this fall Doubleday & Co. will publish "Waiting for the Morning Train: An American Boyhood," the early life and times of Bruce Catton, the Michigan boy who made good without parallel as the historian of the Civil War period.

Fortunately, we need not wait until Autumn to know at least part of what Mr. Catton has to tell us in his new book, for portions of it have already been published in American Heritage under the title, "A Michigan Boyhood." It is a splendid offering, gentle in places, sharp in others, the work of an expert who has the distinct ability to make the past flower and the present wilt in shame.

Mr. Catton, we are told, was born in Petoskey, but was removed at an early age to Benzonia, where his father served as headmaster of the old Academy. Benzonia? Where, you may ask without embarrassment, is Benzonia? Admittedly, the place-name sent me to the map, too.

It is in one of the loveliest sections of our state, a few miles due east of Frankfort and an even shorter distance south of Beulah, which is the seat of Benzie County. Crystal Lake is nearby, it is but a pleasant drive to the shores of Lake Michigan, and the 1970 census showed that the town had 412 residents, which means that it has been holding its own, thank you.

In the "tolerable months," meaning from approximately April through October, Benzonia and environs are smiled upon by Mother Nature, but in the Winter, as Mr. Catton notes, all that separates it from the North Pole are a few radar domes. One gathers that the author, who has a home in the area, flees to sunnier climes when the wind starts howling in from the frozen tundra.

⸻

The impending book's title—"Waiting for the Morning Train: An American Boyhood"—has been drawn from Mr. Catton's recollection of early experiences as a passenger aboard the Pere Marquette, the Ann Arbor and, transferring at Chicago from Minneapolis, perhaps the Northwestern or Burlington lines.

The railroads of Michigan, built primarily to service the lumbering industry, were inferior to the major lines of the Midwest, but O, the joys of a Pullman! Listen:

"Nothing on earth today is quite as snug and secure as a Pullman berth used to be once you were fairly in it, and it seemed to me at the time that to lie there feeling the swaying and jiggling of the car's motion, listening to the faraway sound of the whistle, getting up on elbow now and then to peer out the window when we reached a station, and at last drifting off to sleep, was to know unadulterated happiness." (There will now be "King's X" for five minutes of nostalgia, during which we lament one of the great tragedies of our times—the passing of the Pullman.)

⸻

The serious sides of Mr. Catton's memoirs have to do, in most part, with the manner in which the Indians were maneuvered out of their vast holdings, and the subsequent ravaging of the land by the lumber barons.

Lewis Cass, explorer and politician, did the Red Man in, not through force or whisky, although they helped, but by opening Michigan to civilization.

With a rush, it seemed, the Chippewa was surrounded by a civilization with which he could not cope, and from then on it was a bloodless matter to ease him out of his forests and away from his streams and villages—onto reservations.

As for the lumber baron, he represented a fever of harvesting which bordered at times on blind hatred of trees. In Benzonia, which had been founded as an intellectual community, Bruce Catton remembers a wood lot of second growth in which stood one towering tree "that had somehow escaped the ax and saw when the village was built." A hardwood, it was a creation of beauty, a landmark, a holdout against the on-rush of "progress."

But it did not stand. For a county official discovered that the hardwood stood in what had been platted as a highway, although the street had never been opened. Nonetheless, he sent a crew to fell it, and it went crashing one fine morning to rot in fouled splendor. "Nobody cut it into logs or did anything else with it; nobody had ever intended to do anything with it, it was just a big tree that deserved to be laid low . . . "

Thus, Bruce Catton writing of Michigan, My Michigan. He is one of the jewels in our crown.

The Big City Blues

A headline in the Sunday edition of this megaphone of free speech attracted these jaundiced eyes—"City Life Continues to Lose Its Appeal for Americans." Another beef from a group of whiteys seeking an excuse to flee to suburbia, perhaps?

But no, this turned out to be a report from the Gallup organization, which had come up with a startling figure as the result of a recent survey: Only 13 percent of all Americans, black or white, regardless of present location, would live in the cities if given their druthers. The rest yearn for the wide open spaces.

You have to be a citizen with some mileage on your channels to understand what a turn-around in public opinion this represents. Holy Toledo, I can remember when you couldn't keep'em down on the farm or in the small towns, for love or money.

It was said that only the natural-born yokels, the real yahoos, stayed in the sticks. "Don't sell the old farm, father—give the darned thing away!" Such was the rallying cry of those eager to taste the heady life of the Big City. Well, who is laughing now? Have you priced farm land lately? Hoo, boy.

———◆◆◆——— ———◆◆◆———

In those days it was almost unanimously assumed that city life was better in every respect. If you graduated from a rural, or "centralized," high school, let us say, you were apt to have the feeling that you had been short-changed. Part of this was syndrome—country folk looking up to city folk. But some of it was also true; in the languages and the sciences, for example, we were definitely second best. It was a matter of some conversation in our town when one of our teachers volunteered to start a course in French. What in the world would you do with French besides get your tongue twisted?

If a store in town offered the very same coat or suit as a store in the city, it was better to buy it in the city even if the price was higher. What did our merchants know about style? It was bad enough to be a hick without looking like one, for heaven's sake.

When we were out among 'em as the saying went, we would resort to almost any subterfuge to hide our place of residence. Should someone ask, "Where do you live?" the automatic response was: "Near Toledo." It was 30 miles west of Toledo, actually, and that was a pretty good poke in those days, but we hoped to be accepted as at least a semi-urbanite. We considered it an unfriendly act if our interrogator persisted in trying to pin down an exact place of domicile. "Near Toledo" was close enough!

———◆◆◆——— ———◆◆◆———

As a lad I can remember coming to Detroit to see a ball game, and being absolutely overwhelmed by the bustle and clatter and din of this amazing metropolis. We came up Telegraph Road from Toledo, which was in itself an experience, hooked into Michigan Avenue, and then drove for what seemed endless miles through all of that activity, all of that excitement, all of that challenge! Could you survive, country boy, in such a magnificent maelstrom? One had to find out, one had to discover for himself what hope there was in the world for a yokel. So we cut and ran, most of us, the day after graduation. Away from the sticks, onward and upward. I had $35 in cash and a blue serge suit.

Now the tide is running in the opposite direction. When I was "near Toledo" last spring to reminisce to the athletic association, it was to discover that the old home town has two subdivisions. Honest to Pete. For 40 years the sound of the carpenter's hammer was muted throughout the community—and now they have new houses going up all over the place. It is the same in many sections of the Midwest. The good life is "out there."

Why? Oh, there are many reasons. The cities were cheaply built and now they are wearing out. It is not man's natural instinct to live elbow-to-elbow. Race, which is not a nice thought, but true. Crime. And perhaps too many of us tried to take more out of the cities than we were willing to put in. We were greedy; we refused to recognize that the fires of Paradise, wherever it may be, require a constant supply of fuel. The small towns went to pieces when we neglected them, and now the same thing is happening to the cities. Why are we amazed?

Detroit, an old friend bleeding to death. "A decline in the quality of life," according to Dr. Gallup. If enough of us abandon it, we will create new cities. Then what?

Concentrate on Love

You are warned that this column will not be about Watergate, the energy crisis, unemployment, the travels of Henry Kissinger or Gov. Milliken's new state budget. If you left your bed this morning in the mood for self-torture, you will have to turn elsewhere for inspiration.

Instead, this is going to be a piece about love. Not necessarily kissing-with-your-mouth-open love, although there is much to be said for it. Leastwise, that is what memory records. Neither will it concern love for mother, father or spouse. We will take that for granted. What we are going to deal with is the abundance of love which is apt to be the good fortune of any ordinary citizen as he wends his way through life.

It is being written from personal recollections in an attempt to counteract the prevailing mood, which is that we are trapped in a hate-filled society. I do not believe this. I never have. So here is an ode to love . . .

One of the splendid things about love is that you are never too young or too old to be hit by it, like the proverbial ton of bricks. It is not uncommon for the newspapers to be warmed by the story of the 80-year-old widower who has just been accepted by his 78-year-old sweetheart. Editors have a passion for this tale, especially if the principals parted during their high school days, only to re-discover one another two weeks ago in a laundromat. Invariably, such an account rates the first section, with a two-column picture.

It is much more difficult to chronicle the love of the very young, but it happens. Testimony: At the age of five and one-half years, wearing long black stockings suspended from a garter belt, britches which reached to the knees, a pongee shirt and a flowing necktie, I fell in love for the first time. It was a crashing experience for she was utterly divine, being by name Miss Baker and by profession the first grade teacher. I remember her with the tenderest of emotions and should she come along after all of these years and ask me to hand-wrestle a 400-pound gorilla, I would probably undertake it. Others have doubtless had the same experience. It is love, rekindled by fond memories. It blesses you all of the years of your life.

You can have a love affair with nature, too, and with the creatures large and small which adorn it. I have loved a river—and three dogs.

When I was a lad in northwestern Ohio, there was no stream on this earth as grand and glorious as the Maumee River. Even today, coming upon it, I say to myself: "It is wider than the Ohio." It isn't of course, but it is still "my river," wild and untamed in the early spring, sweet and beguiling in the summer and autumn, windswept and harsh in the winter. The sight of the Maumee rarely affects others in this manner, which is perfectly all right. That leaves more of it to be exclusively mine, and I am a jealous lover.

As for the three dogs who have owned me, for many years I stood leg-to-shoulder with them, hoping by this nearness to transmit to them some of the faith and trust they were imparting to me. Three friends, now gone, but love lingers on.

I have admired several presidents and loved one from a common citizen's distance—Franklin D. Roosevelt. He came into many of our lives at a time when the world had been turned upside down by economic crisis and the rise of tyrants at home and abroad, and he became our leader, our champion, our friend. To us he possessed that intangible something called "class," and no one has ever quite replaced him.

I have loved several other men and one in particular, name of Jake. We sailed the South Pacific as shipmates during World War II and terrorized the natives in a dozen ports. Or so we bragged. And the day he received a "Dear John" letter from his wife back in San Francisco, we cried together.

There has been love for two states, Ohio and Michigan, and for three cities—Toledo, New Orleans and Detroit. And from one who has known many shades of life, from the smallest towns to the largest metropolitan areas, there is this final testimony: Everywhere there have been men and women, rich and poor, worthy of trust, admiration and affection. Love.

While very personal, this has not been an unusual confession. Most lives have been graced with more love than hate. In this respect, today's society is no different than it has ever been. Increasing criminality aside, there may be less hatred in the world than was the case 40 years ago.

Other balances also continue. For every devious politician, scores remain forthright. For every gouging businessman, hundreds serve with honor. Only a few lawyers deserve disbarment; only a few authors traffic in sex; only a few preachers are religious freaks; there are only a few bad apples in the whole barrel.

In truth, there is much good in the world and love abounds. This Sunday morning, think about love. It is good for you.

TEN
The Muse at Work

Spirit of Discontent

An irate female constituent (they are the most interesting of all!) called the other day to report a conversation she had just finished with the Internal Revenue Service. It is that season of the year again . . .

The matter at issue had to do with the deduction from her Federal tax form of Michigan sales taxes above and beyond the amount ordinarily permitted on a joint return. (It comes to $200 as I recall.)

The lady remembered that a few years ago, having purchased a new car, she was allowed an extra sales tax deduction and now she wanted to know if the same privilege would hold for household appliances, on which she had spent nearly the price of a two-door sedan during the throes of kitchen remodeling

—————————

But the IRS told her that the extra sales tax deduction would not be allowed; and when she inquired, perhaps a bit testily, as to how she might gain and additional exemption without buying another automobile, she was told: "Oh, if you purchased a boat or an airplane, we would allow that . . . "

Well, when she came on my line she was flying at about 10,000 feet, full throttle, and we spent the next 15 minutes considering the inequities of taxation and wondering, by turns, where it would all end.

Later, another constituent, a taxi driver caught in the price-tax squeeze, bent my ear while he assaulted the Telephone Company,

281

which is about to mute his service unless he comes up with an arearage of $45.

"I have been a good customer of that outfit for years," he complained, "but when I tried to tell them that I had the shorts and needed a little tender, loving special dispensation, they said it would be 'against policy.' To hell with such a policy, I replied, but it looks as though I am going to lose my telephone, which will make the dear wife exceedingly unhappy . . . " Taxes are killing him, he concluded.

One swallow does not make a spring, it has been noted, and two worked-up constituents do not constitute a revolution, but I will venture the opinion, nonetheless, that as of this moment the country has more confused and or distressed citizens than at any time during my adult span, which included the Great Depression.

Back in the 1930s practically everyone was on his uppers, but we had few illusions about the future insofar as "outside help" was concerned. In other words, we had not yet been told that the government would solve all of our problems. FDR provided some relief and some WPA-type jobs, for which he was roundly cursed by his opponents, but at no time were we led to believe that the New Deal was a substitute for initiative. Individually or collectively, as a citizen or a community, if you were going to make it you had to work, plan, save, build—it was every man for himself and the devil take the hindmost.

This is no particular brief for that system, except to observe that if there is a better one, we haven't yet discovered it.

Since the Great Depression we have gone through more good years than bad in the economic (primarily the employment) sense, but there is the feeling here that it is more difficult today for the Common Man to build for the future than it was in, say, 1948.

There are several reasons for this, one being that so much of what he earns is taken away from him in taxes of all descriptions; and another being that he can no longer be certain that what he has saved or created, such as Social Security or a pension, will sustain him in his later, and final, years.

During this interim the role of government, either through the insistence of the people or the importuning of the politicians, has spread until it is now the Mother Hen for practically everybody. It is involved in medicine, education, housing, transportation, communications, child care, retirement, employment practices—the whole bit. This is all very well except that we are now discovering to our horror that it is terribly expensive—and exceedingly inefficient.

We need a new system, at least to the extent of a revision of priorities, but our leaders are either unable or unwilling to provide the changes. Meanwhile the natives grow restless, and what this will stop short of I do not know.

The Mississippi Mind

As these words are written the sun is shining in Jackson, Miss. I know this because a friend just volunteered the information by telephone.

"It is clear and sort of cool here," he said in the soft Deep South drawl that always pleasures me. "The weather is fine over in Oxford, too, and our boys are standing around in the sunshine with steel helmets and gas masks. They don't have any arms, though. None of our people is armed . . . "

Oxford is the seat of the University of Mississippi, where James H. Meredith has been trying to register. They won't let him. They say, frankly, that "his skin is the wrong color." They say this in many ways—states rights, 10th amendment, interposition, but it always comes out the same. Skin.

So, now, this will become an attempt to interpret what we might call "The Mississippi Mind."

My Friend . . .

. . . in Jackson, Bill, is a wonderful guy. He has that southern gift for making you feel that you are the most important person on the face of the earth. It is more than "hospitality," the way a Mississippian puts it on for you. It is a rubdown with a velvet glove after a shower in honeysuckle-scented soft water. You leave his home, or his office, convinced that knighthood is still in flower.

Yet Bill, who is absolutely typical of middleclass Mississippi, has one fault. Beyond a certain point, he is totally influenced by the color of a man's skin . . .

Up to this point, he "does more" for the Negro than any other man on the face of the earth. If, for example, one of his employes calls at 2 a.m. and says, "Mr. Bill, I'm real sick," Bill will go and get him and take him to the hospital.

He will loan him money; go his bail; feed his family in times of emergency; and, in Jackson, he will clean out the slums, build schools, provide a golf course and a swimming pool, a library, hospital facilities . . . Up to a point, all of this.

But beyond that point, Bill's mind closes. He says, simply:

"Look . . . On a number of matters I have not agreed with Gov. Barnett. But now I am with him 100 per cent. Don't kid yourselves up North. Ross Barnett is not a clown. He isn't trying to become a martyr. He speaks for Mississippi—for all of it."

For all of white Mississippi, that is.

What to Do . . .

. . . with "The Mississippi Mind," how to change it, to bring it into the 20th Century, is one of our gravest problems. The trouble is that Bill's way of thinking is not confined to just one isolated state. At the least, he represents a sectional opinion. And getting James Meredith into Ole Miss, and keeping him there, unharmed, is fraught with dangers.

Even so, I am convinced it must be done. If the federal government retreats now, eight years of progress, some of it earned at the price of blood, will be ended. There can be no turning back.

What is to come will be more difficult for Bill than what has happened in the past. But his way of thinking—"The Mississippi Mind"—is an anachronism in the pathway of all that is now judged decent and honorable.

The literally thousands of Bills must give way. Their time in history has ended. What comes may be worse than what they have given to our system, at least for a while. But it must come, for it is the unrelenting wave of humanity marching forward.

What Is Bravery's Pay?

Notes and Comment . . .

Apology is offered for the fact that immediately there must be a violation of Sunday's promise to abstain from further comment for the nonce on the woeful week that was.

Frankly, I would rather write about something else—almost anything else!— but so many suggestions have come from readers near and far that one more trip around the well-worn track seems necessary.

A constituent in Flint, for example, telephoned on Friday to point out a paradox in the recent life and times of a typical Detroit policeman.

"Less than two weeks ago," he said, "your papers were full of stories of the unhappiness within the department, of how tickets were not being written as a protest against the lack of a pay increase in the city's budget, of how morale was at an all-time low.

"And yet," he continued, "when the riot started your police responded with courage even though they knew their hands were tied, at least in the beginning. There must have been a great deal of devotion to duty left in your officers despite earlier appearances to the contrary."

Indeed, yes. To the best of this knowledge there was no shirking of responsibility. Police are "human" in that some are braver, or more daring, than others; but the level of performance was excellent throughout those desperate days and nights. And the same, of course, was true of our fire fighters, who were frequently exposed to the insanity—what other word is there for it?—of the arsonists and snipers.

Another . . .

. . . citizen has sent along a picture from the July 24 edition of this newspaper, showing a lone patrolman holding a mob at bay.

"You will note," he writes, "that the officer's semi-automatic shotgun is not leveled at the mob even though one member of it can be seen advancing toward him rock in hand. Please honor that man for what he is—a competent and courageous guardian of the peace."

Across the bottom of the picture the reader had written—"Profile in Courage"—and that pretty well did it. What better words are there to describe the bravery of one lone man in the face of adversity?

Detroit has other things to worry about at the moment, but in the near future a fruitful effort should be made to respond to the needs of our firemen and policemen for higher pay. I wonder how many people think now that $10,000 a year is "unreasonable" for service of this nature?

Another call—this one of a rather disturbing nature—has come from a small merchant who spent all of those terrible hours protecting his store from damage. He was successful, but the experience left him shaken and embittered. So now he insists that there should be a public poll on this question:

"Do you think arsonists and looters should be shot on sight?"

If anyone wishes to participate in such a grisly taking of the public pulse, let him write "yes" or "no" on a postcard and mail it to this cubicle. It is noted, incidentally, that in Dearborn the answer is already in the affirmative—Mayor Orvie Hubbard has decreed that his police are to go on the offensive at the first sign of upheaval.

A tough guy and a fine administrator, Orvie, and many people are absolutely taken with his policies. However, it has been pondered here in the past, as it is in the present, if his style of operation hasn't at times contributed to the making of the chaos now besetting the nation. (Maybe we ought to run a poll on that, too!)

Finally, there have been questions as to "Negro leadership," seeing that some of those who hold such positions were obviously out of touch with their own people. Patently, vacuums developed in many areas. Those who became prominent did not always maintain lines of communication. They were as bad off, really, as the poor blind whites.

There is so much to be done, and so little time to do it.

Aftermath of Nightmare

If there is anything new that might be written about Detroit's widely lamented travail, it escapes this attention. Therefore, after the thoughts which follow, this column will be devoted to other subjects, at least for a while.

Man and boy, your commentator has been in the newspaper business for more years than he would now readily admit except under oath. This career, if it may be dignified by such a high-sounding word, has been threaded through the weeklies and dailies of several states, and it has been sustained, sometimes in lieu of cash, by the consistent thought that this is a worthwhile way to spend your allotted time. Pride of profession, you might call it.

Now comes the testimony that never have I been prouder of the Fourth Estate than during these past few hectic days. The reporters and photographers who took to the scenes of savagery and risked head and hide to fulfill their assignments; the inside people who handled a deluge of copy and pictures with professional taste and dispatch; the editors who immediately sensed the need for restraint and fastened upon it without delay; the printers, the pressmen, the mailers, the truck drivers, the carrier boys who functioned under trying circumstances—well, this was some performance believe you me, in this building and down the street as well, and this one, who did nothing out of the ordinary, swells with pride in the memory of it.

There is the conviction at this outpost that the printed record of this tragedy will stand the test of time. I believe that the people charged with the grave responsibility of capturing history as it happened did so with a degree of accuracy and controlled feeling uncommon to such frenzied circumstances.

Some of them are young enough that 20 years from now they may say to the probers and researchers—"We covered the story in full, and we got it straight."

Something should be said, too, about the handling of this frightful event in newspapers at large, especially in their editorial columns.

It was a rather bitter paradox that rarely has Detroit received a "better press." In all sections of the nation there was a sympathetic understanding of what had been done here in an effort to make conditions more tolerable for the Negro—but this knowledge, this comprehension of the city's attempts to make equality a reality, made it more difficult for editors to explain why catastrophe had befallen us.

In no editorial, or news-story, or column, or analysis did the magic of words penetrate the barrier of "why?" The whole country, black and white, remains at sea. Detroit was the last place where such fury and violence were expected. This was the essence of editorial comment, day in and day out, and the elusiveness of an answer to the simple question—"why?"—troubles reasonable men almost as much as the riot itself.

Among the poignant recollections of those terrible days are the expressions of love for Detroit which came to this observer by mail, telephone and word of mouth.

People who have known this city in good times and bad were shaken almost beyond words by the sacking and burning.

Too often we are impersonal about Detroit—we think of it as "the center of the automobile industry" or as a good place to earn a living or have fun.

But to many—the vast majority—it is home, one of the sweetest words in the language. And to see it in flames torn and bleeding, carried those who love it beyond the edge of sadness. They may in time forgive what happened on July 23 and thereafter, but they will never forget.

If what occurred here is to have any rational meaning at all, then out of the rubble must come a better city for everyone. This is going to take patience on all sides, for before long it will be discovered that the weight of rebuilding falls upon those who remain at the scene. The "government" will help, but the task will not be accomplished by the waving of a wand.

The road back is before us. The moment of truth is at hand. Do we have any leaders worthy of the name, really?

Law and Order

Having apparently suffered through the worst of what was a good, old-fashioned race riot in the truest animalistic sense of the phrase, let us speculate about the mood of this community. . . .

If the presidential election were scheduled for tomorrow, who do you think would carry these precincts? Lyndon Johnson? George Romney? George Wallace? There is the thought here that Mr. Wallace would make it hot for all concerned, and certainly for Mr. Johnson.

Remember, please, that we are theorizing about tomorrow—the right now reaction to Detroit's senseless burning. A year hence much of the raw anger will have subsided and the area will have returned to near-normal, politically speaking. But for this moment, there is no inclination to sweep this anarchy under the rug as "just another happening."

In the Days . . .

. . . to come, more and more public attention will be turned to the conduct of those who acted as the commanders-in-chief of the armed forces involved.

Why, for example, did Detroit police ignore looters in the early stages of the uprising? Why did it take the National Guard so long to become functional, and what were the instructions to the troops in respect to looting? And—oh mystery of mysteries!—why were units of the Regular Army withheld for hours on end, first at Self-ridge and then at the Fairgrounds, as the city burned and the in-surrectionists ran rampant?

Another myth that will not hold water is the attempt to sub-scribe the majority of this chaos to "a comparative handful of the lawless." Anyone who has seen any portion of the damage will rec-ognize that it was not caused by just a few malcontents.

Sections of this city were literally ripped and torn to pieces, sacked as though there had been an invasion of the Hun. A few people did not cause $200 million in damages in less than 48 hours. This was an uprising against The Establishment, widespread and ugly, and to avoid the truth because it is unpleasant is to invite an encore at some future date.

It Is Said . . .

. . . that the Detroit burning is causing great concern in the Con-gress, and if this is true then perhaps it has not been in vain.

Certainly, it is high time that the leaders of this nation came to the realization that law and order are in eclipse in the major met-ropolitan centers. Progressively, the streets have become less and less safe, and consistently the hard-core challenges to peace and se-curity have become more and more arrogant.

There is no greater danger to the free world today than this breakdown of our internal security, for unless it is brought under control there is no possibility that America will survive as a major power capable of shielding others from tyranny.

Patently, the first thing we must have is a return to law and or-der. What has happened in recent weeks in Newark and Detroit, and to a lesser degree elsewhere, indicates that the very essence of our social structure is being challenged. The Congress should make available to the cities whatever assistance is necessary to provide police protection adequate to the restoration of peace and security.

The Congress must also recognize that its attempts to upgrade our less fortunate citizens through the so-called war on poverty have been woefully inadequate. It is better to have no program at all than one which promises much on paper, or in the sweet words of the politicians, but offers little prospect of success in reality.

The War . . .

. . . on poverty has been under-committed and over-sold. To the hundreds of thousands—the millions—who need training and education if they are to survive on their own in this complex society, it has offered a success here, a success there—but frustration elsewhere.

The Head Start program is held up to us as the model of perfection, but how many needy children are not included because funds are too few? This is just one example of the "lick and promise" nature of this attempt to bring countless numbers of our citizens out of the economic doldrums.

But before anything can be done, we must have law and order.

The Roots of Our Disease

What does a slum become after it has been subjected to a race riot? A super-slum?

Why not? Super-slum is as good a name as any for the devastated areas resulting from continuing hate spilling. Look upon these ruins, Citizens of Detroit, and make your unbelieving eyes grow accustomed to them. For they will doubtless be with us for a long, long time—mute and ugly testimony to July 23, 1967, the day the beast broke loose in this supposedly well-timed community.

In Monday's . . .

early light, Grand River was a scene out of a nightmare. It hasn't been much to look at for many years, that portion of Grand River which ties in with the Inner City, but just wait until you see it in its new design. Shades of the Four Horsemen . . .

There was still some looting going on when I came to work, and several buildings were on fire, with the smoke blending into the haze which normally hovers at that hour over the Downtown region. Hundreds of Negroes were drifting about and many of them seemed in a carnival mood, as though something unusual had entered their lives after a long seige of drabness.

Where were the police? Oh, they were around, meaning that they were car-patrolling as available strength permitted, but the thing you have to remember about the police is that they lost control of this situation five years before it happened when the do-gooders and the bleeding-hearts within the community fell for all that high-sounding nonsense about "police brutality."

That is when law and order, here and elsewhere, started breaking down, and when you tie that in with the cold and calculating—the "to-hell-with-America-I-am-concerned-with-votes"—attitudes of some of our peerless politicians, why then you have the major causes for the revolution now afoot across this country. Actually, the politicians who over-promised, deliberately and for reasons of personal power, are the major architects of this national tragedy.

What You Have . . .

in Detroit and other major metropolitan areas is really a case of demand for improvements exceeding the capacity for change.

Northern cities have been inundated by Negro immigrants since World War II. As was noted here a few days ago, the "logistics" of this migration, South to North, are staggering—more than four million in less than one generation into six states, Michigan included.

When people move from a low level of potential opportunity to a higher level, it is only natural that their expectations should rise and that they should seek a portion of the "good life."

It was an immediate improvement to come from sharecropping in the South, let us say, to a job on a production line in Detroit, and for a while the shortcomings in this new life—the crowding, the schools which became inferior, the deteriorating neighborhood—were tolerable.

After a while, however, these people wanted some of the economic and social advantages obvious in the white community, and this was when the pressure started, a family here, a family there, building force like a head of steam in a boiler without an escape valve. Why wasn't whitey—and you must remember that the white politician eventually becomes whitey—making good on his promises?

The Reason? ...

Northern cities, and again we include Detroit, have been so weighted with the cost of providing the bare necessities of this immigration that there has been no money for luxuries.

In Detroit in recent years we have had the imposition of an income tax and property values for taxation purposes have gone sky high, but still there is no means for more than the necessities. Now there is a state income tax, plus the possibility of new taxes on gasoline and cigarets, but even so there will be no additional money for the cities.

Lawlessness compounds our problems and plays into the hands of the extremists white and black. The nation is sick of an awful disease and no cure is in sight.

Where Are the Giants of Yesteryear?

The Old Curmudgeon has been reminded that he is now starting his 25th year as a wordslinger for the Free Press. Further, if he can keep this dog-and-pony act going midway through 1984, he will have spent a half-century in what we used to call "the newspaper game. This assumes you will award credit for time devoted in opposition to Messrs. Hitler and Tojo. In any event, Holy Toledo and bring on the Geritol.

The question becomes, are newspapers better than they used to be? Let's have the envelope. And the answer is: Well, some.

Newspapers are larger, easier to read (typewise), better printed when the pressrooms get the color combinations in sync, and they deal with subjects that would have caused a city editor to blush and set his teeth on edge 50 years ago. You will note the use of "his teeth." If there was a female city editor in 1933–34, her light was hidden under a bushel. In those days, city editors were supposed to chew tobacco, swear in three languages, terrorize the police, pet-rify young reporters and brook no nonsense from any source what-soever. It was not then suspected that women were thusly constituted, but fortunately job requirements changed with the times. Today we have a female city editor on this megaphone of free speech, and she is a lady. True, she might be able to swear, sweetly and prettily, if the computers broke down, but otherwise a conver-sation with her is as clean and wholesome as an afternoon tea.

Some will now ask, how's come you don't think newspapers are a whole wagonload better than they used to be, and the answer will be forthcoming in one word: writing. It does not seem to these eyes that the writing has kept pace with technological progress, as it is called.

For starters, there is no national sports columnist who can make the language dance and spit fire, as Westbrook Pegler did before he started making a career of hating Eleanor Roosevelt. There is no Grantland Rice around, for that matter, and Red Smith is mourned for what he was, and for the shoes he left unfilled.

There is no national political columnist who will send you rock-eting into the night, ranting and tearing against injustice, as Hey-wood Broun was capable of doing; and where is the replacement for Walter Lippmann? And while we're asking, what happened to the editorial writers on the old Chicago Tribune, who could raise your blood pressure 40 points when they attacked something you stood for, which was most of the time? They wrote pieces under such titles as "Wherein We Skin a Skunk," and you didn't know whether to roll on the floor laughing or hope the victim sued them for $16 million. Politicians today, including Coleman Young and James Blanchard, think they have it tough. Ha.

What has happened to writing, you old goat? Well, it has been diffused, for one thing. Whereas newspapers were once at least the starting place for most young writers, now they go into television, or public relations, or government; or what you might call "lin-guistic business management," meaning that many corporations keep writers around to do speeches or public statements; or politics, or ghosting books, or one darned thing or another. The magazine field may have been reduced, but the market for writers has expanded.

Even so, the quality of writing has not improved in the great, testing art form—the novel. So much unmitigated junk is being sold that very few novelists are honestly working at their craft. Where is the successor to "You Can't Go Home Again," written by Thomas Wolfe at a young but stricken age and not yet approached in observance, in knowledge of America and the world it was destined to dominate? In one scene, describing the crowd awaiting the departure of a train, he told us more about this Republic, and where it was headed, than you will find in three yards of today's trash.

The Japanese have captured our car market; the Australians have made off with our sailing mug; writing lacks depth and spirit. Never let it be said that the Curmudgeon grew old gracefully.

How Civilized Are We?

How thick—or how thin—is the coating of veneer we call "civilization"? How much—or how little—would it take to drive us back to savagery? Or haven't we left the barbaric state, really?

Of late I have had letters from several readers who have said that they would, indeed, defend their fall-out shelters with guns if that was the only way they could keep strangers, or even neighbors, from trespassing.

"This may be a heartless way to look at it," one Detroiter wrote, "but if it ever came to a survival of the fittest, and if I was one of the fittest because of circumstances or advance preparation, then I would have no compunction about pulling the trigger . . . "

This chap had no shelter at the time, but was thinking of building one. "If I do," he warned, "I will be ready mentally and emotionally to protect it from intruders if need be."

I believe him, if for no other reason than that he, or at least his type, has been showing up in our literature of late years, thus indicating that the novelists, who are supposed to know a good deal about the Inner Man, consider him the logical man of the hour in the event of great disaster.

John Christopher, the Englishman, used Mr. Ruthless, if I may thus name him, to great advantage in "No Blade of Grass," in which the world faced famine, while Pat Frank found worthwhile employment for him in "Alas, Babylon," the story of survival in Central Florida following a nuclear attack.

In both books, Mr. Ruthless turned from a mild, semi-bleeding heart into a merciless tyrant when the safety of his brood was threatened, and that's about the way I think it would happen if disaster came upon us.

Beyond Literature . . .

. . . we may look to history for the "survival pattern" adopted by people in times of stress.

I am told, for example, that in Germany today it is practically impossible to find anyone who knew that Hitler and his goons were slaughtering the Jews, yet this is very strange in view of what actually happened.

Not all of the raids on the ghettos, or beatings at the synagog, took place in the deep of night. Thousands of defenseless men, women and children were carted through the streets like cattle, or were yanked away from their employment, their household chores or their studies in broad daylight, to be vilified openly by the Storm Troopers or other vermin.

Yet, today, the Germans plead that "they did not know what was going on." They knew, all right, but they were afraid to stand up and be counted against such barbarity—and there are times, dear friends, when fear is the worst of all forms of ruthlessness, for in the throes of it all decency is sacrificed to survival.

To a Lesser Extent . . .

. . . we have had some illustrations of "ruthlessness through fear" in this country, too.

For years there were only a few people who sided with the American Indians as they were shunted from one place to another, the victims of broken treaties and worthless promises.

Talk about "imperialism" in Africa! Man, we gave the British, the French and the Belgians lessons beyond their ken in crass deceit and the art of hornswoggling.

And look . . . It has only been a few years, 30 or so, that there has been widespread concern for the plight of the Negroes. Prior to then, you were told, politely but firmly, North as well as South, to "Leave the Negroes alone: There are some things you can't change."

Ruthlessness isn't dead, although I suppose it is true that the world is getting a little better, step by step. But I am not overcome with optimism about the depth of our "civilization." I think some people would shoot their neighbors on the steps of the fallout shelter, and furthermore I believe that the prevailing mood among the survivors would be—"That's just exactly what you should have done, Mr. Ruthless!"

The "Anti-City" Feeling

A good deal of criticism, much of it unbalanced and undeserved, has been directed against the cities of America in recent years and, unfortunately, some of it has rubbed off on our incumbent national administration.

This narrator can not recall when there was more "anti-city" feeling afoot than there is at the moment. It is based in part on the assumption that any large gathering of citizens is bound to lead to crime, corruption, extravagance and the coddling of those who do not want to work. There are politicians in high places who have been feeding upon this assumption. They don't quite say it in so many words, but what they mean is that the damned cities have gotten themselves into this mess, so let them wiggle out of it as best they can, and good riddance in the meantime. They are cheered, alas, when what they really deserve is to be tossed out of office in one sodden heap.

America is unique among the so-called enlightened peoples in that we have lost regard for our cities and are not strongly fevered by their decline. The Japanese love Tokyo, the French are enamored of Paris, the British dote on London, the Dutch rally to Amsterdam, and so forth. But in this country if you happen to harbor a degree of admiration for New York City, let us say, there are circles where you will be considered either touched in the head or a disciple of the devil. It took as much fussing and feuding to get financial help for New York City, remember, as it did to arrange bailouts for Lockheed or Chrysler. When you think about that, you have to wonder what in the world has been going on and what brought it about.

The trouble with the cities is that early on they attempted to shoulder burdens which were actually national in scope and import, and thus far beyond local solution.

Starting with World War II and persisting even now, although on a reduced basis, there has been a shifting of population within this Republic without parallel in world history. No one knows precisely how many Americans changed life-styles, with emphasis on urban influx, but you get some idea of the immensity of this transition from one statistic: between 1940 and 1980, the number of workers engaged in agriculture dropped from 9,540,000 to 3,310,000.

Let us just say, then, that Americans in great numbers poured into the cities, many without resources, undereducated, undertrained, suddenly enveloped in strange surroundings which left them, in a real sense, aliens in their own country. They were the "pioneers" of the mid-20th Century, and surely the time will come when our literature will reflect not only their struggles but their triumphs, for in some respects those who settled an earlier America had it easier.

Meanwhile, the rest of the country looked on as this drama unfolded, without realizing that they were a party to what amounted to a national dilemma. The cities had to beg for money, item by item, to meet the mounting crisis, and as services faltered, tensions mounted, education deteriorated, jobs declined, and crime flourished as it always does when a society is mortally wounded; there was an out-migration also without comparison in the Republic's annals. It became easy to salve the conscience by saying that the cities were hopeless quagmires, that they had nothing to build on, that America had to be reconstituted, and there were those who seized upon this attitude and turned it into the next thing—a political credo.

Whereas Europe and Japan rebuilt their cities after the ravages of war, we subjected ours to something much worse—indifference, distaste, the refusal to admit that urban difficulties were far beyond urban cause or solution, the adoption of a "to hell with them" attitude which affronts even the slightest sense of fair play.

The miracle of these times is that the cities are still trying, that they are developing strong and agile leaders, that the people in them are looking to the future instead of crying havoc. Hurrah for the cities, most of them too tough and determined to die!

A Cardiologist Did It

It has been said that reformed alcoholics and reformed smokers have at least one thing in common—they will bend your ears to the breaking point if given the slightest encouragement—so stand by for a lecture on the use of the noxious weed.

It has been three weeks, one day and seven hours since your narrator took his last puff on a Marlboro, yet to some degree he remains in the throes of nicotine withdrawal. Chiefly, this occurs when he attempts to transfer his thoughts to paper. All at once, the lower case "e" on the typewriter becomes illusive, he has the feeling there is no one here but us chickens when his mind goes searching for a witticism or an expression—this is a form of what is called "writer's block," and there is the constant temptation to bow to it. But he has kept pecking away, and today seems a bit better than yesterday, and tomorrow may be full of sunshine and daffodils. You never know until you give it a whirl.

Against such an immediate background, you might anticipate an indictment of the tobacco trust in general, but such will not be the case. Listen. Man and boy, your narrator smoked for approximately 55 years, and he never met a cigaret he did not like, a cigar he did not admire, a pinch of pipe tobacco he did not enjoy. O, he dearly loved to inhale that smoke and exhale it through nostrils and mouth, and if it was sinful, he is ready to burn for it.

So why has he stopped at this late date—55 years and umpteen million cigarets later?

Well, Sir, one afternoon in Room 1148, St. Joseph Mercy Hospital, Ann Arbor, there was sort of a consortium of experts, all gathered to pronounce the findings after research upon the carcass of your narrator. St Joe's is a mighty fortress of heavy thinkers and the implements of their disciplines, and they do not rush into battle half-prepared.

Anyhow, the cardiologist took to expounding upon his discoveries, which sounded intriguing since they did not seem to be fatal, and finally he was asked the obvious questions—how much had smoking contributed to these misfirings and malfunctions?

The X-rays, he replied, did not show major heart or lung damage as the result of nicotine and its henchmen, and then he paused for a moment before delivering a statement that is now brought to you verbatim: "I think you should know," he said, "that I make my living off people who smoke."

That tore it up. Goodby, Marlboro 100s, tubes of perfection, tributes to the cigaret maker's art. Hadn't felt like smoking in several days and never would again. Never, never, ever, never, ever, ever. With a dog who can eat three cans of Alpo a day, with taxes going up, with Social Security teetering, with budgets out of balance and the Democrats calling for the blood of the non-spenders, who can afford to support a cardiologist?

So the Old Curmudgeon swore off the weed, "wild turkey" as the fellow said, and this is the last you will hear of it, even if he loses complete track of the lower case "e."

One admits, finally, to a major disappointment in this hospitalization. He did not get to see his own gizzard during the gastroscopy, which is a process wherein they slip a camera down your gullet and inspect the caverns and crevasses of the Innerman. Several had described this as something worth seeing, albeit a bit painful.

But progress has taken all the thrill out of it. For when the Old Curmudgeon was wheeled into position, an attendant stuck a needle into this arm, saying, are you getting sleepy? No. Well, you will, the fellow replied. And the next thing the patient knew he was in the recovery room, it was all over, and he had not seen his gizzard or anything else worth reporting.

Live Longer—and Dumber?

Well, dear constituents, here we are in a new year, dragging our old dilemmas behind us. In a way it is akin to moving into a brand new house with the same old furniture, while the neighbors gander at every piece toted by the chaps from the hauling company.

One of the things we would have preferred to leave behind, but couldn't, was the Census Report which showed that we are living longer and getting dumber. In case you missed this revelation which was released a few days before 1977 ended, the pertinent points were as follows:

A girl born in 1974 has a life expectancy of 76 years, while a boy from the same general litter so to speak, will make it to 68, if all goes well. To the best of this knowledge, science has never clearly stated why females live longer than males, but they sure do. And this is one of the things you might keep in mind, mate, the next time she calls you a male chauvinistic pig. Who's hogging the longevity, huh?

"Social Indicators 1976," which was what the report was called, indicated the youngsters who joined us in 1974 will have more leisure time than their ancestors; they will be members of smaller families; crime will be their constant companion, and "While the trend toward completing more years of schooling continues, infor-

302   Lessons Learned During a Wasted Youth

mation on actual achievement as revealed by tests is less optimistic." Older but dumber, as noted.

———————

What is it all about, Alfie? We are spending more money on education than ever before—in some rural counties upwards of 90
percent of all local tax revenues are going to the schools—yet we
do not seem to be matching young people to the jobs available, as
a perusal of Help Wanted advertisements might indicate. Are we
teaching the wrong things; are we, in fact, encouraging a loss of
jobs our people desperately need under the pretext that Americans
are too smart to do that type of work?

This is a good time to bring forth a recent letter from the Hon.
Charles Hampton, professor emeritus from Ferris State College,
who now lives in Marshall. He was attracted by the Dec. 15 column that cited the dangers of unemployment among young people,
and here is his reaction:

"Well do I remember the Great Depression: Ready in hand with
a fresh B.A. I found myself not only out of a job, but in 50 tries in
my home town of Kalamazoo in the fall of 1933, unable to per-
suade anyone to even let me fill out an application for a job! Luck-
ily I was single, and there were 25-cent dances and a 50-cent golf
course and my mother was a wonderful cook.

"However, in 1977, as you well know, we are facing an entirely
different situation. It is my considered opinion that, excluding the
health sciences and service areas such as auto repair and food
preparation, 75 percent of the current crop of college graduates are
job expendable—and for the foreseeable future.

"May I suggest that in some column in the near future you ex-
plore the myth that automation creates more jobs. If it did not eliminate jobs, what employer would spend thousands to introduce it?
Even a cursory examination of two copies of 'Statistical Ab-
stract'—say those of 1966 and 1976—would reveal increase in
population but not a comparable increase in jobs.

———————

"At present," Prof. Hampton concludes, "the public is being
conditioned to automation at the supermarket through the Uni-

versal Product Code (the little parallel lines on the side of each item.) Women are being lulled by the promise that checkout lines will go faster. Nothing is said about the elimination of prices on the package, on the shelf, the elimination of thousands of supermarket employes and the possibility of store fraud.

"Our children will certainly be faced with a revolution from the left or the right. Interesting time!"

Very interesting indeed. The fantasies of earlier years, which we kept with us every step of the way, led to the Great Depression and commercial paralysis in Kalamazoo. And it will be the mistakes of the more recent past, retained with equal fervor (or stupidity) that will accompany us into the next economic collapse.

Twice during 1977, if memory is correct, there were pieces here which attempted to put some dents in the halos worn by the automators, to no avail. As for the educators, they move with all of the speed of cold molasses toward reform of their act. Already 1978 is full of sound and fury, isn't it?

Banks Go for Broke

In the past there have been several snippets in this pillar devoted to the vast changes which have come over bankers in recent years, and this is to testify that my wonder and amazement continue, unabated.

The other evening there was a commercial on the telly dedicated to vacations and how sweet it is to get away from the hot and cruel city during the fever of the equinox, when asphalt turns to syrup and the temper of man runneth short.

You should take a trip for health's sake, said the young lady who was representing the sponsor, and then, gently and sweetly, she turned to the matter of money.

Did you have the shorts? Were there outstanding accounts with the butcher, the baker and the candlestick maker? Were you thinking, perhaps, of foregoing a vacation trip because you really could not afford it?

304 Lessons Learned During a Wasted Youth

How silly of you! How square and utterly old-fashioned! How mean of you to deny your family three weeks at Lake Diddywa-diddy at $40 per day, American plan!

Why, we have the money, she cried, eyes sparkling. Come, let us reason together. Sign the paper, take the money, go forth and be merry, live it up-and pay later. Hotel Toledo!

Well you are horribly out of date if you can remember when a banker would have taken you by the seat of the pants and the scruff of the neck and pitched you into the street had you tried to put the arm on him for vacation money.

Further, he would have passed the word that you were a weakling, a playboy and a candy ankle, and pretty soon every merchant in town would have come down on you for an immediate settlement of bills overdue. A vacation loan, indeed!

Heavens to Betsy, in the times of which we are speaking it was hard enough to get money for what were considered legitimate reasons. If a farmer went in, hat in hand, to get a loan to buy a cow the first thing the banker wanted to talk about was assets.

How many assets you got, Sam?, he would ask, right off the bat, and brother if poor old Sam didn't have plenty it was no dice.

As a townsman, if you had $50 on deposit the odds were no better than even that you could borrow $40, for 60 days at six percent, and the banker would remind you that the hour of reckoning was coming every time he met you on the street.

He wasn't particularly stingy or mean, he was just cautious, which was what bankers were supposed to be. Somebody had to have sense about money and that was his job. It was generally agreed that he was the guardian of the community's nest-egg and the protector of its future. Easy bankers and loose women might be a lot of fun for a while, Elmer, but who could afford them?

The Great Depression just about did bankers in. Leastwise, they haven't been quite the same since. Their image suffered something awful when they couldn't give their customers the cash they had on deposit. Cash was an asset, wasn't it? But what the blazes good was an asset if you couldn't eat it? That's when assets started going to pot, too.

***

Nowadays, the banker plays an entirely different role in our affairs. Instead of sitting back of a big mahogany desk and talking about assets, he is out kicking up the dust in favor of progress. He is strong for progress, the banker is, especially at six percent. Buy that car, purchase that boat, take that trip, educate that child, turn those wheels, oh watch the mare go!

We have reached the point where you can borrow money to pay off money you previously borrowed. It is quite a merry-go-round we have going, and the banker has to keep it whirling or else the whole shebang will fall on top of him.

Losing Their Charisma

In recent months there have been several proposals, including one by Sen. R. W. Packwood of Oregon, which would encourage birth control by limiting the number of tax exemptions the head of a family would be allowed.

The Packwood plan, which attracted wide attention without igniting any perceptible bonfires of support in congress, would limit the number of deductible children to two. Beyond that, babies would have to be loved for the unexempted joy they bring, especially on April 15.

To be the third, fourth or even eighth child on tax day might constitute cruel and unusual punishment, which is supposed to be unconstitutional, but the Senator contends that drastic steps must be taken to curb the population explosion, and there are those who agree.

***

While your commentator does not expect any such restrictions to be adopted in this decade, the mere fact that they are being considered tells us that in one more amazing way American tradition is being challenged.

For up until just a few years ago this was a nation wherein fertility was honored on both sides of the house. The mother was acclaimed for her child-bearing abilities, and the easier she had them the higher her esteem. The father's role, while less spectacular, was nonetheless appreciated. It was generally assumed that a man who had sired and fed ten children, give or take a few, had done a lifetime's good work.

Such reverence for marital productivity was supportable on the grounds that children were useful, at times even essential. What we now forget is that the "labor force" which cleared much of our land and brought civilization to the howling wilderness was in large part under-age by modern standards.

Mere children were hewers of wood, plowers of fields and hunters and trappers of food and fur. Land was cheap but it was without worth unless there were hands to tame it. The answer: children.

In other days, too, the celebrated family business was just that, with a succession of off-spring being utilized at various tasks. There were many things a stripling could do to contribute to the solvency of a grist mill or a weekly newspaper, let us say, so there was a well-defined place awaiting children as soon as they had passed the toddler stage.

In cities and rural areas, families met the world head-on as dedicated units, with each pulling his share of the load. Frequently, probably more often than not, it was a cozy and rewarding arrangement, contributing to the closely-knit family ties with which we were once blessed.

There were additional factors which made large families not only harmless but desirable. The nation needed population—there were all of those countless square miles of territory to be conquered.

There were Indians to be surpressed and foreign powers to be impressed. And the costs were bearable. If a family had several children, as many as four or five, in school at the same time, it would not be for long and meanwhile the teacher was ill-paid and the facilities provided by the taxpayers were crude and inexpensive. Hurrah, then, for human fertility.

Now, of course, all this is changed. Today it costs almost as much to send a child through one year of grade school as it did the late William Kelsey to graduate from the University of Michigan. Large families are frequently not self-supporting where education is concerned, and other taxpayers grow weary of sharing the burden.

Further, when a child is born today someone, at least in theory, must worry about how and where he will fit into society when his school years are over. Industry, once exclusively charged with this responsibility, is no longer able to meet it. Even in boom times the poor multiply despite unemployment or under-employment and now there is a serious move afoot to make welfare "respectable."

The country has changed and so has its need for children. People equal pollution and of both we now have more than the traffic will bear. This is why it is being argued that it is not enough to hold population at its present level: it is said that we must reduce it.

A strange new world, this. Who ever thought that Mom and Pop, producers of bouncing babies, would become Public Enemies?

Death in Perspective

Just as patience was wearing thin, the outline of Ohio's dark hills appeared on the horizon, and there was a flicker of nostalgia for days long past. "Going home," the voice said. But then it qualified itself: "Going home to bury Geneva," and there was no comfort of things remembered in that.

She died, this sister of ours, late last week with the age of 74 nearly in hand. She needed eight more days and wanted them, no doubt, but time marched on without her. She called a son on the telephone and said, "I don't think I am going to make it." By the time he arrived, rushing, horn blaring, she hadn't. From the quick to the dead is a very narrow chasm.

This happened in Flatwoods, Ky., which you reach by climbing Wheeler Hill. Years ago, if you had a car that would make it to the top of Wheeler Hill in high gear, you belonged to the upper middle class. Now even the Common Man makes it in one powerful burst, which is another way of measuring progress.

She had lived in Flatwoods only about a dozen years so they took her down the hill, to Russell for funeral services. Russell was her turf as the saying goes. She lived there from infancy upward, was married there, reared two sons there, went through a shattering divorce there, picked up the pieces late in life and became a licensed practical nurse, and worked in a doctor's office for 23 years and, one suspects, at times practiced more medicine than the law intended.

That was her community, those were her people, and they turned out, a goodly number of them, to see her off.

—————

She looked fine. You may say what you please about undertakers (would they prefer to be called morticians?), but if it solaces you that the features of the deceased should be serene, the coffin glistening, the flowers in tiered array—well, they are worth the money. There is a personal preference for being nailed up in a hurry and cremated, but that is neither here nor there. In extremity, what the family wants, the family should have, within reason. Funerals are among the most ancient of our rituals, and who is to say we would be better off if the form of them was subjected to drastic change? This is another area where the interference of government and all-wise outsiders should be discouraged, so long as the innocent are not preyed upon or bamboozled. Leave the people in peace when it is time for them to mourn and to cry and to pray.

In the evening, members of the Eastern Star Lodge came and conducted their farewell ceremony, based in large part on symbolism. Freemasonry in its various degrees has run through the family for several generations, with even this backslider progressing quite a distance beyond the Blue Lodge. The Stars came out, you might say, on a night given to a cold rain and thick, rolling fog, and they brought with them a connection with the past, a sense of solidarity in a moment of anguished drift.

The service proper was compact, well-organized, with a prelude of organ music that blended the haunting hymns. "The Old Rugged Cross," of course, and then the one with the line that won't go away, "he walks with me, and He talks with me, and He tells me . . . " Ah, yes! And "Onward Christian soldiers," now and always, across all of the years we shared.

———◆———◆———

The preacher, young, sincere from head to toe, wanting to help, came back to the immortal line, not verbatim, "I go to prepare a place for you." He seemed certain that things would work out, that this was only the beginning, but once more Death was a stranger.

Death. We have no particular fear of it, a statement made, you understand, without inviting it. We recognize it as an essential part of the cycle. There might even come a day when we will welcome it. But we do not comprehend it in the "Christian sense."

What has happened to Geneva Hackworth almost 74, of Flatwoods, Ky., dearly departed? The product of the mortician's art was at the funeral home, but she wasn't. Not really. Where did she go? Ah, that is a question!

Winston Churchill referred to the beyond as "the Black Velvet." Others equally as well-informed have been much more optimistic about it. Faith. That is what you need, they say, but it is very illusive.

Death. Whatever there is to it, Geneva now knows. And there are only two of us left in the family to find out, whereas it once seemed that we fairly swarmed around the piano as she played "My Old Kentucky Home."

Broken Illusions

Happy Veterans Day

Veterans Day is a holiday.
What is a veteran?" Word books say,
"Old and experienced—oft in war."
That is a status worth cheering for.
"Life is a battle," or so I've heard;
So it's not odd that this thought occurred:
One who is seasoned in life and wise,

Born as a Veterans Day surprise,
Served in the forces of World War II
Ought to receive this day his due,
Out to be hailed as a special Vet;
— — — SO — — —
Here's to the birthday of Judd Arnett!

—Margaret Rorke

It is an oft-told tale involving the Boy Curmudgeon and his blue Packard roadster, which he was lustily pedaling to and fro on a limited surface when all at once the fire bell started clanging and the church bells joined in, filling that brisk but sunny November morning with a strange and eerie clangor. Then the Old Man came from his store, The Bee Hive, and there was a far-away, wondrous look in his eyes as he said: "The war is over; we have made the world safe for democracy." It has been downhill ever since.

Nations did not recover their equilibrium after the First World War, for reasons the philosophers have been mulling since the Peace Conference fell flat on its backside. One has his own notions as to why the shock never wore off. He believes that the conflict certified what had been rumored out of the distant past—savagery was one of man's leading characteristics. And one other thing. The war showed that stupidity of leadership, in both the political and military arenas, was boundless.

Thus, the First World War had a mindless bloodlust to it that would have brightened the eyes of the Tartars, the Mongols or the Crusaders. Much of it was fought among the debris of mud, slop, odds and ends of human carcasses, mutilated horses and mules, rats and wretchedness wrought by Mars gone utterly insane. At this day, to read of it is to bring vomit to the pit of the throat; and to think that field marshals could have ordered, and politicians could have countenanced, such yard-gained-here and yard-gained-there slaughter is to doubt the balance of the mortal mind on a continuing basis.

Now another "Armistice Day" has rolled around, 1918 to 1984, and those who think savagery has abated and leadership has sharpened are invited to read another chapter of "Alice in Wonderland."

Or, better yet, they might read "Day One: Before Hiroshima and After," a book just brought to the market-place by Peter Wyden and Simon and Schuster. John Hersey, who lifted the veil on the first nuclear holocaust, has said: "Here, quite simply, is what every literate person on earth should know about the start of the atomic age."

You are warned, however, that it may scramble some of your illusions. It halts the rush of Harry Truman toward sainthood; it reveals scientists had no more concept of radiation than your dog does of the bubonic plague and it contains the astounding intelligence that in 1945 the Russians were ahead of the Germans in harnessing the atom.

In this lifetime there have been four miserable wars, so many that "Armistice Day" had to be scrapped for a more general term. And we are headed for the ultimate violence and savagery unless we get smart in a hurry.

One thinks of Nov. 11 as he surely must, and wishes his Mom had pushed a bit harder and had him on the 10th; or had waited a trifle longer and presented him on the 12th. Or better than that he wishes that much of the world had not gone crazy in 1914.

ELEVEN
The Best Is Yet to Come

Heading for Friarship

Oh, dear chums, there is the possibility the Old Curmudgeon will have to give up drinkin', at least for a while. So long Old Slippery Elm, the whisky that slides down like a noodle; farewell noble martini, the classic of the bartender's art; goodbye wine and beer, even though you were never strongly favored; hello soda pop and all the rest of that swill. Holy Mackerel.

There have been no strict doctor's orders to this effect, understand, but you don't have to be too smart to recognize when you have potholes in your digestive tract. Booze will tell you. All at once, the evening cocktail that took the throb out of your feet and the jangle out of your nerves is putting bile in your gizzard. The dollop of Old Slippery Elm that once flowed like honey throughout the deepest recesses of the Inner-Man takes on the consistency of road tar, and you find yourself fumbling your way in the darkest of night to the medicine cabinet, there to gulp a half-tankard of antacid. Oh, that damn antacid. Surely that is what the chute to Hell is greased with.

All of this is very vexing to one who has dearly enjoyed a good lusty snort without becoming addicted to it. He will have much less trouble quitting booze than quitting cigarets. He will miss the conviviality of clicking glasses, of saying here's to your health, of listening to the chitchat, some of it marvelous, at bars, of sensing the camaraderie common in a good middle-class saloon. The Europeans knew what they were doing when they established the pub, and its transfer to these shores was one of our smarter imports.

313

Much has been said of late about drinkin' and its evil influence on the passions of men and automobile drivers in general, but take a little advice from Ol' Arn, who has lived on both sides of the fence: If you really want to see this Republic flip its lid and become downright unbearable as a place to draw breath, bring back Prohibition.

———

What we still need to do is teach moderation, which is easier to say (and do) in the country than it used to be in the city. When the Curmudgeon was functioning as a scribe in the concrete canyons, he would customarily have a blast, and sometimes two, at lunch. Then he would wend his way back to compose prose so deathless it was fit only for cremation.

Since moving to the outback, however, he has done little drinkin' at noon. Fern was one of those with the firm conviction that the sun did not come over the yardarm until 5 p.m. Eastern Standard Time, and it took a cataclysmic occurrence, such as a reversal of the Japanese current, to reduce her conformity to that tradition. It was not that she took verbal umbrage at violations. She would simply fix a steely gaze upon a noon martini, let us say, and all the ice would melt, the gin would curl up and die, and the vermouth would take on the odor of disinfectant spray. Our intrepid assistant, Bonnie, has been taught the rudiments of martini making, but she, too, seems to have a streak of purity where drinkin' before near-dark is concerned—so, as you can see, your narrator lives a life verging on such chastity as to cause him to comtemplate the additional steps needed to become a friar.

Wherever he has been, the Old Curmudgeon has rarely done any tippling after dinner. After he has had his victuals, all the spark goes out of his system where alcohol is involved. He believeth, more or less, that a fellow ought to do his drinkin' between five o'clock and the call to dinner, and this is what he has enjoyed, and this is what he is moanin' and bewailin' about, simply because it seems to be riling his innards.

———

For that matter, he is still supposed to be on a very tender diet, free of anything a civilized man would deliberately choose to eat, so bland that when you chew it, you can't tell whether it is cardboard or old mattress cover. You know something? This world is full of absolutely inexcusable cooking, and most of it was invented by dieticians. God love the Italians, the Mexicans, the French, the Polish, the Germans, the Hungarians, and all others with a natural-born instinct to make of eating a dazzling experience as long as your stomach holds out—and then to hell with it.

A Walk for Peace

Washington—the affairs of man having reached the point where a "non-conformist" is an individual who carries a sign advocating peace, it is only natural those gentle souls, the Quakers, should be attracting a good deal of attention these days.

Officially known as the "Friends Witness for World Order," nearly 1,000 Quakers have been picketing the White House on behalf of such ancient virtues as brotherly love and overcoming evil with good.

Washington has had a spate of "peacemongers" of recent months, but the city has been able to brush most of them off.

With the Quakers, however, it is something different, for at least a few of those who have come here are ancestors of the Americans who have been living on Cloud Nine, peace-wise, for hundreds of years—and making it work.

———————

The old-line Quakers lived in harmony with the Indians of Pennsylvania at the time when residents of the Eastern seaboard were huddling in blockhouses, keeping their powder dry, in an effort to retain their scalps.

Incongruous as it seems, the modern Quaker feels that what worked once is worth another try. "Peace is more than the absence of war," they say. "It is the practice of love and respect for others."

"With the Russians?" you ask.

"With the Russians," they reply.

And then they take up their "vigil for peace" once again, carrying placards that read: "Grapes from thorns? Figs from thistles? Peace from armaments?" . . .

Coming upon these people in Washington, which at times vibrates with the A-bomb jitters, is a good deal like walking into the corner saloon to find an itinerant preacher holding forth against the wages of sin.

You don't know whether to laugh, or cry—or join 'em. The latter wouldn't be too hard, for this is a pretty high-class bunch of citizens, running to college professors, lawyers, doctors and successful businessmen.

A spokesman for the group in front of the White House was Roscoe Griffin, a professor of sociology at Berea (Ky.) College. He was neither on the muscle, nor on the defensive. He just talked.

"We believe in working to meet the needs of people, regardless of where they live," he said. In this connection, he recalled that a few years ago, after the American Friends Service Committee had won the Nobel Peace Prize, they used the money to buy penicillin that was sent to Russia.

The vigil at the White House and the State Department has been based on an appeal for "disarmament under the reign of law" and here too, the Quakers have been deliberately disconcerting. They have chosen as their text these quotations from the preamble to the charter of the United Nations:

"To save succeeding generations from the scourge of war; to reaffirm faith in fundamental human rights, to establish conditions under which justice can be maintained; to promote social progress and better standards of life in larger freedom; to practice tolerance and live together in peace . . . "

One leaves the Quakers with the feeling they do not consider themselves hopelessly old-fashioned. To the contrary, they act as though they were about 10 years—and an atomic war—ahead of the rest of us.

Men or Peacocks?

A constituent who had better remain nameless reports that a few weeks ago he was invited to lunch at our new Ponchartrain Hotel, which was convenient to him inasmuch as he had been doing some supervisory work that morning on an exhibit at nearby Cobo Hall.

"I was not dressed exactly formally," he now admits. "I was wearing slacks, sport coat, sport shirt—all garments fairly expensive, in good taste and from one of our finer specialty shops. My face and hands were clean and my hair was combed—but I was not wearing a tie. . . . "

———————

"As my friends and I approached the dining room," he continues, "we were met by a hostess, a young lady wearing a skin-tight dress, very high heels, considerable make-up, a towering hair-do, and with a manner of moving and standing that suggested she might have had her training on a theatrical runaway. She turned me away coldly: without a necktie I was personna non grata, in spades . . . "

The point this gentleman now raises—he has obviously been smouldering over this incident for many days—is that the rejection of a potential diner because he does not happen to be wearing a necktie is rank discrimination.

He asks: "Isn't it just as much segregation to bar me from the dining room because I am tieless, as to bar another person because of his color?"

He thinks so, and now he proposes a monster parade down Woodward Avenue "of men who are not wearing ties, and maybe women who are not wearing girdles, and we will carry signs and sing songs and march into the Pontchartrain lobby and sit-in all over the place . . . "

If he can get this demonstration organized, I will be inclined to join it.

Not because of discrimination, which I consider the weaker of the evils in this situation, but because I am against the necktie as a form of peacockery and as a symbol of mass conformity. Be gone with it!

There is the recollection of the first evening spent some years ago at the sedate old Holly Inn, in Pinehurst, N.C., with Robert Hefty, a golfing buddy.

In preparation for dinner, Mr. Hefty donned a sport shirt which had been designed, no doubt, by a far-gone impressionist painter. It featured polka dots within polka dots, and there were leaping fingers of flame as though to warn you of what might happen if your garage caught on fire. Over this, Mr. Hefty clapped on a sport coat of elegant cut and vivid hue, being thus garbed fit to kill, as the saying goes. Or, in the more modern vernacular, he was ready, baby.

But when we arrived at the door of the dining room a large lady responsible for admissions refused to honor him. Was she exercised about his shirt, which challenged that evening's sunset? No. Did she have a beef about his coat, which would have stood out in a roomful of neon signs? No.

She repulsed him, rather, because he wore no tie, a deficiency she immediately corrected by offering him the choice of several she kept for such emergencies. He selected, as I recall it, a purple one.

Now the point in all of this is that the necktie has become a symbol of respectability all out of proportion to its true place in the mainstream of human affairs. Conformity has seized us by the throat, and something must be done to shatter its grip.

Who made the necktie respectable in the first place? The dictionary blames it on the Croatian militarists, who wore scarves, or cravats, at their necks. The British, one suspects, adopted cravats for their sailors, who were issued blouses with gaps at the neck. Rather than design a new blouse, the tars were given puckering strings. See how silly this whole thing is?

Anyhow, conditions have descended to a pretty pass indeed when a hostess takes the measure of a gentleman by what he is, or isn't, wearing around his neck. Let us start that march along Woodward Avenue!

Behind The Sign

Deshler, Ohio, which played a small role in your commentator's checkered past, attained the pinnacle of its fame on Wednesday when it was mentioned coast-to-coast during the victory proclamation delivered by Richard Nixon.

It was in Deshler, Mr. Nixon recalled, where he saw the sign that touched him the most. Held high by a teenager, it read: "Bring Us Together Again." This occurred at dusk—there were hundreds of people gathered at the railroad station, it had been a long and tiring day for the candidate and his entourage—then, suddenly, like an omen of the future there appeared The Sign, the one out of the millions, held in the warm and eager hands of a youngster appealing for brotherhood . . .

A fine story that, and it should have ended right there for the sake of the history books. But it didn't. For now comes the Associated Press with the details.

It seems that Vicki Lynne Cole, 13, an eighth grade student, first showed up at the rally with a sign which read: "LBJ Convinced Me To Vote Republican." But she lost it. How? The Associated Press doesn't say. Who can tell how or why youngsters lose things? Not even their mothers.

———◦—◦——   ——◦—◦——

Anyhow, as Mr. Nixon's train approached Deshler, Miss Cole realized that she was signless. Holy Toledo. So she picked one up off the ground, where it had probably been lost by another teen-ager. She didn't even know what it said but she held it aloft and waggled it with enthusiasm. "Bring Us Together Again . . . "

In the good old days, Deshler was a railroad town. Trains stopped there to gather strength before venturing onward and outward into the wide, wide world. This activity—towns leaned heavily on railroad taxes—produced a degree of community affluence.

It was at Deshler, in 1922, that your commentator, then in knee britches, saw his first basketball tournament in an honest-to-John auditorium-gymnasium. Liberty Center won it. We were in the same county, Henry, and we made a practice of stomping the daylights out of such as Deshler.

Well, times have changed. Now the surviving Iron Horses whiz through Deshler without pausing for vitamins. In such search as it has made for new industry, the town hasn't had much luck. But it has coined a slogan even if the story behind it leaves something to be desired: "Bring Us Together Again . . . "

One wonders how much luck Richard Nixon will have as he attempts to give meaning to The Sign of Signs. At this moment the election returns, still trickling in like a creek about to run dry, tell us that while he has won in the electoral college, Hubert Humphrey leads in the popular vote.

This may change. But nowhere are there indications of a mandate. Indeed, in some of the great industrial states—New York, Pennsylvania, Michigan—it was a bleak Tuesday for our President-elect.

Mr. Nixon's problems are complicated by the fact that in order to be nominated and elected, he had to consort with and depend on politicians and community leaders who are almost totally removed from the realities of urban life.

Publically, for example, Mr. Nixon said he would need the votes and support of at least 10 percent of black Americans in order to govern, but he made not the first move toward winning such allegiance.

In Detroit and elsewhere, he studiously avoided the ghettoes. Today, there is no cheer in these areas as the results of the election sink in. "Bring Us Together" has a very hollow ring among millions of people who were deliberately ignored.

Perhaps more than for any other President-elect in our history, the interim period into which he is now moving will be vital for

Richard Nixon. If he is to succeed in his goal of wound-healing, then he has to show a degree of awareness and courage far above that which led to his selection of Spiro Agnew and his embracing of Strom Thurmond.

Richard Nixon's election has not reduced a single problem: only his actions from here on out will be pertinent to where America is or where it is going. In short, he can have the support of an over-whelming majority of our people—but he still has to earn it.

A Unique School

There are several unusual institutions of higher learning in this fair land and this will be devoted to one of them—Berea College.

A few months ago your commentator spent several days on the campus located in what is called "The Athens of Southern Appalachia," Berea, Ky. It is a quiet town of 4,000 in the foothills of the Smoky Mountains, 40 miles south of Lexington. Berea was founded before the Civil War for one purpose—to educate the young people of a vast and hard-pressed region—and it still persists in that commitment.

The motto of the college is "God Hath Made of One Blood All Nations of Men," which wasn't very popular immediately before and after slavery, as you will see.

Southern Appalachia, as defined by Berea, embraces 230 mountainous counties in Alabama, West Virginia, Kentucky, North and South Carolina and Georgia. The region has been described as the "Scotland of America," and many of its residents have one thing in common: They are poor but proud.

Anyhow, Berea College thrives today despite the fact that it was once considered dangerous. Slave owners closed it by force in 1859 because black students were being registered, but it came back stronger than ever in 1865. Then, in 1904, the Kentucky legislature passed a law forbidding interracial education and the school was in trouble again. It responded by raising $400,000 to endow an all-black college, Lincoln Institute, located near Louisville, and then it started concentrating on a "grand new subdivision," as President William G. Frost defined Southern Appalachia.

Today, Berea College has an enrollment slightly in excess of 1,400 and it is unique in that all of the students work. That is a requirement of enrollment—willingness to work at least 10 hours a week at a job supplied by the school.

Among other activities, the college owns and operates Daniel Boone Tavern, so fine a place to eat and sleep that the memory of it warms your commentator on this cold, cold day.

In the restaurant the pretty waitresses come at you in waves and the "dignity of labor," as it is called, is so highly ingrained that no tipping is permitted.

The students receive an hourly wage of 65 cents in cash as "take-home pay," while the balance of their remuneration (it is said to figure out at approximately $4 an hour) is applied against their expenses.

———————————

The basic "term bill" for students comes out at about $1,000—$686.40 for board, room and fees (there is no tuition); $344 for books, supplies, clothing and other expenses. A comparable liberal arts education elsewhere would run in the neighborhood of $3,000. (1968 figure.)

Berea College is able to sustain its students without tuition because it has one of the largest endowments—about $50 million—of any small school in America. Many Michigan citizens have contributed over the years and it is not at all uncommon for Berea to be included in wills.

According to one administrator, "the students are more idealistic than ever before. Many of them are thinking, 'Help the home land instead of myself,' and this is good."

Surprisingly, I found almost unanimous opposition to the consolidation of Southern Appalachia's grade and high schools. Several students were downright vehement about this, claiming that consolidation has "set education back 30 years in the mountains."

"Many mountains kids," one professor said, "just can't cut it in the consolidated schools because they are graded on the social standards set by the middle class youngsters and teachers of the towns and cities. It isn't long before a youngster gets to thinking that he is 'different' and therefore perhaps worthless. And you can't teach a child, let alone keep him in school, if he thinks he is worthless . . . "

This sounds familiar, doesn't it? Perhaps we need to "re-think" some of our approaches to education.

San Francisco

Well, dear friends, your "prodigal pundit" has returned to the scene of his crimes. As the fellow said the other afternoon as Flight 192 took off from Los Angeles: "California, here I go; right back to that slush and snow!" Button up your overcoat and zipper your galoshes, Big Daddy, for the ball is over . . .

But it was a heap of fun while it lasted and during the next few days I will attempt to re-create some of it for you. Like it or not, you are going to hear about that Republic within a Republic, the one, the only, the glorious and the chaotic State of California, where the sun has yet to set on Ronald Reagan.

On a late September afternoon in 1945 your commentator boarded the San Francisco-to-Oakland ferry and stood out to sea, as we old salts put it, for the last time. There were orders to return to Toledo, of all places, for discharge from the United States Navy, thus terminating the "career" of a Chief Yeoman, Permanent Appointment.

It was a day to remember. The sun was shining, the water of the Bay was the color of a colleen's eyes, the gulls were wheeling and calling, the war was over, we had won, God was kind.

I stood at the rail and looked back at San Francisco, with the buildings forming white cliffs against the backdrop of the green hills, and I thought of something Westbrook Pegler had written: "San Francisco," he had said, "is the only civilized city in America." And I smiled and quoted Douglas MacArthur to no one in particular: "I shall return . . . "

Twenty-five years and a few months later, on the occasion of our 36th wedding anniversary, we made it back. It was all there, and more, too, much as we had remembered it, although time had wrought some changes. But it is still a great city, San Francisco, although I will not go as far as Mr. Pegler did and endorse it as the only civilized one extant.

But San Francisco has a charm, a grace, a tempo, a style all of its own. It is a very special place and as is usually the case in such surroundings, they charge you for it. Take money—help keep California green. Wow!

One evening, for example, I had a yen for oysters on the half-shell. They were available—five for $3.35. The fish chowder turned out to be very nice.

We were there, of course, just a few days in advance of Christmas and that undoubtedly had something to do with the volume of traffic in the downtown area. The streets were jammed, the stores were packed, the mood was festive. But what we would call the "inner city" remains vibrant and vital, I was assured, at all seasons of the year. If so, hurrah for that—such is the way cities should be.

———————

There are some obvious reasons for this vitality. Downtown San Francisco has always been "fun-land" without resorting to too much honky-tonk nonsense. The commercial interests, the fine hotels, the restaurants and apartments, the shops and theaters are centered in a hill-studded region which presses against the Bay, providing a vista on a clear day which is almost without parallel among American cities. Downtown is where the action is, it is where much of the beauty is—it is where the natives as well as the tourists want to be.

And San Francisco, at least to the casual observer, has a fine transit system. You can ride from the airport to a central gathering station for $1.10, and thereafter you have the immediate choice of bus, street railway or taxi. The rates are reasonable, comparatively speaking.

For 25 cents, for instance, you can board a cable car and have an amazing ride up hill and down dale, clanking along at about eight miles an hour while the "grip man" toils at his levers and the conductor rings his warning bell and shouts instructions. "Left turn!," he will bellow, or "Going down hill!"—and the passengers hang on for dear life, laughing and squealing, seeing the sights in a style they will always remember. A few years ago the politicians wanted to get rid of the cable cars but the people of San Francisco said "no," emphatically, and as usual the people were right.

San Francisco has its poor, its oppressed, its downtrodden and its forgotten: It is not paradise. But if a city can be magnificent in these parlous times, then it is magnificent; and seeing it again after all of those years was a joy and a delight, thank you very much.

Somebody Say It Isn't So

Into the radio shack during the lonely hours of the early morning would come the wireless report which capsuled the news of the previous day. This was our only contact with the outside world, and it was considered so important that the chief radioman, whose name has slipped into limbo, stood the watch himself.

Patiently, quite often feeling his way through static, he would pick the letters, the words, the sentences out of the Pacific sky, and before dawn the frequently garbled text would be in the hands of the chief yeoman, this narrator, who served as editor, publisher, typist and mimeographer of the ship's newspaper.

"The Pirate," it was called, which was fitting inasmuch as the ship itself was the SS Jean Lafitte, leased by the Navy from the Waterman Steamship Co. and converted to wartime use. The constant cargo was troops, 1,500 or so at a whack, two stand-up meals a day and all the salt-water showers their hides could stand. There were circumstances during those years when just getting to the fight was worse than the fight was apt to be, or so said the passengers. Tell it to the chaplain, they were told, as a watery furrow was plowed toward the Philippines, or somewhere. The Navy did not operate on the theory that the customer was always right.

The chief radioman, who had been recalled from retirement and perpetually looked as if he had just dined on sauerkraut juice and lemon slices, was extra grim the morning in question.

"It has finally happened," he said as he handed over the news report. "We have invaded France."

His gleanings from the wireless, supplemented by a crudely drawn map and augmented by numerous editorial opinions, formed the nucleus of that day's edition of "The Pirate." All of the copies were gone within 15 minutes and a few may have wound up amidst family keepsakes, as is the case at this house.

That was how we learned about the long-awaited Second Front, and it occurred 37 years ago to this instant, if you take into consideration the International Date Line. Ancient history and ancient feelings of being out of it, of being headed in the wrong direction, away from the real action. Or so some of the troops said. Then they were called to chow and they immediately reverted to cussing the Japs and the Navy, but not necessarily in that order.

It has been said that old soldiers do not die, they just fade away, and the same is no doubt true for old sailors, although it is difficult to imagine how they will exist in hereafter harmony, especially if some old marines show up. Old pilots and old bomber crews probably have their separate never-never land, else all hope of tranquility would go glimmering.

But of late we seem to have sensed a widespread stirring among old warriors of all descriptions, altered by the news that the Pentagon is on the prowl again and banded together by a common question: "How could we fight another major conventional war? It's impossible."

Old sailors are told that battleships may be taken out of mothballs, and they shake their heads in disbelief. Old soldiers and old marines study the silhouettes of modern tanks, consider the expanded firepower of howitzers and shiver in the noonday sun. And old pilots and old bomber crews, aware that the sound barrier has long since been punctured, wonder whether bomb sights have kept pace with speed.

And there is another shared wonder: "How would they get us to a war if we were going to fight it somewhere else?" These are the old-timers who remember convoys spread across the oceans as far as the eye could see, protected by busy little destroyers and assorted other escorts, but still vulnerable to determined fighters and bombers. What would happen to a whole convoy if one—just one—atomic bomb plopped into the middle of it?

Surely the Pentagon has something new in mind, the old warriors think to themselves and sometimes say to one another. Of all of these, the old sailors are perhaps the most skeptical. They can remember, after Pearl Harbor, when some of the admirals were hell-bent on building more battleships. And now there are those who want to bring back the USS New Jersey, or whatever. It gives an old sailor pause, this sort of intelligence.

Still, you have to think the Pentagon has something new up its sleeve. Surely it is not going to spend all of that money on a new line of Edsels, so to speak.

Say it isn't so, somebody!

This nation, and this world, may have one more major war in its collective system, but after that, what? This is the pure-quill question: After that, what?

And it may be high time for the old warriors, joined by the new legions, to pose the question at every turn. Numerous members of this audience have lived through four wars, and when you recall how easily we got into them, and how terribly hard it was to get out of them, and at what price glory, you cry again inside for all of those who either did not make it or suffered all out of proportion to what should be expected of one of God's children.

Old warriors, in short, should stop fading away, except when summoned by a Higher Authority. Let us be strong, yes, but let us be sensible about it. And let us ask the Pentagon officials just what it is they have in mind that is new and different, in keeping with the times.

An Old House and an Outhouse

That old house . . .
Some pictures taken by Irish on Armistice Day came in from the developer a week or so ago, and they included views of your narrator's boyhood home in Liberty Center, Ohio. Nostalgia is a powerful force, as you shall see.

But first a few words about the photographer and her camera equipment. She is on her third snapshooter since our marriage, the other two having either been lost, strayed or stolen, and she does well with it. She has a sense of the unusual, such as the old man snoozing in a chair with his glasses hanging off one ear.

En route home from Florida last winter she lost her second camera in either St. Augustine or Savannah, Ga., and to quiet her remorse there was a personal vow to find a replacement: An American-made, neat little pocket camera; that's the stuff.

Alas. The man in Birmingham said there is no such animal. Japan, yes, to be sure; Europe, of course; America, no dice. True, there is one bearing the name of Kodak, which is about as native as any product you can think of, but it is assembled in Japan. Well, if you can't make a ringer, settle for a leaner. Irish carried the Kodak to the old hometown.

So now we have a picture of yours truly standing in front of his boyhood home. He is coated, capped and gloved and a keen little wind is nipping at his knees. He is numerous years younger than the house, but it looks better that he does. It was on the market (and still may be) for about $35,000, and if we could haul it up here and add a few licks of paint and a board or two, it would fetch another hundred grand.

There is the recollection of awakening one early morning and looking out the window at the butternut tree, which was showing a bit of recovery from winter's mauling. The kid slept under two quilts and whatever else was necessary to ward off chilblain, for the only warmth in the room filtered upstairs from the radiators hooked into the hot water system. Shoot, most of the time you could sit on the radiators without raising blisters.

There were nights during severe weather when remnants of driven snow fought their way past window casings, and the boy would look at them and whisper "jeepers!" (Now a painful memory intercedes. There is the recollection of Mom coming home one evening after a long painful session with the town's dentist, and she sat on a stool in front of the radiator, put her face on her arm and cried. She is hurting bad, he thought. She is getting old, he also thought, perhaps for the first time. He resolved to do better, but he didn't . . .)

Man, that heating system. There was a large water tank, almost the size of what horses drank from, in the attic, and it fed the system that eventually went through the coal-burning furnace in the half basement. Thus was heated the water that percolated through the radiators on the first floor — living room, parlor, dining room, main bedroom. The kitchen had its own cookstove, or range, kindling and more coal, with the kid in charge of logistics. He also fired the furnace, and hauled out the damned ashes — when he was old enough to use such language.

There was another bedroom upstairs, reserved for company, and in the kitchen there was a trapdoor and steps leading into the root cellar, where Mom stashed enough canned vegetables and fruit to withstand a siege by Chief Pontiac. The boy was always pleased when asked to go down and fetch a jar of this or that. The trap door; the semi-darkness of the cellar; the dim reflections from a single light bulb; the modified colors of the food—pickled beets, for instance, always tasted better than they looked. There was mystique involved, something chancey that only a youngster would ordinarily sense, but one has a whiff of it now, hunkered over his writing machine as Poppy sleeps on the davenport while her mommy is out shopping.

There was no bathroom. None. A Chic Sale sat about three first downs away from the kitchen door, snuggled against a sizable woodshed, and it was protected with ferocity on Halloween night.

You weren't considered out of knee britches in Liberty Center until you had assisted in the annual barricading of Main Street with an assortment of outhouses, and woe to the householder who slept in sweet innocence through dawn's early light.

That was the house many years ago. It has probably been "upgraded," as the real estate agents say. We did not ask to go inside. Memories are worth keeping if they're worth anything at all.

Greengrocer Turns Me Purple

Notes and Comment . . .

In the good old days—meaning up to three or four years ago—it was considered dangerous around our house to take me shopping, for I was the gadfly type who loved to drift around the store, picking up a goodie here and a choice morsel there. High-on-the-hog-type, that was Ol' Arn.

Cheese; olives; smoked oysters; bottle of wine; rye bread; packet of beer; special hot mustard—oh, no kid ever had more fun in a toy store; and what great sport it was to pile all of this loot in the dear wife's shopping cart and then stand by, full of savoir faire, casually thumbing through a magazine, while she paid the bill out of her household allowance. It was almost as exhilarating as outfumbling the Town Howler for a luncheon check, which takes a tremendous heap of doing, believe me.

Well, once more it has been decided that it is dangerous to take me to the store. In the aftermath of last Saturday's expedition, it has been agreed that shopping is hazardous to my health. I might suffer apoplexy . . .

Perhaps because of pre-conditioning, things went smoothly enough until we reached the produce department. I had heard that meat prices were high, and the rumor turned out to be well-founded. Cheese, olives, smoked oysters and assorted other delectables had also taken off into the wild blue yonder, it was noted. But, then, one can live without them if one has to. Sacrifice, that's the thing. Bucks you up, gives you the sense of contributing to a worthy cause, reminds you that such was the stuff that made America great. Carry on, little man, and this, too, will pass.

Finally, however, we got over among the tomatoes, and that was when I like to died. Give that fellow some oxygen before he keels over! Quick, Henry, the smelling salts.

For there was this one special tomato, you see, which had been wrapped in cellophane and mounted in a plastic container. It was about the size and shape of an old-time baseball after it had been run over by a dray truck. It sat there in all of its pristine glory, this tomato did, shimmering under the lights, you could literally taste a slice of it draped over a hamburger, fortified by a slab of onion with a rasher of dill pickles—and the price was 63 cents.

Sixty-three cents! The enormity of it staggered me. I clutched at the dear wife and pointed, speechless. She arched her eyebrows as if to say, Where have you been all of this time, big boy? It is true: Women are stronger than men. She could accept that tomato in stride, as part and parcel of a way of life, whereas I kept thinking: My God, I can remember when you could buy a bushel of them for 63 cents, and the farmer would throw in a mixed collie pup for good measure.

En route home I kept saying: 63 cents for a tomato, 63 cents for a tomato, 63 cents for a tomato! Like Captain Queeg in the Caine Mutiny, rubbing those steel balls together. Basket case.

It was then we decided—she insisted, really—that I wouldn't go shopping anymore. Ol' Arn has been grounded, dear friends, but not among the tomatoes.

Past Is a Dream World

A constituent in Oak Park, Howard Green, recently purchased a special album of records devoted to the music of the "big bands" of yesteryear—Guy Lombardo, Benny Goodman, Kay Kyser. Oh, how sweetly they played!

But when Mr. Green invited his son, Dennis, and some of the latter's college friends to listen to the records, their response was rather stunning. "The music," they announced, "all sounds the same . . . "

"What stunned me," Mr. Green later reported to this department, "was that this was exactly what I had been saying about their music—rock 'n roll: 'It all sounds the same.' I can't tell one number from another. But I thought the music from my youth was distinctive and highly challenging. Perhaps I was wrong . . . "

Perhaps, but if so, it was not a trail-blazing error destined to establish a dangerous precedent. As a matter of fact, man has been worshipping the past in preference to the present since the dawn of time. Socrates may have set the style for all of this when he looked around Athens in 363 B.C. and then wrote:

"The poorer citizens have captured the government and have voted the property of the rich into the coffers of the state for redistribution . . . Politicians have strained their ingenuity to discover new sources of public revenue. They have doubled the direct taxes, such as customs due to imports and exports. They have continued the extraordinary taxes of wartime into peacetime. They have broadened perilously the field of the income tax as well as the property tax . . . "

In morality as well as in politics, in sports, in economics, in patriotism, it has always been the custom of the generation then in adulthood to consider its ways and beliefs superior to those of the young people verging on the threshold of authority.

During the early stages of the Civil War, there were serious doubts among Northern leaders as to the willingness of the young men at their command to bleed and die for the Union.

A DiMaggio or a Mantle must pass into retirement before baseball fans will accord them the reverence reserved for Ruth or Cobb, while our modern writers are never admitted to greatness until they have been mouldering for at least 20 years.

And most absurd among our customs of eulogizing the past is the tendency to say: "Lincoln would do so-and-so if he were here today" . . . Or Washington . . . Or Jefferson.

There is a saying that "there are horses for courses," and some-body ought to amplify this a bit further: There are also men for their times.

The truth is that if Lincoln, or Washington, or Jefferson—indi-vidually or collectively—came back to this vale of tears, he or they would be horribly out of place, and dreadfully out of step.

What in the world would Lincoln do with Vietnam; how would Washington deal with NATO; and how would Jefferson handle Adam Clayton Powell?

To have been a giant in one era of history does not necessarily assure similar greatness in another, for circumstances, events, and bounce of the ball, so to speak, are part and parcel of the genesis of greatness and these things do not repeat themselves in the same or-der or with the same emphasis. Ancestor-worship is all right if not carried to the extreme of wishing they were back running things.

Succeeding generations must make their own music, their own literature, their own successes—their own failures. That is what makes life challenging and worthwhile, from one period to another. If the present and future were dictated by the past—how dull things would be!

Interpreting the Labels

Labor Day having passed in an election year, politicians by tra-dition are now free to assault our ears and affront our eyes.

Why this is so is beyond me. Somewhere along the line we should have been at least as smart as the English or French and passed a law which would have kept office-seekers invisible and mute until the first of October. But we didn't—so here they come . . .

Roughly speaking, politicians come under two labels, Democra-tic or Republican, but wise observers also realize that they break down into four delicious flavors—Conservative, Liberal, Moderate and Radical.

In truth, the flavors are more important than the labels, so to-day—as a public service without extra charge—we are going to discuss these predominant qualities in some detail. It is hoped that this lecture will help you separate the sheep from the goats in the trying days to come . . .

CONSERVATIVE—This flavor is sometimes ascribed by reporters to politicians they do not particularly like. When used in this connection, you can smell skunk from just over the next hill. The fellow in question, one gathers, would cancel a widow's mortgage and send her kids to reform school.

Actually, by and large, Conservatives deserve a better fate for some of them are decent sorts. They are patriotic and they believe in Home, Mother, Church and a Balanced Budget. While they might insist that the widow get her financial house in order, with a little help at eight percent, they would not send her kids to reform school. But they wouldn't send them to Harvard, either. They would try and find a place somewhere in between, with an opportunity to work after school.

The great strength of Conservatives is that they believe in what you might call The Orderly Process. They want the country to move ahead but they don't approve of a lot of loose ends flapping in the breeze. As a result, they prefer to tackle one problem at a time and grind away at it like an icecap pulverizing a mountain. Conservatives also worry a great deal about their country, which is a plus for them.

The weakness of Conservatives is that they refuse to believe there is anything The System can't accomplish. We had an economic boom a while back (remember?) but still there were people without jobs. The Conservatives had no plan for these folks that I can recall. They assume that everyone is capable of coping in this complicated society and this, unfortunately, is not quite the case.

Nevertheless, Conservatives are all right and we need some of them. How many I will leave to your own taste and imagination.

LIBERAL—When a reporter uses this flavor to describe a politician, you are in the presence of a fine fellow. The scent of jasmine is everywhere and the widow and her kids are home free. Somebody will have to foot the bill for their reclamation, of course, but we will worry about that tomorrow.

The Liberal is also patriotic and he supports Home, Mother, Church and a Balanced Budget. The latter he would attain by raising taxes, if necessary. It usually is. He tries to make out that such an increase will not affect the widow or working people in general, but he has never been able to prove this.

The Liberal is sore about the way things are going and he wants instant reform. His assault on the country's problems resembles the Detroit Lions going off tackle when the blocking breaks down.

The strength of Liberals is that they want everyone to have it good; and the weakness is that they can't figure out how to do it. We need the Liberals, but again in unstated quantities. This is for you to decide.

MODERATE—This is a fellow caught between the Conservatives and the Liberals, both of whom hate his innards. When in power, the Moderates have to call on outsiders for help and they usually wind up holding the biggest sack in the snipe hunt. Moderates are all right but sometimes you wonder if their suffering is worth the effort.

RADICAL—He wanted perfection yesterday which is the reason he will be so unhappy tomorrow. Bad company as a rule, given to hollering and pounding the table. Of the four flavors, the Radical is least appreciated.

Best Is Yet to Come

Jesse Spalding, the farmer's farmer who lives up the road a piece, came by the other day bearing a gift—a sturdy, lusty-looking tomato plant for which he predicted a brilliant future.

It will produce fruit the size of shaving mugs sometime in July, he said, so room for it was found in a garden already stuffed with young flowers that seem to be suffering from a common ailment— double pneumonia. Jesse is the perfect guest. Not only does he bring plants and shrubs for which he guarantees high performance, but he provides his own trowel and does his own planting. And between times he exudes optimism.

The sweet corn for which he is justly famous in Livingston County and environs is only about two inches tall, which means it is going to have to pick 'em up and lay 'em down if it is to attain "knee high by the Fourth of July," which is supposed to be the standard of excellence. His flowers haven't been growing much, either, and he admits that May was a cantankerous month in many respects, with June showing similar proclivities to this point.

But it is not to worry. Mother Nature will stop sulking one of these days and Michigan will bloom from stem to stern, up and down, hither and yon and sideways, as Sonny Eliot used to say. This glorious commonwealth has not within the memory of living man been guilty of a complete crop failure and this is not the year for it. That is what Jesse Spalding, graduate student of the outdoors, thinks, and you can bet on it. It is money in the bank.

The corn will grow and one of these sweet days you will be buttering it and imitating the motions of a harmonica player as you devour it row by row. The flowers will stiffen their spines, dig in their roots and soar to pristine beauty, as pretty a sight as ever you saw.

What we need is patience, a trait lacking in many Americans. Mother Nature will not be fooled or rushed, but she will not abandon us. It will be the same in other categories that constitute life in this Republic. The future isn't as dark and dreary as some pessimists would have us believe.

It tests the memory of a wizened citizen to recall when we were not in some sort of a cold war posture with the Russians. We have lived on the edge of strain since the 1940s and on several occasions, as with the Berlin airlift and the Cuban missile crisis, we have verged on diplomatic impasse and all of its consequences. In two other instances, first in Korea and then in Vietnam, we went to war to halt what was considered communist aggression.

Yet it is worth remembering that in all of these confrontations there was no publicized instance of an American taking a deliberate potshot at a Russian, or of a Russian sighting in on a Yank. It may have happened in the air, particularly during the latter stages of the Korean conflict, but if so neither side wished to make an issue of the incident.

Our ships and submarines have "tracked" their fleets and they have returned the surveillance. Their agents have violated our homeland security, and our CIA has retaliated.

But there has been no shooting and there may never be. Each passing month adds a glimmer of hope to the prospect of peace, for everywhere the people, all of them God's children, are asking the burning question—"Why war?" Why, indeed? There is no answer in favor of war that contains a grain of logic.

It is estimated that there are now 33 million unemployed workers in what are called the Western democracies, and the United States has certainly contributed its share, and more, to this tragic statistic. But here, too, there is hope for the future, especially since the realization grows that recovery must be general.

Wendell Willkie was among the first to use the phrase, "One World," and he was hooted for it. But that is what it has come down to—one world: mankind is in recession together, and it must recover in concert.

It will. Somehow the staggering debts of improvident nations will be handled. Somehow our own budget deficits will be brought under control. People everywhere are better at "somehow" than they used to be, and that is the hope of mankind. Jesse Spalding knew that when he brought the tomato plant. Somehow it will grow.

Virtue Rewarded

It is presumed that you have heard and read enough about holes-in-one to last you through this life and whatever follows. After all, the golfer and the fisherman share a common weakness: When good fortune strikes, the truth is not in them, they are apt to smell of strong drink before the day is over, and they keep telling you about it forever, and ever, and ever.

There is the recollection, for starters, of the hole-in-one registered some years ago at the Meadowbrook Country Club by Rapid Robert Reynolds, the noted sportscaster. A strong following wind prevailed that day and Mr. Reynolds selected a seven-iron for the shot. The ball took off like a wounded gull, witnesses testified, and fell to the green with a sickening clunk. Then it bounced into the hole and since then we have had constant reminders of the magnitude of this achievement, of the sheer beauty of the flight of the spheroid as it soared heavenward with the after-burner aglow. Hoo, boy.

Further, from that moment forward Mr. Reynolds always used a seven-iron on that hole. He might be hitting into the teeth of a gale with sufficient velocity to alarm a Gloucester boat-swain, but still he persisted in his club selection. It became a standing wager at Meadowbrook that he could not hit the ball off the tree and onto the fairway, let alone to the green. Frustration finally prevailed— Mr. Reynolds quit golf and took up tennis, where every stroke is accomplished with the same instrument.

———————

And then, of course, there was the interminable saga involving J. P. McCarthy, our voluble wordsmith, who synchronized his lurch and his lunge one morning at the Detroit Golf Club, speared the ball with a three-iron and scalded it into the cup on the seventh hole. We have heard a few million well-chosen phrases about that one, haven't we?

Witnesses included the aforementioned Mr. Reynolds, the Hon. Jerry Rideout of Flint, your commentator—and an unidentified on-looker whose reaction shrouded the event with mystery beyond comprehension. For this gentleman, who was standing to the right of the green, pin-high, surely saw the ball roll into the cup. Yet he did not wave his arms; he did not shout; he did not await our arrival at the scene. He simply turned and walked away as though witness to a common, everyday, run-of-the-mine occurrence, and we did not see him again.

———————

Perhaps he had a premonition of what was to come. For Mr. Mc-Carthy spent the rest of the day galloping around the course, interrupting perfect strangers in the midst of their backswings with the glad tidings—"I got a hole-in-one! I got a hole-in-one!" What he did not mention was that he also "got an eight" on the next hole and posted 96 or thereabouts for the round. With a partner like that you do not need the yips.

Fortunately, some of the elation seems to have gone out of Mr. McCarthy this season, and one suspects it relates to the fact that his handsome wife, Judy, also banged home an ace at Orchard Lake shortly after the frost had departed the greens. It would probably lower the steam in your boiler if you had to give equal time to your ever-lovin' whenever the subject of holes-in-one came up. For whatever reason, ol' J. P. has been less ebullient and the tranquility has been beautiful—to this point. And now we will do our level best to shatter the calm with a velvet glove.

Which is by way of warning that on August 6, 1977, at 10:08 a.m., under overcast skies and in the aftermath of night-long showers, your commentator was graced with a hole-in-one after 40-plus years of hacking and slashing. Glory be!

This cataclysmic event was recorded at the third hole of the Chemung Hills Country Club during the final round of the annual invitational. Immediate participants included John Gnau, partner, who went into orbit, and Tom Cull and Gary Havolich, opponents, who fell into a state of shock, as though struck by an act of God. We did not actually witness the miracle, for the green towers above the tee, 185 yards as the crow flies, and the final stages of the flight were obscured. But those at the scene, who whooped and hollered, said the ball landed near mid-green, bounced several times, thudded against the pin and dropped into the cup. A four-wood, swung from the heels, provided the propulsion and the final score was 84.

Addenda: J.P. McCarthy is dead and there is no joy in these precincts.

Reagan in a Sentence

O, unfurl the flag, matey, and run it up the pole, and watch it flap in the breeze for a minute or two, then find yourself a nice warm place to hide for Ronald Reagan is about to become "it"—like when we used to play Run-Sheepy-Run and someone had to be "it," and then he had to chase the rest of us all over 40 acres until he could catch someone else to be "it"—only this time the game is reserved primarily for the Republicans, who haven't had a real pure-quill "it" of their own since Herbert Hoover, what with Dwight Eisenhower having been coveted by the Democrats, and Richard Nixon having turned out poorly, and Jerry Ford being an accident, sort of a shot-gun president, you might say; so this is going to be a day for the true-blue stalwarts of the Grand Old Party, who will quaff vast quantities of Old Slippery Elm, and whoop and holler, and dance the two-step, and fall into the orchestra pit, some of them, and make speeches about how they are going to save the Republic, and practice lechery, if they have steam enough left for it, and sing the Battle Hymn, with special emphasis on that part where it talks about marchin' through Georgia, and tomorrow morning there will be such a run on stomach easers and headache powders as we have not seen since the end of Prohibition—and you remember the one, sure you do, about Franklin D. Roosevelt saying on radio, "We need bee-ah," and the drunk in the speakeasy turned to the bartender and said, "What the hell is bee-ah?"—and there won't be any place in all of this for you, matey, you old mugwump; and then there is the possibility the Irish will get into it, for Ronald Reagan is half-Irish, you know, and if they do they may drag another hundred million citizens along with them, like on St. Patrick's Day, God help us all, and in that event the whole country will be potted until Saturday; but that isn't likely to happen, when you think about it, for shortly beyond noon, after he has been sworn in as "it," our new president will be called upon to deliver his inaugural address, that being the custom, and thereafter there may not be enough Old Slippery Elm around to get four Republicans and two Irishmen snockered, for things are not good, matey: the stock market has the quivers; and the automobile business is sicker than a pup with distemper; and you have the sneaking suspicion that the Sheiks of Araby, those OPEC-ers, will bushwhack us again one of these days; and one of the coldest winters on record has us by the ears; and the minorities, some of whom voted 90 percent for Jimmy Carter, are uneasy; and if you need a loan from your friendly banker he starts talking in Roman numerals, like this—

XX; and the states are running out of money; and the cities are flat-broke and worse; and the unemployment lines break your heart; and poor ol' Doug Fraser of the UAW is wondering how soon Ford and General Motors will take out after him now that he has given another piece of his workers' hide to Chrysler; and all of the miracles of the New Deal have been galloped around the track until they are sore of hoof and strained in the withers, wherever that is; and yet very shortly, matey, there will stand Ronald Reagan, a country boy from Illinois, basically, with the eyes and ears of the nation and most of the free world at his command, and no matter what he says, or how well he says it, there will be some, and perhaps many, who will ask, "Is that all there is?" for what you have to remember is that the myth prevails where the President of the United States is concerned—all he has to do is grip the magic wand and wave it a few times and miracles occur, there is peace and prosperity at home and abroad, so why doesn't he quit stalling around and do it?; which is why the presidential honeymoon the reporters keep talking about is usually shorter than when a movie queen marries a rock 'n roll singer; and then the muttering starts, and Congress gets on the muscle, and you hear people saying, "Bring back the other guy!," and after a while it is just like it used to be, only maybe worse; but this is Ronald Reagan's day, nonetheless, he is "it," and in honor of it, matey, you have just read the longest sentence ever to appear in an American newspaper, God help us all again.

For Those Who Waited

Memorial Day

Lord, hear this prayer
From us who share
The memories of war,
Who know the price
Of sacrifice
And "goals worth dying for."

Who boldly brag
About our flag—
The symbol of our pride—
And realize
She rides our skies
Because so many died.

"Their loss—our gain"
Is truly plain.
We are because they gave!
To that bestowed
A debt is owed
To cherish and to save.
To fill this need
Without war's wasteful way.
Give us the love
To rise above
What needs Memorial Day.

—Margaret Rorke

Those who waited . . .

One remembers "marching off to war," to use the phrase which has inherited more pride and circumstance than it deserves. But mostly these days he thinks of those who waited, and cried inside, and put flags with stars in their windows, and prayed in the deep stillness of the night, and whispered "thank you, God!" when the news was good, and stood straight, stunned but straight, when it was bad.

Perhaps not quite, but almost, Memorial Day is as much for those who waited as for those who went away. In a true sense, the day belongs to all of us.

In the cold early spring nights of the first year of our all-out commitment to the Second War to End All Wars, he would balance himself in the taut hammock—only chiefs, blast their mean hides, rated bunks in those days at the Great Lakes Naval Training Station—and try to will himself to sleep.

Falling out of hammocks, which were stretched as tightly as a string on a fiddle, was as common as the snoring, coughing, sneezing and other less pleasant sounds associated with a barracks full of recruits.

He fell an average of twice a night, which was probably slightly above par for the course, and invariably he tried to find sleep again by thinking of his last day at home and those who waited.

Mom had cooked his favorite of all favorites, beef and noodles, with the noodles a half-inch wide and almost two inches long, swimming in gravy and begging to be ladled over mashed potatoes. No wonder he would lose 19 pounds in the next four weeks.

Then he would recall standing in the living room of their neat little home in Napoleon, Ohio, hands on Fern's shoulders, he said: "I'll be coming back," and she had replied, "I'll be waiting somewhere." And with Pat, our dog, between us, Fern drove to the bus station where he caught the Greyhound for Detroit and, ho, the war.

Those first four weeks in the Navy, he wrote letters while standing—only the card players had facilities for sitting—and one of them to Mom, dated May 6, 1942, was found the other day during the sorting-out process before movers arrived. Perhaps you will permit a portion of it, since it has to do with those who waited . . .

"Dear Mom: . . . The Navy, having many sons to look after, isn't as considerate of my welfare as you used to be, but I am getting along nicely, nonetheless. I am still fat and sassy, although I have learned to 'button my lip' and do more listening and less talking. That hasn't hurt me a bit . . .

"You were always a swell mother and I want you to know that I am deeply appreciative of all you have done for me. Thank you, too, for looking after Fern and Pat while I am away. After this is over and Old Glory is again secure, I will try to make it up to you for your goodness . . . "

She died that late autumn, sitting in her favorite rocker and reading another letter from the sailor whose star was in the window.

Oh, the millions who waited—fathers, mothers, siblings, sweethearts, wives. Some aching for the son who had been born and called and some aching for the son they hoped to bear. This was a nation on hold, the arsenal of democracy, some called it. But more than that, it was an arsenal for waiting, hoping, reaching out.

Fern was in the thick of it, battling her way to the West Coast, when his ship would return from ho, the war. How many more times he said, "I'll be coming back." And she replied: "I'll be waiting somewhere."

She is gone now. Surely she smiled when Irish came to the typewriter a few minutes ago, put her hands on his shoulders and said: "I'll go get lunch." Time marches on, yes, but Memorial Day lingers for all who waited, as Irish did for her brother.

TWELVE
The Last Round-Up

Four Phases of Life

Heaven help us, but this is one of those heavy-thinking days when the wheels are creaking and the marbles are slowly dropping into their designated slots. It was on such a day that Sir Isaac Newton was hit on the noggin by an apple. Yeah, man.

What follows will be a discussion of the Four Phases of Life, with a capstone of comment that shall be called the Sublime Condition, first recognized last Saturday evening through the bottom of a glass of Scotch and ice cubes at a birthday party for Tony DeLorenzo.

The First Phase of Life, probably the meanest of all, embraces the ages of 1 to 21. The best judgment of youth was written by George Bernard Shaw: He simply noted that childhood was wasted on children. Things haven't been getting any better. Kids approaching puberty seem to have the giggles and hee-hees when in groups, but when you meet one of them on the street he/she is apt to act as though there had been a huge fire at school—but all 12 of the books in the library would be replaced. During this phase you can get in an awful bunch of trouble with cars, sorry grades, clutching (which is basic training for sex), and the drugs that Mike Royko contends are beyond control. So many things can happen, in fact, that unless there is steady guidance, you are apt to be so far over the hill at 21, you may never make it back.

However, if you do survive the First Phase, which vast numbers seem to accomplish despite the dark mutterings of us ancient foofs,

345

the Second Phase—ages 22 to 35—may be the peachiest of all. For suddenly, as though magic had occurred, it dawns on you that there is something to the saying, "Life is real, and life is earnest." So you set about escaping intact from college, getting a job, playing office politics, wooing a beauteous female and making sex count, saying so-long to convertibles and hello to sedans or mini vans, edging a little money into the stock market, and discovering that hitting a golf ball straight wins more "skins" than knocking it out of sight. You also have focused your eyes on a career, and you go home at night instead of slopping it up at the corner bar. And somehow things seem simpler when Republicans say them than when Democrats do. Then all at once you are taking the wife and kids to church—and next year you may wind up as a deacon. Holy Toledo.

You're cruisin' now in the Second Phase. For obvious reasons you are more family-centered and security-minded, which partially explains the Republican-Democrat thing, and before you know it you have moved into the Third Phase, the 36-to-50 time slot, which is occasionally referred to as men's menopause.

* * *

The Third Phase is the Second Phase with all the stops pulled out. Now you are really thinking about "getting ahead," and scheming to bypass two or three numbskulls who have your pathway to the top bouldered; and even though every once in a while you get tired of everything, you aren't silly enough, one hopes, to play around a little with that sweetie over in sales who could spot Cher a head start and beat her to the davenport. You'd better not, boy, something tells you, because you might lose the wife, the kids, the house, the bank account, and all of those lawyers' fees, not to mention that you might never become a vice president.

So you settle in some more, and tote that bale, and if you work like a piano mover you may make the bonus list, and the years sort of swim by as though they were using the Australian crawl, and the first thing you know you are in the Fourth Phase, ages 51 to 65.

* * *

The Fourth Phase is the hardest of all. Maybe you feel in the pit of your gizzard that you are not going to make it; or it could be, you think, that if you keep working your fanny off you may keep ahead of those fire-eating jerks who are pushing up from below. When you are 30 you think 62 is the cutoff age when old geezers should be fed to the alligators; but when you are 62 the golden goal is 65 and retirement—full benefits.

So you retire. And maybe you are born to it—it won't be any nicer in heaven. Then again, not having enough to do can turn out worse than having too much to do; or you travel and, as the fellow said, "Arn, all of the Italians speak Italian, even the kids!" Or perhaps better yet you start a little business of your own and keep it under control and sort of cozy along until one day you are 75, the saints be blessed.

At long last you are in the Sublime Condition. You are surrounded by children and grandchildren and by old friends, some of such horsepower that once they were chairmen of the board where you worked so long and skillfully; and they make speeches, and so does your great wife and partner, Jo; and now it is your turn, there is no way out of it. You do well for maybe a dozen words and then you clasp a handkerchief to your eyes and sit down; and that is when glasses are raised and through Scotch and ice one sees the Sublime Condition to the refrain of "Happy Birthday," dear Tony.

Born Too Soon

To strolling back to the office the other day from the Detroit Press Club, where tasty viands and bracing elixirs may be obtained at prices levelled to the purse of the Common Man, and to being joined by a gentleman whose daughter has at least a passing interest in journalism.

She is a sophomore at one of our institutions of higher learning, her father revealed, and she has been offered a summer job on the school paper at $80 a week. He was proud of her, obviously, as well he might be, and we parted without his noticing that Ol' Arn was having a hard time catching his breath . . .

Eighty dollars a week for summer work on a school newspaper! Holy Toledo, it is true what they say about having been born 30 or 40 years too soon!

In the rural community where your orator was drug up our school year was geared as nearly as possible to the whims and requirements of the farmers. This meant that the teachers let the monkeys out, as the saying went, by mid-May, at the latest, in order that they might assist in the plowing, harrowing, planting and other activities connected with the horticulture of that era.

This also left the town kids foot-loose and fancy-free while the madness of spring was upon us, so some of us would start thinking about finding a piece of work to do.

In this we were encouraged by our parents, most of whom were seized by the conviction that if you were big enough to play football and ogle the girls, why you were also big enough to earn an honest dollar or two.

Parents were very trying in those days, as they are reputed to be at present, although for somewhat different reasons.

Anyhow, there was an unwritten rule that the more prosaic jobs, such as working in the grocery store or serving as water tender on the threshing machine, were reserved for underclassmen, whereas it was anticipated of seniors-to-be that they would invade the outside world and gather experience for the future. Largely, this meant they would go to Toledo and get a job in the Willys-Overland plant.

In those days automobile workers were not protected by the union, the Hon. Walter Reuther having not yet reached the age of puberty, so in the spring Willys-Overland would be deluged by an influx of cheap but eager hirelings.

Employment was arranged through a central hiring hall, where at the crack of each dawn a swarm of young refugees from surrounding small towns gathered in anticipation of a place on the payroll.

A gentleman seated behind a battered desk would shuffle through a stack of cards and call out—"We need two experienced flamdoozle fitters," whereupon everyone in the hall would stand up.

Patently, the woods were full of flamdoozle fitters. So the chap behind the desk would sigh, select two prospects at random (usually the biggest and strongest-looking), then pass on to the next job.

One morning in the spring of 1928 he called out for "an experienced knotting machine operator" and your correspondent, desperate by then, jumped to his feet with alacrity. Marvel of marvels, he was hired on the spot.

A knotting machine operator, it turned out, was the fellow who knotted the ends of the small coiled springs which fitted into the front and rear seat cushions. You stuck the coil of wire into a slot, pressed a foot lever and whammo!—a steel finger tied it. Then you turned the coil over and did the same thing to the other end. They paid more on a piecework basis for fine wire than for heavy, but feeding the former required rare skill and timing, being somewhat akin to fitting a wet noodle into a keyhole.

The summer passed at about $22 a week, knot by knot. Great experience was gained in many fields, for Toledo was a gay town in those days. It was not until about 15 years later, however, that your commentator came upon a newspaperman who was making $30 a week. Which shows you how times have changed.

The Good Executive

Many long and pulsating years ago (it was in the late 1950s, actually), your narrator decided he no longer wished to be an executive. Hell with it. Better to dig ditches or sell vacuum cleaners door-to-door.

He was then the editor of one of the oldest dailies in the Deep South, a midwesterner whose notions concerning the constitutional rights of all Americans were not popular in the community. It was the time, if you will remember, when the civil rights movement was gathering momentum, and the chasm separating those who believed in it and those who didn't grew wider by the day. Violence had not yet flared, but you did not have to be a genius to recognize that the irresistible force was galloping head-on toward the immovable object.

There was a black doctor who had the audacity to announce his candidacy for city council. He was a gentleman of true learning, of culture, of compassion, eminently worthy of widespread support. Outside of his own precincts, where voting was still a strange and curious white man's custom upon which severe limitations had been placed, he received two percent of the total ballots cast.

Those in the North who stood for equal rights have no idea to this day of the gumption it took to adopt a similar stance in the Deep South. The Voting Rights Act, just recycled by Congress, is one of the miracles of this age. God be praised.

But we digress. It was not the controversy which swirled around the editor's noggin that caused him to say farewell to the executive suite, such as it was. What brought this decision was simple arithmetic. One day he figured out that he was spending one-third of his time in committee meetings; one-third in arranging budgets and assignments for the staff; one-sixth in answering mail and in public appearances, including luncheons where there was much off-key singing, and only the final one-sixth—usually late at night when he was worn out from his other chores—in contributing to the product which landed on the doorsteps of subscribers.

Farewell, then, to the sanctum sanctoriums. Your narrator has since spent years at the Free Press, in charge of no one and responsible only for the production of a column, and he considers this the wisest decision he ever made.

Hurrah for publishers, executive editors, editors, managing editors, city editors, and so forth. They are essential to that wonderland known as management, and the paper would never get out on time without them. But in this business, as in all others, they are a different breed of cats, and trying to emulate them without possessing their special qualities will drive you bonkers and you may wind up drinking three martinis for breakfast.

Glaring examples of this are common in other fields. A super salesman, let us pretend, is rewarded by being made manager, and a year later the staff is breathing rebellion and he, personally, could not sell Lake Erie to Saudi Arabia.

Or a brilliant surgeon, again let us pretend, becomes chief of staff and pretty soon the other doctors are sticking scalpels in his back and the nurses are talking about joining the union.

A professor whose resume reads like Who's Who In Smarts becomes president of a college, and shortly thereafter the faculty is muttering and the students are planning protest rallies. The keenest scientists, the cleverest engineers, the snappiest lawyers—all have been known to whiff with the bases full when burdened with management.

Why is this? Well, if we knew the answer and published it we would ruin the talent-seeking industry, which is in constant, and quite often futile, search for managers. Even in a time of recession they are having difficulty matching individuals to responsibilities.

There is a "gift," let us call it, to directing the efforts of others. Don't get too chummy, don't get too aloof. You have to know what you want done and be able to articulate the essence of it. And in the process you must retain respect, if not always affection.

Tricky business, management. Cherish a good manager, for he or she is rarer than you may think.

The "Right" To Work?

A lady raises a fascinating issue. In response to a recent remark by the president on the subject of welfare, she suggests someone ought to tell him "that the people have a right to work."

Do the people have any such right? If so it must be a moral rather than a Constitutional right, for the latter document does not have a word to offer on the subject.

Neither does the Declaration of Independence, beyond Jefferson's listing of "certain unalienable rights," including the "pursuit of Happiness." Did the rich planter from Virginia equate the right to work with happiness? Let the scholars argue that point while we agree that our lady constituent is leaning on a moral right, which will be difficult to enforce.

But under certain circumstances I might be enticed into leaning with her. After four (or is it five?) recessions and one Great

Depression, I am prepared to argue that one of the foremost rights should be the right to work. If this means modifying the system so that people are no longer considered "commodities," like steel ingots or bales of cotton, I am listening. Now we are entering a mine field, to be sure, but it is high time we found a way through it.

One of the disappointments of this existence has been the discovery that our economic system was no better prepared to deal with this recession than it was 45 years ago when the Great Depression started. (Note: It has become the custom at least in newspaper usage to capitalize Great Depression. This attests, no doubt, to the lasting impression it left on us.)

When Wall Street took the pipe in the autumn of 1929 and the economy collapsed, the response was to fire everyone in sight. This included $18-a-week filing clerks, of which I happened to be one. So what happened a while back when the still-lingering recession hit us? Why, the brass canned everyone in sight, although they had trouble finding anyone earning as little as $18.

At the time it was written here that you could have gone out on the street and hired a tiger for $80 a week to handle industry's plan for meeting the emergency, and this did not sit well in board rooms nor will it now. But it was and is the truth.

Since then we have been patting ourselves on the back because of how much better off the unemployed are than their forefathers were in the 1930s, but you have to remember that the lion's share of credit for this improvement belongs to the politicians, the labor leaders and their friends and associates in the legislatures and the Congress. Industry originated very few of the measures which are now restraining the jobless from their constitutional right to starve to death.

The point is that basically the worker is still a commodity, subject to being shunted onto a side track when his presence on the main line becomes unprofitable, unseasonable or undesirable.

We need to do better than this if for no other reason than it is grossly unfair for any of God's children to be treated in such a fashion. Ah, we have arrived at the moral right to work, haven't we?

Assuming that there is such a right, how do we put it into practice? Always such an embarrassing question follows an outburst in
favor of a better world. The reformer does not have an easy time
of it, does he?

We return to the nasty word "planning," for which no palatable
sugar coating has yet been found. Industrialists hate the very
thought of it, referring to it as "interference," and vow to die a
thousand deaths rather than accept it. But something says it will
become part of their diets.

One believes the time will come when you will purchase your
new Ramrod Eight on a planned production and delivery basis.
You will order the car in November and receive it in April, let us
say, and if this seems an unreasonable delay then remember that
much of today's business is being done on longer lead-times. The
intent, of course, will be to take the peaks and valleys out of employment, which just might stabilize profits as well as jobs.

The time will come, too, when society will look back on "welfare" as a bad dream. Instead there will be "workfare," although I
do not suggest that name for it. "Workfare" will be utilized to accomplish improvements now going undone throughout America.

Do not be frightened by the right to work. It is a noble thought
long overdue in our society.

Are Girls Smarter?

Intelligence relayed by the weekly newspaper on which this observer served as a printer's devil, The Press at Liberty Center, Ohio,
is to the effect that 80 seniors have received their diplomas at graduation exercises. Further, of the 10 honor students, five are boys.
What in the world is going on down there?

While no precise statistics are available, a casual accounting
maintained at this outpost over several years indicates that scholastic awards have been running at a ratio of approximately 7–3 in favor of the girls. Not too many seasons ago, in fact, the score was

10-0 at one Livingston County school, and other lopsided tallies have been noted in Michigan and elsewhere.

It comes as a surprise, then, that the boys have broken even at the old alma mater. One suspects they have been building character while caught in a prolonged slump on the basketball court.

―――――――――――――――

If you will permit one more slippage into the dim and distant past, it will be related that for the Class of '29, which numbered 32, scholastic honors probably ran (memory is shaky) 8–2, females winning. This despite the fact that the Tigers didn't have a very good basketball team that year, either, although character had little to do with it. The basic trouble was that the varsity averaged approximately 5 feet 9 inches in their stocking feet, and several of the starters could not have hit a barn door with a handful of buckshot.

All of which begs the question. Why have girls walloped the daylights out of the boys in the race for good grades? This has been mulled over at considerable length, and the following is offered without the substantiation of facts or figures. No proof, in other words.

―――――――――――――――

Girls have been more regimented than boys, for a variety of reasons. Leastwise, this was once the case, and we suspect that it still applies, although there may be arguments to the contrary.

Virtue, for one thing. Society has always been lopsided on behalf of virtue among females, probably out of desperation, the primary penalty for infraction being what it was, and still is. Pregnancy prior to wedlock remains a scourge, the best efforts of the pharmaceutical companies to the contrary notwithstanding. So girls have been kept under close surveillance while boys have gone helling around all over the place until the wee hours of the morning. Thus restrained, girls have given more time to their studies. They have even been known to read the whole manuscript before turning in book reports, a practice which has impressed their instructors all out of proportion to reality, let alone fairness, in the eyes of the boys.

Anyhow, so much for the preservation of virtue, a delicate subject which stirs the passions of parents, preachers, equal rights advocates and, in particular, those of our cohort in this vineyard, the Hon. Ms. Nickie McWhirter, who takes great umbrage at the suggestion that she ought to be more virtuous than anyone else, especially males.

————————   ————————

Let us move along. Why else are girls more apt to win scholastic honors?

Well, girls seem to possess the innate knowledge (again, this is an assumption) that if they are going to get along in the world, overcoming the handicaps of prejudice and centuries of knuckling under, then they are going to have to be keener, brisker, more dexterous and faster on their feet than boys. This was true in 1929, and some things never change.

In those days there was a segment of instruction known as "commercial courses," featuring typing, shorthand, bookkeeping and allied subjects, and the girls just plain knocked the socks off the boys. They could type faster and with few errors; they could read their shorthand two hours after they had taken it, which amounted to a miracle in these eyes; and they were quicker, more accurate and much neater in the keeping of ledgers and marshalling of figures. It was no contest: girls 10, boys 0.

The commercial courses, you should remember, offered girls the fastest—in some cases the only—escape from their small-town or completely rural surroundings. If they didn't become secretaries, how were they ever going to see Toledo, Ft. Wayne or—wonder of wonders—Detroit? So they worked at it and plotted and planned, and several of them became absolutely top-flight secretaries, totally independent of the vagaries of a male-oriented society.

————————   ————————

This might be the appropriate place, incidentally, to recall that some years ago, an essay was fashioned to the effect that in the average business, if you fired half the executives but kept the secretaries, the company would survive; whereas if you canned the secretaries but kept the executives, it would collapse. The author still considers this a fair statement of how business is structured and conducted and bows to no one, male or female, in his admiration of secretaries, God bless each and every one of them.

We reach the point of departure in this epistle without having touched on what may be the real reason why girls may be grabbing off more scholastic honors than boys. Could it be that they are just born smarter? Or if you won't accept that, could it be that they start off even in intelligence, then work harder because that is the only hope for survival left to them? Something is happening, that's for sure.

Try Touching Your Knees

That creaking, snapping noise you heard a few moments ago occurred when your correspondent stood at attention, stretched his arms heavenward as far as they would go, then bent over and touched his knees.

His knees? Yes, his knees. You say you can reach over and grab your ankles, or maybe even put your hands flat on the floor? Well, hurrah for you, and may you live to be 100. But first you have to get past 50, or 60, or 70; for if you don't watch out, stress or one of the other goblins will get you, and then being as limber as a dishrag won't butter any parsnips, will it?

All of this was brought on by a glance at the calendar, which shows that it was just about a year ago that yours truly was carted off to St. Joseph's Hospital in Ann Arbor and introduced to the mysteries of angioplasty. That is a process through which arteries (this time in the chest) are reamed out, with patches of sludge being penetrated by a manipulated balloon on the end of a wire, the action having the general appearance of a shark eating its way through a school of minnows with hardly a pause to swallow.

It is a sophisticated technique that substitutes for open heart surgery when conditions are proper and expertise is available. It is said that the process can head off a heart attack, or perhaps even a stroke, if applied in time. In any event, this patient also returned to St. Joe's three months later and submitted to angioplasty on his lower arteries. That is how he became an ancient athlete, able to bend over and touch his knees or walk a mile with Irish and Schultz, even though his left leg has a tendency to tighten, or freeze, sometimes, necessitating brief time-outs. Angioplasty—the shark—could not reach all of the blockages in the nether regions of the left limb; it would take knife surgery to get at them. Let well enough alone, it says here.

———⟫◦⟪—— ——⟫◦⟪———

A similar reserve applies to exercise, which has become a national craze supporting large industries. But we have never answered some of the major questions connected with all of this activity, such as: How much muscle-stretching or joint-bending should one do, and should it be self-imposed or professionally directed?

There was a short segment on national television a few nights ago showing an aerobics dancing class of mostly young women, going through their gyrations full tilt, arms flying, legs thrashing, hips pivoting, sort of a tribal stomp-out, you might say, lacking only the beat of a tom-tom. Facial exhaustion was obvious, and later the announcer said there had been muscle injuries and bone damage to earlier participants who had not been physically ready for the strenuous flailing and pounding.

———⟫◦⟪—— ——⟫◦⟪———

The prevailing professional view is that each of us has a "heart-beat range" which should be attained and maintained for protracted stretches—say 10 minutes—if exercise is to be meaningful. Your narrator's range is between 72 and 78 (he has a low pulse rate), and sometimes he makes it and sometimes he doesn't. Either way to heck with it.

For it is a personal view that exercise should be rewarding, not just demanding. You should enjoy the people who share the program; you should get some fun out of the various contortions to which you are subjected; you should be free of the stress of competition or "doing better than last week"; and you should go home feeling refreshed and ready for a wee drop of scotch, a nice dinner with your dearly beloved and a romp with the dogs.

When exercise becomes a "serious challenge," it adds to the wear and tear with which life is already overrun, and you would be better off playing gin rummy or bobber fishing in the Rouge River. This has been, as indicated, the personal regime of the past year and 20 pounds of blubber have been shed, enriching the tailor who has altered the britches that would otherwise have fallen to half-mast.

At the Barnum Health Center sponsored by William Beaumont Hospital, an exercise specialist, Scott McClintock, collects "sayings" that are chalked on the bulletin board. Last week the line was: "People do not fail; they give up trying." The truth, no doubt. But people also fail because they can't handle stress, competition, the rat race. How about a new motto: "Do it, but take it easy!"?

Taxpayer Revolt

Dandelions

Yellow buttons dot the lawn—
Sprinkled there last night!
Nothing could so quickly spawn
Fully blown and bright.
Random tossed as if mere tots
Dropped them toddling 'round,
Smiling sunward all these spots
Fasten down the ground.

—Margaret Rorke

Diary of a Country Correspondent . . .

To re-reading some of the famous "Monday pieces" written years ago by Henry L. Mencken for the Baltimore Sun. While he never said it, one suspects that dandelions might have reminded him of politicians: Bright on top but ugly otherwise. Both are, in his language, the pusillanimous poltroons in what remains of the Garden of Eden, and the lawn-tender cries out against them and fights them claw and fang.

If there are those in the audience who feel that the Old Curmudgeon sometimes accords government, bureaucrats, and politicians too little respect—well, they should have been around when Mr. Mencken was in full voice. He was a caution.

Once he wrote: "Perhaps on some doomed and distant tomorrow it will become the custom, when news arrives that this or that man has been invited to the White House, to throw him out of all decent clubs."

Again; "My private belief, long ago set forth in this place, is that it would be an excellent idea to hang half a dozen . . . idealists . . . every year, in good times as in bad, along with a like number of judges, the whole current corps of Prohibition agents, and maybe 10,000 or 15,000 head of lawyers."

Finally: "The More Abundant Life charlatans, in fact, have got their machine running at such velocity that stopping it will be almost impossible; it will have to run down. They have convinced millions of the lazy lowly that the taxpayers owe them a living—that every cent he earns by hard labor is, and of a right ought to be, theirs. They have brought up a whole generation that has been taught only one thing, and that is to hold out its hands. It will not be easy to dissipate such romantic notions. It will take a long time, and it may also require some rough stuff. But mainly it will take time, and while time is running on, the taxpayer will have a lot to think about."

These essays, and others containing an equal amount of potassium cyanide, were written in the 1920s and 1930s, when it was still considered normal among newspaper folk to look upon politicians as the arch enemy and to treat them accordingly. Times were hard then, in the sense that three billion dollars were considered more than sufficient for the federal budget, and charity began and ended at home. Compassion on the editorial pages, and among columnists, consisted in the main as support for private philantrophy. No one dreamed of entrusting politicians with the feeding and care of the downtrodden and the dismayed.

This began to change with the advent of the New Deal, and it was accepted as standard procedure at the end of World War II when it became the popular notion that the country was so rich, so powerful, so blessed with inexhaustible resources that even poverty could be stamped out here and abroad. Until Jimmy Carter, no president since Harry Truman had been threatened with voter reprisal for spending too much money on social reform, and none had given more than lip-service to the old-fashioned idea of balancing the budget. The press, with rare exceptions, accepted this change in philosophy. It is no longer considered sinful for a journalist to have kind thoughts toward a politician bent on shaking another half-billion simoleons out of the Washington money tree.

———————

But there is a cloud on the horizon. We are verging on a taxpayer revolt, or so it is said, and if it reaches gale force, what then of the relationship between press and politicians? Shall we return to the era of Henry L. Mencken, when knives flashed and noggins were bashed?

In Michigan, at the moment, centered in the Owosso area, there is a drain commissioner, one Robert Tish, who is talking the language of Mr. Mencken, albeit in a more brutish and earthy style. He says politicians are scoundrels, and he is intent on doing them in by removing the source of their power—tax money. The press is having trouble getting Mr. Tish in focus, which shows how times have changed. Shoot, that's the way newspapers sounded before the Age of Enlightenment, or whatever it was!

Words For A Helpmate

Thirty-five years ago as the crow flies your commentator bounded out of bed, shaved, showered and shampooed, took a deep breath, looked the world straight in the eye—and went out and got married.

He has been married ever since. To the same woman, by grabbies. Deserves a medal, he does. What she deserves may not be attainable on this earth, for like most husbands your commentator has not been worthy of all of the nice things that have happened to him.

Oh, we have had our little differences. Wouldn't try to kid you about that. She is part Pennsylvania Dutch, you see, and she can get a goodly amount of dander up when tormented to the lengths of her patience, but by and large we have done reasonably well, a small triumph here, a reverse there, which is life, and under the same set of circumstances we would take another whirl at it.

At this juncture your commentator does not want to get too preachy about marriage, for it takes a lot of luck to put one on the track and keep it there. In the first flush of love, which is a vastly overworked and misunderstood word, two young people may feel absolutely certain that they were "made for each other"—and wind up a year or so later discovering that they have much less in common than they thought.

There is just no guarantee that marriage is going to live up to its advance billing. The only way you can make sure is try it and tough it out. Unless you are a couple of angels, who are scarce on this mortal coil, there will be some good days, some mediocre days and some punk days.

You put 'em all together and they spell m-a-r-r-i-a-g-e, and if you are very fortunate you look up one day at the calendar and ask yourself: "Good heavens, where have all of the years gone?" Then, finally, you are hooked, for once and for all.

If you will permit an observation on why marriages fail, then I will say it is because an old-fashioned word has fallen out of common usage.

The word? "Helpmate," which Webster defines as "one who is a companion and helper." In marriage it works both ways, although I am not going to argue with you if you insist that it applies more to the wife than the husband.

Life is a gruelling test for many people. Making a living, the primary responsibility of the husband, is quite often a difficult assignment. And keeping the home together, the basic charge of the wife, is not easy under stringent financial conditions. So unless they are helpmates, full of understanding and concern for each other, they are apt to end up throwing the crockery while the kids hide under the bed.

There have been several occasions when your commentator was so full of admiration for his wife that he almost burst with pride.

Once, during World War II, when Navy pay was $80 a month, she became an airplane inspector in New Orleans. My God, an airplane inspector! To the best of this knowledge, she hadn't even ridden in one of the contraptions to that time. But she carried it off, riding street cars in the dark of night to the factory where she was employed and hanging red tags on the work that did not please her. Helped win the bloody war, she did.

Again, after we had bought our first newspaper, she took over the advertising solicitation. Didn't know which end of the press the paper went in. Would go around town saying to the merchants: "You don't want to run an ad this week, do you?" And would come back with so much business your commentator would throw up his hands and wail: "Where in the hell we going to run all that stuff this week?"

She really didn't like the newspaper business. Hated writing "personals" and detested press day, when she was in charge of mailing. But kept her grousing to herself, didn't demand a place on the regular payroll, was proud of what progress we made. A helpmate.

You could have put her in the jungles of Africa, in the middle of the Sahara or aboard a tramp steamer, and she would have said: "All right, if this is what you really want to do." The only thing was, it had to mean something to you. A great one for purpose.

And now it has been 35 years and your commentator has to go out and rustle her up some jade, which is traditional for this date. Darned if she hasn't earned it!

(She died in 1983, and now Irish totes the load.)

Pleased To Meet You

Once more we are easing into the season of endless delights. This is the best of all times in Michigan, My Michigan, with a rich greenness upon the landscape and glorious tumult generating in the gardens and orchards.

Cucumbers as big as fungo bats are ready for the plucking. The sweet corn is passing from adolescence into maturity. The finest pie apples in captivity, yellow of skin and semi-tart of taste, glut the marketplace. Scarcely a day passes but what a new culinary sensation, the tender gift of Mother Nature, reaches the table. Munch and crunch, with little damage to the waistline. One revels in the midst of abundance and has but one regret—that he lived so many years before being introduced to kohlrabi.

You have known kohlrabi for a long time, you interpose? How lucky for you! In contrast, we met it only a week or so ago through the grace of Fran Kizer, but already we are fast friends.

Webster says of kohlrabi that it is of the cabbage family, "having a greatly enlarged, fleshy, turnip shaped edible stem," and that is fair enough if you want the mere descriptive facts of it. Chilled and sliced, however, and served with either salt or a dip to your taste, it passes from the realm of language into chin music without parallel. Single-handedly, your commentator can polish off a kohlrabi the size of a softball at working day's end while Old Yeller, who has no taste for it, looks on in amazement.

This is also the point in time, as that fellow used to say, to run off a batch of Gazpacho Soup. We did it the other day, using the following ingredients:

One-half cup of diced celery; one-half cup of green peppers; one-half cup of diced onions; one-half cup of thinly sliced cucumbers; one half cup of diced tomatoes; $1\frac{1}{2}$ cups of cocktail vegetable juice; one $10\frac{3}{4}$-ounce can of tomato soup; one can of water; one table-spoon of wine vinegar; one tablespoon of commercial Italian dressing; garlic salt to taste; one-eighth tablespoon of pepper, and four dashes of Worcestershire sauce.

The solids were first run through the food chopper and then everything went into the blender. Chill for four hours, it is recommended, and then you have servings for eight. Actually, we made a double batch, substituting a can of Mexican sauce for the soup in one batch, and rations of it have been adding zest to evening repasts.

Ah, the good old summertime! Revel in it while you may, for the harshness of reality reminds us that we are only about six weeks away from the first frost.

In the interest of efficiency of operation, and in the hope of contributing a mite to the conservation of energy, the venerable Ramrod Eight recently was submitted to an internal checkup. It was thought to be suffering from low blood pressure, leading to gasoline mileage in the 15-to-16 per gallon range.

New spark plugs were inserted, with comment from the attendant to the effect that the old ones were the worst from the standpoint of wear and tear he had ever seen.

The points were replaced, and again there was the observation that never, but never, had he been witness to such overuse of original equipment. The air filter was switched, and he shuddered as he dropped the old one into the refuse can. The oil and its filter were changed; the tires were inflated; and finally there came the climactic moment when a marvel of electronics, with dials and flashing lights, was hooked to the engine and adjustments were made to the satisfaction of all concerned.

Drive it, the attendant said as the bill was paid, and enjoy yourself.

We have. A tankful of gasoline now has gone through the reconstituted innards of the Ramrod Eight and the figures have been tabulated. Alas, they do not lie. The old buggy is still getting 15-to-16 miles per gallon, right on the button.

We Are America's "Magic"

" . . . America has no magic, only what we the people impart to it. In the last analysis, it is what you and I do in our daily lives that, taken together, constitutes the idea of America."

>—James M. Roche, chairman of the board of General Motors, in a Christmas message to fellow workers.

While it is always dangerous to attempt to read meaning into what a board chairman has said, one suspects that James Roche is of the belief that the American people must "rise to difficulty."

The phrase, "rise to difficulty," appears in a book just written by Wilferd A. Peterson of Grand Rapids.

Mr. Peterson, a gentle soul with a fine mind, has presented a series of small tomes devoted to "the art of living" and now he is with us again on "The Art of Living in The World Today." To date his works have sold in excess of 800,000 copies, indicating a considerable rapport with the reading public.

"The Art of Living in The World Today" is the sort of book you can devour in 90 minutes—and draw strength from for upwards of a year. There is much in it about God and the brotherhood of man, and there is a general theme to the effect that if man wishes to improve his lot, then he will have to work at it. Santa Claus makes one shuttle run each year, Mr. Peterson seems to be telling us, and after that life becomes real and earnest for us earthlings.

"Rise to difficulty" is a phrase he borrowed from Erwin Haskell Schell, the late head of business and engineering management at Massachusetts Institute of Technology, and Mr. Peterson comments on it in this fashion:

"Those who rise to difficulty have a quality in life which might be called 'lift.' It's the quality airplane builders seek to build into their ships to make them climb faster. It is upward drive. It is going out to meet difficulties instead of running away from them. It is a heroic acceptance of the challenges that come our way. It is the conquering attitude. It is refusing to be buried by troubles, not letting other people get you down, constantly climbing."

———————

The spirit of man, Mr. Peterson assures us, "is supreme. All the blows with which life may pound you cannot break your spirit. There is only one way that your spirit can be broken, and that is if you break it yourself by surrendering . . . "

In different words leading to the same general conclusion, Wilferd Peterson and James M. Roche seem to be telling us that once again we have reached one of those plateaus in human affairs where the determination and dedication of the individual will shape the future of America.

Neither is saying that we should gallop off in 20 million directions, and neither is pretending for whatever reasons that collective action through government is a thing of the past.

Rather, what I gather from their words is that all of us must put more of our faith, our concern, our affection and our time and energies into the conduct of our nation if we expect it to thrive in the years to come. They are saying, too, that the individual is not just important, he is all important, and upon his sturdiness and dependability rest the hope of the future.

This is "old-fashioned" dogma, of course, but there is evidence that more and more people are either turning or returning to it.

Since 1932, this observer can recall no other period during which there was less enthusiasm for innovation at the federal level. Congress, but recently adjourned, reflected this mood: the bulk of its activity was centered around essentials—the new tax bill, for example. Further, when our lawmakers reconvene they will be concerned with the reform of existing reforms—welfare comes to mind.

In a very real sense there is a pause in the course of our affairs, but this does not necessarily mean that we are standing still. It could be, if we the people insist on it, a time during which priorities will be reconsidered and new goals established.

We desperately need a new set of values and only individuals, acting in the concert which comes out of widespread national concern, can bring this about. Now is the moment to be heard: already the "silent majority" has outlived its usefulness. One way or another, collar your Congressman.

What magic would you impart to America? Rise to difficulty!

The Ailing Refrigerator

At the moment your correspondent is suffering from a dreadful case of the North Country Blues. There is a sudden longing to be free of the city, to stand where water and woods mingle in magnificent solitude, to share the commonest of thoughts with those unhurried and unspoiled. In truth, there may not be such a place left on the face of this continent, but I keep thinking of Leland. Good morning, Leland! Have a splendid day . . .

As is the case with most ailments of the soul, the North Country Blues may be brought on by most anything. If you are susceptible to such a "virus," the news will give it to you—murder, rape, thuggery, drugs, man's inhumanity to man.

Sometimes a glimpse of the Detroit River from an office window will remind you of greater glories; or the sound of wind in the trees, that will do it, too. Little things. And all at once you have the North Country Blues so darned bad you can't hardly stand it.

The case started, I do believe, a few days ago when we decided that the motor in the kitchen refrigerator was laboring on start-up. You know how a notion such as that grows in your mind. It is a little noise at first, no more than a slight hum, but after you wait for it for a while, and listen to it with ears cocked, it becomes as loud as a jet whistling in for a landing.

Anyhow, we took to reading the manual and discovered that the condenser at the rear of the refrigerator should be cleaned "periodically," how ever often that means. In any event, we hadn't tended to it since the installation in 1971, primarily because we didn't even know it was there. What happened was that they pushed that big lunker against the wall, flush with the floor, with no clearance on one side and less than half-an-inch on the other, and when I tried to budge it you would have laughed at the grunting and straining. Nearly popped four arteries and never moved her an inch.

Obviously, I gasped, you are going to have to get somebody in here with hydraulic rollers, or a hoist of sorts, to pull this dad-burned monster away from the wall so the condenser can be cleaned. She said she would take care of it.

Well, sir, I called a while ago for a progress report, and here it is: There is a man who will do the work on a sliding scale. He gets $18.75 for the first 15 minutes, plus $1.75 for each additional five minutes. What do you think: she said. And that's when I said: Baby, I think I've just come down with the North Country Blues. A real bad case . . .

Things may have changed over the years, but when we were living in "rural America," as it is now called, there was always a fellow around town who could fix anything for a price you could bear. In two communities we came upon absolute geniuses who grasped the intricacies of linecasting machines after no more than a few hours of fooling around with them.

One of them repaired an automatic press abused by a printer, standing astride it and beating at the mechanism with a hammer while my heart turned flip-flops. Instinctively, they knew metals and what they would stand under given circumstances, and between them they kept everything running in the commercial establishments and found time to come to the aid and comfort of countless householders.

Either would pull that blasted refrigerator away from the wall and clean the condenser for five dollars in cash plus a bottle of beer or a piece of pie, depending on the time of the day and the season of the year.

Occasionally it has been written here that what public education really needs is a required high school course called "Fix-It I, II, III and IV." In it students of both sexes would learn the rudiments of appliance repair and maintenance, plumbing upkeep, wiring and how to use and preserve simple equipment. No other studies would be worth more to them over a period of years.

Having said all of this, having fumed and fussed to such an extent, the North Country Blues still weigh upon me. Probably the only cure will come from going back up there one of these sweet days.

The Brave and The Stupid

A few days ago the Congressional Medal of Honor was bestowed upon Capt. Roger H. C. Donlon, United States Army, for heroism in South Vietnam. It was the first such award since the end of the Korean War.

When you come upon a Medal of Honor winner, take off your hat or salute—you are in the presence of an honest-to-goodness hero. In contrast, some of our other awards have gone on at least rare occasions to rather cheesey warriors. Generals have been known to receive official accolades for being in the proximity of, or for flying over, combat areas. It is said that this sort of thing used to give the dogfaces and the gyrenes extreme nausea.

But This Is Not . . .

. . . intended as a piece on valor, phony or otherwise, or even about the war in South Vietnam. However, there is an interesting statistic concerning the latter and this is as good a place as any to drop it in. Someone has figured out that the seven billion dollars we have spent over there would have provided $70 million worth of education in each of our 50 states—plus another $70 million each in back-up money for such things as buildings, books and the like.

But we wouldn't think of doing such a thing with our money, would we? Horrors, man, quit promoting socialism!

When It Comes . . .

. . . to war—and this is a piece against war, dear heart, in case you haven't caught the drift of it—Americans have been about as dumb as they come.

Prior to 1917 we were content to fight among ourselves, or to rally against the British, or to take on outsiders only when they had something close by which we either wanted or needed—one thinks of the Mexicans and the Spanish. We were belligerent, but still in the minor leagues.

In 1917, however, we went big league in war, sticking our noses into the holocaust then sweeping over Europe, and since then hardly anyone has been able to fight a war without us—and some shimmering myths have been created about our prowess in the field, particularly in respect to the quality of our leadership.

As a youngster, for example, this one was made breathless and bug-eyed by accounts of the fighting at Belleau Wood, which was where our Marines made their first offensive thrust against the

Germans in the summer of 1918. You were left with the impression that this was the military planner's finest hour, a magnificent demonstration of heavy thinking in the face of the enemy.

Actually, we now know that Belleau Wood was one of the most stupid maneuvers in the annals of war-making. The field commanders should have been cashiered out of the service.

For in violation of the one great lesson of the war, that neither man nor horse had any chance against the entrenched rifleman or machine-gunner, our lads were sent head-on against fixed German positions.

A British writer, Barrie Pitt, describes the scene this way: "Five yards apart, in four ranks, 20 yards between each rank, the Marines advanced. Nothing has been seen like it, in mass innocence . . . since the British attack on the Somme . . . " There were 5,711 casualties.

Mr. Pitt mentions the Somme in 1916. The flower of Europe, 600,000 French and British, were lost there in a matter of days. For slaughter caused by pig-headed leadership, there was never anything to equal it. What was learned?

Very Little . . .

. . . really. For in the late summer of 1918, in the Retz Forest, the French actually staged a cavalry charge with crested helmets, lances, sabers, the whole bit. The Germans mowed them down by the hundreds.

Since then, sketchily, we have had Pearl Harbor, the blood bath at Tarawa, the Yalu river, the battleship versus the airplane, and one may be excused for wondering what they will do about the atomic bomb. Bravery? Yes! But oh, sweet heaven, the stupidity!

Solar Heat—V-8 Juice

Uppen atem in good time (7:35, really) to what promises to be sunshine. Can't tell for sure yet because we haven't had any for so long it is not easily recognizable.

But if it does turn out to be sunshine, bright and steady, we may get some use out of the passive solar system for the first time in at least six weeks. Haven't had the door which separates it from the family room open since late November, and it may have taken root. Will try it later. Keep fingers crossed.

Diary entries show we had passive solar system by Pella added to house in summer of 1981 at cost of $8,620, not including furniture. There was much hurrah about it at time, for it had been featured at annual Detroit Home Show, or whatever it is called, and given "media exposure" elsewhere. Neat package, actually, with glass roof, windowed sides and tile floor on foundation of boulders and concrete. In this location it also has an absolute southern exposure by compass reading.

Well, now. There is still much hoopla about solar heat, with current Reader's Digest containing an article which extols its virtues. Reaction here, based on personal experience, is more reserved, to put it mildly.

———————————

Solar heat may be the right stuff in some parts of the country such as Arizona, Florida and other regions where rattlesnakes and gila monsters thrive, but in Michigan you had better have a darned good back-up system or you are going to freeze your tootsies.

Further, we doubt if our little system (it is eight-by-12) has saved 20 gallons of fuel oil. What you must keep in mind is that we get a steady run of gloppy weather from November through March, and when overcast predominates a solar system is kaput. It just sits there, as useless as an umbrella in a hurricane.

This is not to say that we have not enjoyed our addition on occasions. It has been a great place to relax in the late afternoons and evenings of spring, summer and autumn. The Old Curmudgeon has a favorite chair tucked into a corner and there he has spent countless hours reading, with Schultz snoozing at his feet. Splendid times, those.

There have also been occasions in the dead of winter when bright sunlight has sent the mercury zooming into the 90s—bingo. It is amazing how swiftly those glass panels will magnify the sun's rays into broiling heat.

But it happens all too seldom, without benefit of consistency, to make solar energy a dependable source of warmth, or so is the result of this experience, and this is the last report. Now that the unit is in place, we wouldn't want to give it up. But from the standpoint of reduced fuel bills, a much better bet would be an airtight, wood burning stove.

It is said that many of the great cooks—"chefs" is probably a more appropriate word—are men. There is no statistical proof of this at hand, but the fact that the rumor abounds leaves the Old Curmudgeon down at the mouth, for he is no ball of fire in the kitchen.

Still, illness in the family has forced him to assume at least an auxiliary role in the culinary department, and he has learned a thing or two in recent months.

One of his discoveries is this: that if you do not know what else to do to add zip, or flavor, to a dish of leftovers, give it a shot of V-8 juice. Or two shots, for that matter. Pour with a heavy hand, stir repeatedly.

This column is not often given to testimonials, but we would say of V-8 juice that it is one of the finest concoctions man has wrought since he stumbled onto the secret of bourbon whiskey.

The other day, as an example, we came upon a collection of bean soup which had been congealing in the refrigerator. What to do with it, since it had the appearance of old and rare wallpaper paste?

Why, V-8 juice! Stirred in half-pint or so, added water, simmered, served with a flourish, won Cook of the Day accolades from Fern and Schultz. That may not sound like much, but it sure beats being Bum of the Day, take it from one who has been there.

Life's All Backwards

Your commentator went out and delivered the commencement address at Clinton High School the other evening, sending the graduates into the bright blue yonder with thoughts of war, high taxes, slums and corruption in government. As someone has said, there is nothing like a cheerful beginning . . .

In advance of the delivery of those remarks, these rheumy eyes had fallen upon a line in the advertisement of an automobile maker: "A Convertible—Everybody's Dream Car." This led to the conclusion that the trouble with life is that it is run backwards, and the thought left me in a glum mood . . .

Upon graduation from high school, your humble servant would have given ten years off his life for a convertible. This would not have been as bad a bargain as it seems; a convertible would have been of great utility in those days, what with moon and June and spoon and all that glorious nonsense.

Today, there is a convertible in the garage, but it has come at least 30 years too little and too late. At best, it is a sop to the memories of youth, which rattle like corn husks in the winds of reality. Last season, the top was down once, leading to a cold in the head.

After the bloom is gone, Junior, a convertible is simply an automobile with a cloth dome . . .

At this stage in his advanced development, Ol' Arn can lecture for at least 90 minutes on the mechanics of the golf swing. He has consorted with experts, he has taken lessons, he has read learned tomes, and on a good day, with a following wind and a favorable lie, he can hit a five-iron 140 yards, including a downhill roll. Again, too little and too late.

For during the time of his sweet innocence, when the sap was bubbling within him and the steel springs were coiled in his sinews, Young Arn could propel the pellet 170 yards uphill with a five iron from a sandy lie. The only trouble was that he did not know where the ball was going, or why—and there was no money to hire advice on the subject. Today, paying the pro for help and succor does not make much more sense than our government giving Nasser another 40 million.

It is somewhat the same way with the other good things in life. We now have it rigged so that when a fellow reaches 65, or thereabouts, he is relieved of his daily burdens and given leave to do as he pleases. But the heck of it is that what would please him most he ran out of a long time ago and what is left to do he did not enjoy in the first place.

This is why you find so many retirees full of aches and pains and bordering on churlishness. A few days ago I asked a fellow who is very dear to me how he was feeling—and 45 minutes later he was still expounding. He felt poorly, or at least he thought he did. What is wrong with him, really, is that leisure has come much too late.

I do not know how you would go about turning life around, making what comes last be first, but it is a brilliant idea, if I do say so myself.

The young could be happy doing what the young do best, sort of horsing around and living it up on big pay, while the old, after being beautifully young, could settle down and run the store with no worry of being tossed into discard because they had a touch of the dodders.

You know something? There is almost as much brainpower retired today as we currently have in government, politics and business. It is a guess that 80 percent of these gaffers would just love to be back in the thick of things, wheeling and dealing. But they are on the sidelines while the young-in-years, who would still like to kick the gong around, are in the harness, pulling and tugging.

Something is mixed up.

Ah, Sweet Memories

And Now Christmas . . .

Always on a day such as this when she had her brood around her there would come a time, finally, when she would ask: "Well, I wonder where we'll all be a year from now?"

Someone would laugh and reply: "You ask that every year, Mom. Relax—we'll be together."

But now we aren't. She has gone to whatever high reward awaited a woman of fidelity and courage, while the rest of us scattered, some in Ohio, some in Kentucky, some in West Virginia and this one in Michigan.

More than any other day, Christmas is a "family day," and it can be a lonely time if you are separated from those you love.

I Remember . . .

. . . some Christmases from the dim and dear past . . .

You came downstairs well before dawn, tippy-toe, tippy-toe, and from the hug-yourself-to-keep-from-being-scared darkness you stepped into a room aglow with Christmas lights and scented, so richly and so memorably, with an admixture of things green, the tree and the wreaths; and things freshly baked, the bread and the cookies.

It was one of the magnificent moments of life, one you shall treasure forever, and even now it enfolds and enchants, warm and rich, soft and fine, balm for the aches and hurts in between.

You walked a few steps toward the lights, little boy awed, on the verge of the understanding of many things, the real Christmas story included, and then you stood there making photographs with your eyes, preserving for the posterity that is you all of the beauty and loveliness. For a second you wanted to cry—not eyes-cry, but heart-cry.

Then you rushed forward, squealing in delight.

And it was yours, all of it, or at least most of it, and you pulled it to you, the brightness and the sheer wonder of it, the giddiness and the beginning-of-possessiveness of it, and that was the advent of a Christmas, long ago.

But you remember, don't you?

Really, Though . . .

. . . it was just the beginning. For after the unwrappings, and the geeings, and the rememberings-to-say-thank-you, there was the family, the best part of it, really.

There was Big Brother, sort of standing on the perimeter of Christmas, for he had given the most and expected the least;

There was Little Sister, who played the piano for the carols;

There was Big Sister, who sang so sweetly;

And there was Mom, who cooked, and smiled, and beat a path between the living room and the kitchen, reveling in her brood, and exclaiming, finally:

"This is one of the best Christmases we ever had! . . . I wonder where we'll all be a year from now?"

That seemed sentimental-sweet-silly of her, didn't it, for families are always together, aren't they?

Not always, little boy—not forever.

About the Author

Judd Arnett was born on November 11, 1911, which inclined some to refer to him as old 11/11/11. He has a one track mind as the result of a lifetime spent in the newspaper game. He has been a typesetter, reporter, editor, owner of two weeklies and for 30 years was the lead columnist for the Detroit Free Press. He served sea duty in the South Pacific during WWII and escaped as a Chief Yeoman.

His assignments have carried him around the world and his writings have been featured in dozens of major American and Canadian newspapers.

Mr. Arnett and his wife, Rosemary, currently live just outside of Detroit, Michigan.